Susman & Chambers, American History

Selected Reading Lists and Course Outlines from American Colleges and Universities

American History
Vol. II: Selected Topics in Cultural, Social and Economic History

edited by Warren Susman and John Chambers
Rutgers University

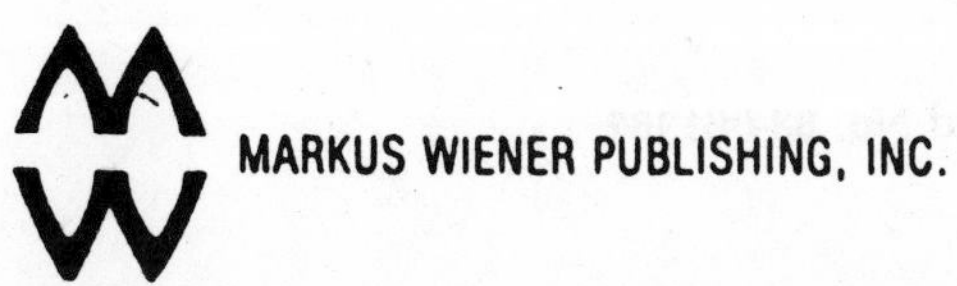

Second Printing 1986

ISBN 0-910129-05-3
Library of Congress Card No. 83-061362
Printed in America

TABLE OF CONTENTS

VOLUME II

SEE PAGE 197 FOR TABLE OF CONTENTS

OF VOLUME I, VOLUME III AND WOMEN'S HISTORY

UNIVERSITY OF ROCHESTER

Christopher Lasch

History 245
American Cultural History, 1830-1890
Syllabus
Fall Term 1981

Students should buy the following books:

Perry Miller, ed., The American Transcendentalists

R. W. B. Lewis, The American Adam

Henry Nash Smith, Virgin Land

William R. Taylor, Cavalier and Yankee

George M. Fredrickson, The Inner Civil War

Henry James, The Bostonians

The following books will be placed on reserve:

Richard Hofstadter, The American Political Tradition

D. H. Lawrence, Studies in Classic American Literature

Michael Rogin, Fathers and Children: Andrew Jackson and the Subjugation of the American Indian

Horace Bushnell, Christian Nurture

Suggested topics for term papers will be distributed later. The papers should be no longer than 2000-2500 words (about 8-10 pages, allowing 250 words to the page) and are due on December 2. No extensions will be granted for any reason. Students not meeting the deadline will automatically receive a grade of E for the paper.

Before writing these papers, students will find it a good idea to buy a copy of The Elements of Style, by William Strunk, Jr. and E. B. White, and to master the contents of this eminently useful book.

PART I: THE DESTRUCTION OF THE OLD ORDER

1. Cultural Foundations of the Old Regime (Sept. 9-18)

   Hofstadter, American Political Tradition, chs. 1-3

2. The Crisis of Religion: Experiences of Deconversion (Sept. 21 - Oct. 2)

   Miller, The American Transcendentalists, chs. 1, 2 (part 1), and 3

   Bushnell, Christian Nurture, chs. 4-5

PART II: INDIVIDUALISM ASCENDANT

3. The Psychology of Colonization (Oct. 5-9)

    Lawrence, Studies, ch. 1

    Rogin, Fathers and Children, ch. 1

    Holiday: Oct. 12

4. The American Adam (Oct. 14-21)

    Lewis, The American Adam

    Miller, American Transcendentalists, ch. 2 (part 4), ch. 4 (parts 2, 6), ch. 6 (parts 1, 2, 3), ch. 7

    MID-TERM EXAM: Oct. 23

5. Symbolism of the West (Oct. 26-30)

    Smith, Virgin Land

    Hofstadter, ch. 5

PART III: THE FEAR OF CHAOS AND THE SEARCH FOR A NEW PRINCIPLE OF ORDER

6. The Romance of the Old South (Nov. 2-6)

    Taylor, Cavalier and Yankee

7. Civic Religion (Nov. 9-13)

    Edmund Wilson, "Abraham Lincoln: The Union as Religious Mysticism"

8. Reconstruction, Reform, and the Origins of the Progressive Movement

    George Fredrickson, The Inner Civil War

    Henry James, The Bostonians

    Thanksgiving vacation: Nov. 27

    TERM PAPERS DUE: Dec.

    FINAL EXAM

Christopher Lasch UNIVERSITY OF ROCHESTER

HISTORY 245: AMERICAN CULTURAL HISTORY, 1830-1890

TOPICS FOR TERM PAPERS

1. The United States as seen by Foreign Travelers

What drew so many European observers to the United States? What did they find when they got here? Are there significant disagreements among them? Which accounts seem most reliable? It might be desirable to focus on a single aspect of American society as seen by foreign travelers: for instance, the position of women, to which most of these travelers devoted a good deal of attention; race relations; slavery; the West; class and social structure. Some of the best known accounts are Frederika Bremer's Homes of the New World, Harriet Martineau's Society in America, Michael Chevalier's Society, Manners, and Politics in the US, Mrs. Trollope's Domestic Manners of the Americans, Charles Dickens's American Notes, and of course Alexis de Tocqueville's Democracy in America.

2. Regional Elites and Aristocracies

One of the first questions here is whether there is any class in American history that can properly be called aristocratic. The closest approximation seems to be the regional elites which still flourished in many places at the outset of the 19th century but lost power thereafter. On what forms of property were these classes based and how did they exercise power? Did they really "decline"? Did they have any enduring influence on American politics? Did they articulate a genuinely conservative ideology? Did these regional elites later become the basis of a new national upper class? These are complicated questions and it is unlikely that any single paper could address itself to all of them, but they indicate the kinds of issues that need to be raised. The bibliography is spotty, and most of the works listed deal only indirectly with these questions. See Roland N. Stromberg, "The American Patrician Class: A Field for Research," American Quarterly, summer, 1963; Dixon Ryan Fox, The Decline of Aristocracy in New York (Carl Becker's Beardian study, The History of Political Parties in the Province of New York, deals with the 18th century but throws much light on later developments in New York); Geoffrey Blodgett, The Gentle Reformers, and John G. Sproat, The Best Men, for the New England mugwumps; E. Digby Baltzell, An American Business Aristocracy (originally published under the title, The Philadelphia Gentleman). One might also consult some of the books on the South listed under #11 and #12 below. On the "Southern mugwump" see also William R. Taylor, Cavalier and Yankee, a work that is strongly influenced by the theory of the "status revolution."

3. Ideas about and Treatment of Insanity in 19th-century America

One way of organizing this paper would be to use the thesis of Michel Foucault in Madness and Civilization, a thesis developed from European materials, as an interpretative framework for understanding developments in the United States; or rather, to ask whether this thesis does in fact provide a satisfactory framework for American developments or whether it is contradicted by the facts. In searching for the empirical data, it is important to remember that the following works, however neutral their tone may seem, embody an interpretation of their own, one radically different from Foucault's: Norman Dane, Concepts of Insanity in the US; Gerald Grob, The State and the Mentally Ill; Albert Deutsch, The Mentally Ill in America; David Rothman, The Discovery of the Asylum.

4. Origins of the Asylum

In the early part of the 19th century asylums for the insane, criminals, paupers, and other deviants sprang up all over the country. What was the rationale behind this movement? What were the social forces behind it? Did it represent the triumph of humanitarianism or a new type of repression? The recent study of Rothman, mentioned under the previous topic, is the best place to begin. See also the chapters on this subject in Alice Felt Tyler, Freedom's Ferment. On prisons see N.K. Teeters and John D. Shearer, The Prison at Philadelphia; W. David Lewis, From Newgate to Dannemora: The Rise of the Penitentiary in New York; and the contemporary account by Alexis de Tocqueville and Gustave de Beaumont, On the Penitentiary System in the United States and Its Application in France. On insanity see the bibliography listed under the preceding topic. Erving Goffman's sociological study, Asylums, is not historical, but it is very helpful in identifying exactly what is distinctive about the asylum.

5. American Drinking Habits and the Temperance Movement

As in the case of other 19th-century reform movements, one question to ask is whether the sudden upsurge of reform agitation starting in the 1830's was simply a response to an intensification of the problem in question--in this case, drinking--or whether it sprang from other sources; for example, middle-class anxieties about social disorder, fear of the working class, fear of immigrants, etc. In the case of the temperance movement, one therefore wants to know whether American drinking habits were in the process of change (was there a sudden increase in drunkenness?), whether there was any correlation between the incidence of temperance agitation and the incidence of manufacturing, etc. Comparative perspectives would be useful here: comparisons of the temperance movement in the US with temperance movements in other countries; a comparison of the temperance movement in New England in the middle of the 19th century with temperance agitation in the South at the end of the century, etc. The literature on this subject is not very good. See John A. Krout, Origins of Prohibition; Tyler, Freedom's Ferment (ch. XIII)

Ernest H. Cherrington, The Evolution of Prohibition in the USA; David M. Ludlum, Social Ferment in Vermont, 1791-1850; Gilbert Seldes, The Stammering Century (ch. XV); and, for primary materials, Temothy Shay Arthur, Ten Nights in a Bar Room (1855); Lyman Beecher, Lectures on Political Atheism and Kindred Subjects, together with Six Lectures on Intemperance (1852); Henry William Blair, The Temperance Movement, or The Conflict between Man and Alcohol (1888); Benjamin Rush, An Inquiry into the Effects of Ardent Spirits upon the Human Body and Mind (179-?) On the prohibition movement in the South see James B. Sellers, The Prohibition in North Carolina; and W. H. Patton, "History of the Prohibition movement in Mississippi," Publications of the Miss. Hist. Soc., 1909; Brian Harrison, Drink and the Victorians; Norman Clark, The Dry Years: Prohibition and Social Change in Washington; Joseph Gusfield, Symbolic Crusade.

6. The Rise of the Common School: Liberation or Repression?

See Lawrence Cremin, The American Common School: An Historic Conception; Sidney L. Jackson, America's Struggle for Free Schools; Rush Welter, Popular Education and Democratic Thought in America; Michael B. Katz, The Irony of Early School Reform; Colin Greer, The Great School Legend.

7. A Comparative Study of the Abolition and/or Antislavery Movements in England and the United States

One object of such a comparison might be to test Stanley Elkins's thesis (in his Slavery, ch. IV) that the American abolition movement had a distinctively American character, moralistic rather than pragmatic, immediatist rather than gradualistic, and that the special character of American abolitionism derived from the special quality of American society. For the English movement, see Frank Klingberg, The Antislavery Movement in England, and William Mathieson, British Slavery and Its Abolition; also Eric Williams, Capitalism and Slavery. Examination of the American movement might begin with the collection of primary materials edited by Louis Ruchames, The Abolitionists, and the collection of secondary essays edited by Martin Duberman, The Antislavery Vanguard. There is also an extensive bibliography of the subject in Elkins.

8. Contrasting Views of William Lloyd Garrison

See, for a start, John L. Thomas, The Liberator, and Aileen Kraditor, Means and Ends in American Abolitionism. The object, here, should be not merely to discuss Garrison but to get at the antislavery movement as a whole by way of Garrison, as in fact both these books try to do.

TOPICS FOR TERM PAPERS

9. Social Origins of the Antislavery Movement

See, for strongly contrasting interpretations, David Donald's status revolution theory in his Lincoln Reconsidered, and Leonard L. Richards, Gentlemen of Property and Standing: Anti-Abolition Mobs in Jacksonian America. This last work, as its title indicates, deals with anti-abolitionism but throws light on the social incidence of abolitionism as well. See also the older study by Gilbert Barnes, The Antislavery Impulse. For primary sources see the Ruchames collection, mentioned above, #7.

10. Communitarian Societies

A great variety of utopian communities were founded in the 19th century. What did these have in common and how did they differ? Why did some succeed and others fail? In what ways did they challenge the surrounding society and in what ways did they reflect it? There are two useful contemporary accounts: John Humphrey Noyes, History of American Socialisms, and Charles Nordhoff, The Communistic Societies of the US. See also the bibliography in Alice Felt Tyler's Freedom's Ferment.

11. Social Origins and Significance of Jacksonian Democracy

The literature on this subject is very large. One way of approaching it might be to read the essays in the collection edited by George Rogers Taylor, Jackson versus Biddle (Amherst Problems in American Civilization), especially the contributions by Bray Hammond and Arthur Schlesinger, which are elaborated more fully in their books, Banks and Politics in the US from the Revolution to the Civil War and The Age of Jackson. Other works bearing on the subject are Edward Pessen, Most Uncommon Jacksonians; Lee Benson's study of New York politics as a test case of the concept of Jacksonian democracy; Michael A. Lebowitz's essay-review of Benson, "The Significance of Claptrap in American History,"(Studies on the Left, 1965 [?]); and the relevant chapters in Frederick Jackson Turner's The United States, 1830-1850 (see especially chapters II and IX).

12. Southern Ideology

Did the South, in trying to formulate a rounded defense of slavery, articulate an anti-capitalist ideology reflecting the peculiar needs of the planter class, or did considerations of race override those of class? The poles of debate on this question now seem to be represented by the works of Eugene Genovese on the one hand, especially the essay on George Fitzhugh in The World the Slaveholders Made, and those of George Fredrickson on the other, especially The Black Image of the White Mind. For primary sources see two collections edited by Eric McKitrick, Slavery Defended, and Harvey Wish, Ante-Bellum: Three Classic Writings on Slavery in the Old South. Winthrop Jordan's White Over Black, is also relevant to this controversy.

13. The Nature of Southern Society

This question is closely related to the preceding one. In its starkest form the question may be put: was the South a feudal (or "seigneurial") society or a capitalistic one? Genovese's The Political Economy of Slavery once again represents the clearest statement of one position; for the other, see Kenneth Stampp's The Peculiar Institution and ch. II of Stanley Elkin's Slavery. Fredrickson's Black Image in the White Mind takes a position different from either of these, as (to a certain extent) does W. J. Cash's The Mind of the South.

14. The Comparative Study of Slavery and Patterns of Race Relations

There is now an extensive literature on this subject, including Frank Tannenbaum, Slave and Citizen; Elkins, Slavery; Marvin Harris, Patterns of Race in the Americas; Herbert Klein, Slavery in the Americas; Harmannus Hoetink, The Two Variants in Caribbean Race Relations; and part I of Genovese's World the Slaveholders Made.

15. The Southern Lady

The position of women in Southern society; the sentimental cult of womanhood; the possible connections between this and the institution of slavery--these are some of the questions that come to mind. See Ann Scott, The Southern Lady and William R. Taylor, Cavalier and Yankee; for primary materials see Mary B. Chestnut, Diary from Dixie.

16. Changing Interpretations of the Causes of the Civil War

Compare the interpretations in Charles A. Beard, The Rise of American Civilization; Avery Craven, The Coming of the Civil War; and Allan Nevins, The Ordeal of the Union.

17. Changing Interpretations of Reconstruction

Compare the interpretations in William A. Dunning, Reconstruction; James Allen, Reconstruction; and Kenneth M. Stampp, The Era of Reconstruction. See also Bernard Weisberger, "The Dark and Bloody Ground of Reconstruction Historiography," Journal of Southern History, 1959. It might also be useful to compare the 1937 edition of J.G. Randall's Civil War and Reconstruction with the 1961 revision by David Donald, which incorporates many revisionist perspectives.

18. Reconstruction as Presented in High School Textbooks

Almost any textbooks could be used; here again, it would be useful to compare successive editions of the same books, in order to examine changes in the way the subject is presented, Some popular textbooks are David S. Muzzey, Our Country's History (1960); Ruth Gavin and William A. Hamm, The American Story (1945); I. James Quillen, Living in Our America: History for Young Citizens (1956); Howard B. Wilder, Robert P. Ludlum, and Harriet M. Brown, This Is America's Story (1948); and Everett Augspurger and Richard A. McLemore, Our Nation's Story (1956). In most cases the editions I have cited have probably been superceded by more recent editions.

19. The Negro in Reconstruction

William A. Dunning, Reconstruction; Kenneth Stampp, The Era of Reconstruction; W. E. B. du Bois, Black Reconstruction; and Joel Williamson, The Negro in SC during Reconstruction, are the books to start with.

20. Origins of Racial Segregation

A considerable controversy has grown up around the origins of segregation in the South after the Civil War--about the chronology of segregation (just when was it introduced?); the purposes behind it; the social and political pressures behind it; and the social distribution of support for it and opposition to it (or at least, indifference to the alleged urgency of its need). The literature includes Vernon Lane Wharton, The Negro in Mississippi, 1865-1890; George Brown Tindall, South Carolina Negroes, 1877-1900; Albert D. Kirwan, Revolt of the Rednecks: Mississippi Politics, 1876-1925; Charles E. Wynes, Race Relations in Virginia, 1870-1902; and, of special importance, C. Vann Woodward, The Strange Career of Jim Crow. Since its publication in 1955, this book has been twice revised to take into account criticisms of its thesis; it is instructive to compare the earlier and later editions.

21. Uncle Tom's Cabin in Various Adaptations

This famous novel became an equally famous melodrama and also underwent a number of other adaptations. It would be interesting to compare these with the original book, to see in what way the book's meaning

22. Feminism

A variety of approaches to this topic might be taken. Why did feminism arise when and where it did? What was its relation to other reform movements? When and why did the movement come to concentrate on the demand for the vote? What were the reasons behind the split in the suffrage movement? Another approach would be to concentrate on feminist thought.

To what extent did feminists criticize and to what extent did they reflect 19th-century culture? To what extent were they Victorians? Basic books are Andrew Sinclair, The Emancipation of American Women; Eleanor Flexner, Century of Struggle; Alan P. Grimes, Puritanism and Woman Suffrage; the collection of primary sources edited by Aileen Kraditor, Up From the Pedestal; Kraditor's Ideas of the Woman Suffrage Movement; and William O'Neill, Everyone Was Brave. The last two are the best, but unfortunately they deal mostly with the period after 1890.

23. Beginnings of the University

Since the American university did not assume its definitive form until the early yeas of the 20th century, this topic extends beyond the chronological limits of this course. The beginnings of the transformation of the college into the university lie, however, in the 19th century. Why and how did this transformation take place? Several conflicting conceptions of the university were advanced; what were they and how did they influence the institution that finally emerged? Reading might begin with Frederick Rudolph, The American College and University, and Laurence R. Veysey, The Emergence of the American University. For the development of the elective system at Harvard see Samuel Eliot Morison, Three Centuries of Harvard. Richard Hofstadter and Walter P. Metzger, The Development of Academic Freedom in the US, contains material on the 19th century. So does Oscar and Mary Handlin, Facing Life, if one can ignore their polemical chapters on the university today. See also Jurgen Herbst, The German Historical School and American Scholarship. For a comparative view see Abraham Flexner, Universities, German, English, and American.

24. The "Sentimental Revolution"

This term has been used to describe certain aspects of American popular culture from the 1830's to the Civil War and, more broadly, a general change in sensibility (reflected in art, literature, drama, journalism, social life, etc.). Such changes are elusive; part of the problem here is to define sentimentalism and identify its characteristics. Another part (most difficult; this is really a subject for a paper in itself) is to explain the relation between "sentimentalism" and romanticism; the most obvious answer, probably too obvious, is that the former represents a popularized and debased version of the latter. (On romanticism considered as a distinctive and historically rooted sensibility, see Mario Praz, The Romantic Agony.) Another possibility is to deal with the influence of sentimentalism on the quality of political discussion in the middle of the 19th century. Edmund Wilson touches on this in Patriotic Gore; so does William R. Taylor in ch. IX of Cavalier and Yankee. Other works on sentimentalism include E. Douglas Branch, The Sentimental Years; Herbert Brown, The Sentimental Novel in America; Helen Papashvily, All the Happy Endings; Alexander Cowie, "The Vogue of the Domestic Novel," So. Atlantic Quarterly, 1942; the first sections of Leslie Fiedler, Love and Death in the American Novel; Meade Minnegorode, The Fabulous Forties; and Carl Bode, Antebellum Culture (also published under the title The Anatomy of American Popular Culture, 1840-61).

25. The "Dangerous Classes"

This is tricky. For one thing, distinguishing the "dangerous classes" from the working classes presents a difficult theoretical problem, especially since contemporaries often failed to make the distinction themselves. Moreover, material is scanty. The rise of an urban lumpenproletariat, however--or, better, the changing character of this class under industrialism,--presumably tells us many important things about the industrial city and industrialism in general. One interesting approach would be to compare two contemporary classics, Henry Mayhew's London Labour and the London Poor and Charles Loring Brace's The Dangerous Classes of New York.

26. Horatio Alger and the Myth of the Self-Made Man

One of the reasons this topic is interesting is that the Alger novels themselves don't always say exactly what they are commonly supposed to have said; there is a discrepancy between Alger and Algerism. Any of Alger's novels (there are about a hundred) may be sampled; some of my favorites are Andy Gordon, Andy Gordon's Pluck, Making His Way, and Risen From the Ranks. Biographies include Herbert R. Mayes, Alger; John Tebbel, From Rags to Riches; and Ralph Gardner, Horatio Alger and the American Hero Era. See also John Cawelti, Apostles of the Self-Made Man; Irwin Wyllie, The Self-Made Man in America; and Richard J. Walsh, "The Doom of the Self-Made Man," Century, Dec., 1924.

27. The Self-Made Man in Reality

See William Miller, ed., Men in Business, and his "American Historians and the Business Elite," Journal of Economic History, Nov., 1949; C. Wright Mills, "The American Business Elite: A Collective Portrait," ibid., Dec., 1945 (supplement); C. Wright Mills, "American Historians and the Business Elite," ibid., Nov., 1949; and E. Digby Baltzell, An American Business Aristocracy (also published as Philadelphia Gentleman).

28. Organized Religion and Social Issues

Some have seen the churches as a conservative influence; others have stressed the links between evangelical religion and social reform. John R. Bodo, The Protestant Clergy and Public Issues, 1812-48; Timothy Smith, Revivalism and Social Reform; and Arthur Schlesinger, Jr., Orestes Brownson: A Pilgrim's Progress, bear on this issue; one might also consult Richard Niebuhr, Social Sources of Denominationalism.

29. Social History of the American Family

Most historians and sociologists have seen the history of the family as a movement from the extended to the nuclear family and from patriarchal to egalitarian arrangements. See, for example, the second volume of Arthur Calhoun's Social History of the American Family. This view is challenged by Philippe Aries, Centuries of Childhood, which, although it deals with France, it is indispensable for anyone interested in the American family. Works dealing with the latter subject in the 19th century,include William C. Bridges, "Family Patterns and Social Values in America, 1825-1875," American Quarterly, 1965; Anne L. Kuhn, The Mother's Role in Childhood Education: New England Concepts, 1830-1860; and Ernest R. Groves, The American Woman. The first chapter of William O'Neill's Divorce in the Progressive Era, is a critical review of sociological concepts of the family.

30. The Labor Movement before the AFL

The usual interpretation is that reformism weakened the movement and that it was only with the emergence of Gomper's bread-and-butter unionism that labor began to make real gains. See Gerald Grob, Workers and Utopia, and Norman Ware, The Labor Movement in the US. Montgomery's book, on the required reading list, represents the beginnings of a new interpretation; see also Herbert Gutman, "The Workers' Search for Power," in H. Wayne Morgan, ed., The Gilded Age: A Reappraisal. For the condition of the working class see Norman Ware, The Industrial Worker; Caroline F. Ware, Early New England Cotton Manufacture; and Hannah Josephson, Golden Threads (the mills in Lowell). For comparison, consult Frederick Engels, The Condition of the Working Class in England in 1844.

31. The City

The difference between the old urban history and the new is explained by Moses Rischin in the spring, 1972, issue of the Journal of Social History, in which he reviews Blake McKelvey's The Emergence of Metropolitan America, 1915-1966, and Sam Bass Warner, Jr., The Private City: Philadelphia in Three Periods of Its Growth. See also Arthur Schlesinger's Rise of the City; Eric Lampard's "American Historians and the Study of Urbanization," American Historical Review, 1961; and Warner's "If All the World Were Philadelphia: A Scaffolding for Urban History, 1774-1930," ibid., 1968.

32. Abraham Lincoln: Symbol for an Age

An interesting attempt could be made to apply the method of John William Ward's Andrew Jackson: Symbol for an Age, to the study of Lincoln. The best biography of Lincoln is by Benjamin Thomas. There are numerous collections of Lincoln's own writings, of which the most complete was edited by Roy Basler and published in 1953 by Rutgers University Press.

33. The Adams Family

Of a voluminous literature, the most important books are Henry Adams' Education, the two-volume biography by Ernest Samuels, and the careful study by W. H. Jordy, Henry Adams, Scientific Historian; Brooks Adams' Degradation of the Democratic Dogma and the biography by Arthur F. Beringause. See also Henry and C.F. Adams, Chapters of Erie. For the preceding generation see Martin Duberman, Charles Francis Adams.

34. The Mark Twain Controversy

The studies by Van Wyck Brooks, The Ordeal of Mark Twain, and Bernard DeVoto, Mark Twain's America, set forth opposing positions; these are analyzed by Dwight Macdonald's "Mark Twain: An Unsentimental Journey," New Yorker, April 9, 1960, itself a contribution to the debate. See also Justin Kaplan, Mr. Clemens and Mark Twain.

35. American Architecture in the Gilded Age

The general opinion, that the architecture of this period was tasteless, vulgar, and ostentatious, is vigorously disputed by Wayne Andrews, Architecture, Ambition and Americans and, on different grounds, by Lewis Mumford, The Brown Decades. It informs the useful history by John Burchard and Albert Bush-Brown The Architecture of America. Montgomery Schuyler, American Architecture, is a contemporary view, published in 1892. Carl Condit's American Building is a corrective to the usual tendency to define architectural history, and architecture itself, too narrowly.

36. Nativism

Basic are Ray Billington, The Protestant Crusade; David Brion Davis, "Some Ideological Functions of Prejudice in Antebellum America," American Quarterly, XV, 115-25; and for the period after the Civil War, Barbara Solomon, Ancestors and Immigrants; and John Higham, Strangers in the Land.

37. The Culture of New England after Transcendentalism

The literature includes Ferris Greenslett, The Lowells and Their Seven Worlds; Geoffrey Blodgett, The Gentle Reformers; John Sproat, The Best Men, the Solomon book referred to under the preceding topic; Henry James, William Wetmore Storey and His Friends; Van Wyck Brooks, The Dream of Arcadia: American Writers and Artists in Italy; the same author's New England: Indian Summer; and Kermit Vanderbilt, Charles Eliot Norton: Apostle of Culture in a Democracy. This topic could be approached largely through novels; two of the best are Henry James' The Bostonians and William Dean Howell's Rise of Silas Lapham.

Addendum to No. 21, Uncle Tom's Cabin.

For bibliography see Richard Moody, Dramas from the American Theater, a collection of popular plays, and his America Takes the Stage; Bernard Hewitt, Theater USA: 1668-1957; Arthur Quinn, American Drama; Glenn Hughes, A History of the American Theater.

UNIVERSITY OF ROCHESTER

Christopher Lasch

History 246
U.S. Cultural History, 1890 -
Fall Term 1982
Syllabus

Please buy the following books.

Robert S. Lynd, Knowledge for What?

Sinclair Lewis, Main Street

Malcolm Cowley, Exile's Return

Lionel Trilling, The Middle of the Journey

Philip Slater, The Pursuit of Loneliness

The rest of the readings will be placed on reserve.

PART I: THE PROGRESSIVE COUNTER-REFORMATION

1. Legacy of the Civil War: The Strenuous Life and the Search for a Moral Equivalent of War (Sept. 8-10)

William James, "The Moral Equivalent of War"

Randolph Bourne, "A Moral Equivalent of Universal Military Service"

Theodore Roosevelt, "The Strenuous Life"

2. The "Managerial Revolution" and the Bureaucratization of Benevolence (Sept. 13-24)

Walter Lippmann, Preface to Politics

3. The Rise of Social Science & the Progressive Synthesis (Sept. 27 - Oct. 8)

Lynd, Knowledge for What?

PART II: CULTURAL MODERNISM: THE AVANT-GARDE AGAINST MAIN STREET

4. The Pre-War Cultural Revolt (Oct. 13-15)

Lewis, Main Street

5. World War I and Its Aftermath (Oct. 18-20)

   Bourne, war essays; Mumford, "The Pragmatic Acquiescence"

   MID-TERM EXAM (Oct. 22)

6. The Dialectic of Alienation and Return (Oct. 25 - Nov. 12)

   Cowley, Exile's Return

   From Partisan Review:
   Meyer Shapiro, "Populist Realism" (1937)
   ——, "Looking Foward to Looking Backward" (1937)
   F. W. Dupee, "The Americanism of Van Wyck Brooks" (1939)
   Morton Dauwen Zabel, "The Poet on Capitol Hill" (1941)
   Dwight Macdonald, "Kulturbolschewismus Is Here" (1941)
   Richard Chase, "The Armed Obscurantist" (1944)

   Philip Rahv, "Proletarian Literature: A Political Autopsy," Southern Review, 1939

   ——, "Twilight of the Thirties," PR, 1939

   James Agee, "Late Sunday Morning"; "Near a Church"; "A Country Letter: I" [departure of Emma]; "Some Questions which Face American Writers Today," in Let Us Now Praise Famous Men

   Lewis Mumford, "The Corruption of Liberalism," New Republic, 1940

   ——, The Condition of Man, chs. 9, 10

PART III: PLURALISM AND THE LIBERAL CRITIQUE OF LIBERALISM

7. Cold-War Liberalism (Nov. 15-24)

   Trilling, The Middle of the Journey

8. The New Left and Its Legacy (Nov. 29 - Dec. 15)

   Slater, The Pursuit of Loneliness

   TERM PAPERS DUE: December 6

   FINAL EXAM: date to be announced

UNIVERSITY OF ROCHESTER

Christopher Lasch

History 246
Topics for Term Papers

1. The US in 1893, as seen by Baedecker

In 1893 the firm of Baedecker, long famous for travel guides of the European countries, for the first time published a guide to the United States (reprinted in 1971 by Da Capo Press, New York). Using this source alone, as if it were the only one available, try to reconstruct a coherent picture of American society at the time.

2. The 1890s

What were the characteristics, the successes and failures, of the literary culture of this period, and what does this culture reveal or suggest about American society as a whole? For a beginning, consult Larzer Ziff, The American 1890's; Thomas Beer, The Mauve Decade; and the relevant parts of Lewis Mumford's The Brown Decades and Henry Steele Commager's The American Mind.

3. The Cult of the "Strenuous Life"

The emergence of a martial ethic is one of the characteristic features of the American scene at the turn of the century. Examine its social origins, its social and political content and implications, and its relation to the rise of imperialism. See the last chapter of George Fredrickson's The Inner Civil War for an introduction; also, for a very different interpretation, John P. Mallan, "Roosevelt, Brooks Adams, and Lea: The Warrior Critique of the Business Civilization," American Quarterly, 1956.

4. Nativism, Anti-Semitism, and Populism

A great deal of controversy has been generated by the attempt to link populism to nativism, characteristic of the essays in Bell's Radical Right and, to a lesser degree, of Hofstadter's Age of Reform. See Walter T. K. Nugent, The Tolerant Populists; Norman Pollack, "The Myth of Populist Anti-Semitism," American Historical Review, Oct. 1962, and the rebuttal in the same journal, April 1963, pp. 910-11; John Higham, Strangers in the Land; Oscar Handlin, "American Views of the Jews at the Beginning of the Twentieth Century," Publications of the American Jewish Historical Society, June, 1951, pp. 323-44; E. Digby Baltzell, The Protestant Establishment.

5. The Anti-Imperialist Movement, 1898-1900

For conflicting interpretations see Robert L. Beisner, Twleve against Empire; Daniel Schirmer, Republic or Empire; Elinor Fuchs and Joyce Antler, Year One of the Empire; and Christopher Lasch, "The Anti-Imperialists, the Philippines, and the Inequality of Man," J. So. Hist., Aug. 1958.

6. The Professionalization of Social Work
Why did charity become a profession, what kinds of anxieties and social tensions generated this movement, what did it promise to achieve? Roy Lubove, The Professional Altruist and David Pivar, Purity Crusade are useful introductions to this topic.

7. The Anatomy of the Upper Class
How does the upper class define and perpetuate itself and how does it rule? To what extent is this class based on family and to what extent is it based on money? How has it changed since the turn of the century? C. Wright Mills, The Power Elite; G. William Domhoff, The Higher Circles; E. Digby Baltzell, An American Business Aristocracy; Cleveland Amory, The Last Resorts; and Ward McAllister, Society As I Have Found It will help to answer these questions.

8. The Emergence of the University
The best study by far is Laurence Veysey, The Emergence of the American University; for a contemporary critique, see Thorstein Veblen's The Higher Learning in America. (Where does Veblen fit into the spectrum of opinion described by Veysey?) It might be asked: has the university changed in any essential respects since 1915? Again, it might be asked, what is the role of the university in the economy, particularly in certifying people for jobs? Two recent books b that bear on this issue are Robert Paul Wolff, The Ideal of the University and Ivar Berg, Education and Jobs: The Great Training Robbery.

9. The Emergence of the High School
This institution derives in part from the same ferment that produced the university. Edward A. Krug, The Shaping of the American High School; Raymond E. Callahan, Education and the Cult of Efficiency; and Joel H. Spring, Education and the Rise of the Corporate State deal either directly or indirectly with this topic, as does Cremin's Transformation of the School, with which these accounts should be compared.

10. The Americanization of Sigmund Freud
This essay might focus on the reception and popularization of psychoanalysis in the United States or, at a more academic level, modifications of Freudian doctrine made by American psychoanalysts. See John C. Burnham, "Psychology, Psychoanalysis and the Progressive Movement," American Quarterly, 1960, and his Psychoanalysis in American Medicine; Fred Mathews, "The Americanization of Sigmund Freud," Journal of American Studies, 1967; Frederick J. Hoffman,

Freudianism and the Literary Mind; Nathan G. Hale, Jr., *Freud and the Americans*, deal with one or another aspect of this subject. The essay on Freudian revisionism at the end of Herbert Marcuse's *Eros and Civilization* does not bear directly on the subject but is extremely suggestive.

11. The Strange Career of Walter Lippmann

Lippmann's career as a commentator on American life and politics stretches over half a century. He has changed his positions many times (while maintaining an underlying consistency, it could be argued); and an analysis of these changes would presumably tell us something about changes in the larger political climate. The high points are *Drift and Mastery* (1914), *A Preface to Politics* (1913), *A Preface to Morals* (1929), *The Good Society* (1937), and *The Public Philosophy* (1955); for more recent opinions, one might consult *Conversations with Walter Lippmann* (1965); see also Clinton Rossiter and James Lare eds., *The Essential Lippmann* (1963).

12. The "New Woman"

She appeared, trailing clouds of controversy, around the turn of the century, the product, perhaps, not so much of feminist ideas as of underlying changes in woman's condition--these latter, I think, should probably be the focus of this essay. Andrew Sinclair, *The Emancipation of the American Woman* (originally published under the title *The Better Half*); Page Smith, *Daughters of the Promised Land*; and Christopher Lasch, *The New Radicalism in America* (ch. 2) discuss this phenomenon, at least in passing. For contemporary comment, see *Harper's*, *The Atlantic*, *Harper's Bazar*, and other periodicals, from, say, 1900 to 1910 (with the help of *The Reader's Guide to Periodical Literature*, which lists articles by subject).

13. Changing Fashions in Literary Criticism: The Case of Mark Twain

Dwight Macdonald, "Mark Twain: An Unsentimental Journey," *New Yorker*, April 9, 1960, is a good introduction. The major documents in the controversy are cited in this article. Papers on this topic should try to relate the ups and downs in Twin's critical reputation to larger cultural changes; in other words, to see them as symptomatic of larger movements of opinion and feeling.

14. The Reputation of Henry James

This topic invites a treatment similar to the last. See Van Wyck Brooks, *The Pilgrimage of Henry James*; Philip Rahv, "The Heiress of the Ages" and "Attitudes toward Henry James," in his *Image and Idea*; Lionel Trilling, *The Liberal Imagination* (essay on The Princess Casamassima); F. W. Dupee, *Henry James*; Maxwell Geismar, *The Cult of Henry James*; and Philip Rahv again, "The Henry James Cult," *New York Review of Books*, Feb. 10, 1972.

15. Waldo Frank
Once an extremely well known writer and critic, this interesting and gifted figure has fallen into oblivion. A study of his career, however, although his career has very little in common with Walter Lippmann's (above), might proceed in something of the same way; this is, offer a chance to examine broader changes in American intellectual life and in American society, over a period of several decades. Frank's main works are Our America (1919), The Rediscovery of America (1930), Chart for Rough Waters (1940), and his Memoirs, edited by Lewis Mumford and recently published by the University of Massachusetts Press.

16. The Harlem Renaissance
What was this movement, why did it arise when and where it did, and what influence did it have? How was the movement influenced by white patrons and by genteel definitions of "culture"? How did black writers seek to escape from these influences? For a beginning see Nathan Huggins, Harlem Renaissance, and Harold Cruse, The Crisis of the Negro Intellectual.

17. Rise and Decline of the Social Gospel
Charles H. Hopkins, The Rise of the Social Gospel in American Protestantism, and Henry F. May, Protestant Churches and Industrial America deal with the period before World War I, and Paul Carter, The Decline and Revival of the Social Gospel, 1920-1940 and Donald Meyer, The Protestant Search for Political Realism, with the twenties and thirties. The Meyer book is by far the best of them.

18. The Humanist Movement
See Irving Babbitt, Rousseau and Romanticism and Democracy and Leadership; Paul Elmer More, Shelburne Essays; Norman Foerster, ed., Humanism and America and Toward Standards; C. H. Grattan ed., Critique of Humanism; L. J. A. Mercier, Le mouvement humaniste aux Etats-Unis.

19. The Jewish Intellectual
Since the thirties, Jews have played an increasingly important part in American intellectual life. How has intellectual life changed as a result? This is a difficult topic, and most of the writing, such as it is, either focuses on the implications for the Jewish community--the dangers of a complete assimilation to American life and the loss of Jewish identity (which some Jewish writers, in turn, have seen as a paradigm of the modern condition in general); tries, on the other hand, to trace the emergence of a peculiarly Jewish literary tradition in America,

or ignores Jewish themes altogether. Memoirs by Irving Howe, Alfred Kazin (Walker in the City), and Norman Podhoretz (Making It) might be a good place to begin. Much could be done with two magazines, The Menorah Journal, which flourished in the twenties and early thirties, and Commentary, a product of the forties and fifties. See also Allen Guttman, The Jewish Writer in America: Assimilation and the Crisis of Identity.

20. The City of the Future
A study of the rise of city planning and the critique of city planning would probably reveal a great deal about how intellectuals tried to deal with the problem of technology and of "modernism" in general. See, for example, Frank Lloyd Wright, The Living City; Paul and Percival Goodman, Communitas, and Jane Jacobs, The Death and Life of Great American Cities.

21. The Nashville Agrarians
A group of Southern poets, writers, and critics, associated among other things with the emergence of the "new criticism," at the end of the twenties turned to more political questions and produced an interesting defense of regionalism and critique of industrialism, the famous manifesto I'll Take MY Stand. See also Louise Cowan, The Fugitive Group; John M. Bradbury, The Fugitives; and John L. Stewart, The Burden of Time: The Fugitives and Agrarians. One of the problems here would be to see whether there was any direct connection between their literary work and their political.

22. The Dream Factory

Movies can be approached in many ways; the one suggested by the heading is to study Hollywood as the creator and purveyor of popular fantasies and to ask what these fantasies reveal about American life. See Martha Wolfenstein and Nathan Leites, Movies: A Psychological Study; Frederick Elkin, "The Psychological Appeal of the Hollywood Western," Journal of Educational Sociology, 1956; Parker Tyler, Magic and Myth of the Movies and The Hollywood Hallucination; Evelyn T. Riesman, "Movies and Audiences," American Quarterly, 1952; Hortense Powdermaker, Hollywood, The Dream Factory; Leo C. Rosten, Hollywood.

23. What Has Television Done to American Society?

It might be advisable, instead of getting lost in generalities, to concentrate on some particular aspect of television, e.g., its presentation of news, melodrama, "comedy," soap opera, advertising. See Marshall McLuhan, The Mechanical Bride and Understanding Media; Robert Shayon, TV and Our Children; Leo Bogart, Age of TV; Joseph T. Klappner, Effects of Mass Communication; Daniel Katz et al.. Public Opinion and Propaganda; W. L. Warner and William E. Henry, "The Radio Daytime Serial: A Symbolic Analysis," Genetic Psychology Monographs (1948), and most important of all, the essays in Bernard Rosenberg and David Manning White, eds., Mass Culture--the best introduction to the popular arts in general. See also Jerry Mander, Four Arguments for the Elimination of Television.

24. Advertising and Public Relations

See Robert Merton, Mass Persuasion; Vance Packard, The Hidden Persuaders; Edward L. Bernays, Propaganda and The Engineering of Consent; Ivy Lee, Publicity. Boorstin lists other works in The Image.

25. The Professionalization of Sports

The secondary literature on sports is generally poor; those who choose this topic will be largely on their own. Much can be learned, providing you already have an analytical framework, from recent memoirs by athletes, the best of which, probably, are Jim Bouton's Ball Four, Jerry Kramer's Right Guard; Dave Megeysy's book on the football Cardinals, and Jim Brosnan's books on baseball. For a broader perspective on games and play and their role in culture, see the superb book by Johan Huizinga, Homo Ludens, also the chapter on "Puerilism" in his In the Shadow of Tomorrow.

26. The Controversy about Mass Culture

The Rosenberg-White reader, cited above, is a good introduction. See also Dwight Macdonald, Masscult and Midcult; D. W. Brogan, "The Problem of High Culture and Mass Culture," Diogenes, winter 1954; Edward Shils, "Daydreams and Nightmares: Reflections on the Criticism of Mass Culture," Sewance Review, 1957; Irving Howe, "Notes on Mass Culture," Politics, spring 1948; Louise Bogan, "Some Notes on Popular and Unpopular Art," Partisan Review, Sept-Oct. 1943; Clement Greenberg, "Avant-Garde and Kitsch," ibid., 1939; Leslie Fiedler, "The Middle against Both Ends," Encounter, 1955, and "Cross the Border," Playboy, 1970.

27. Modern Revivalism

See William McLoughlin, Modern Revivalism, and his Billy Sunday Was His Real Name, for a beginning; also the works listed below, no. 34.

28. The Ideology of Sexual Emancipation: From Heresy to Orthodoxy

O'Neill's chapters on "The New Morality" in his Divorce in the Progressive Era trace the beginnings of the ideology of emancipation-through-sex. In the twenties these ideas began to be widely popularized: see, for example, Margaret Sanger, Happiness in Marriage; Bertrand Russell, Marriage and Morals; Floyd Dell, Love in the Machine Age, and the 1929 symposium edited by V. F. Calverton and S. D. Schmalhausen, Sex in Civilization. Recently those ideas have permeated American society; see, for example, Natalie Gittelson, The Erotic Life of the American Wife; and for the latest "scientific" statements, Albert Ellis, The American Sexual Tragedy, and the studies by Kinsey and by Masters and Johnson.

29. Recent American Conservatism

Papers might focus on the "new conservatism" of the fifties or on popular movements like McCarthyism or the Goldwater campaign. See Irving Crispi, "The Structural Basis for Right-Wing Conservatism: The Goldwater Case," Public Opinion Quarterly, winter 1965-66; David Danzig, "Conservatism after Goldwater," Commentary, 1965; Raymond English, "Conservatism: The Forbidden Faith," American Scholar, 1952; Vincent DeSantis, "American Catholics and McCarthyism," Catholic History Review, 1965; Russell Kirk, The Conservative Mind; Frederich A. Hayek, The Road to Serfdom; Ludwig Von Mises, Human Action; Peter Viereck, Conservatism Revisited; Clinton Rossiter, Conservatism in America; Richard Hofstadter, The Paranoid Style in American Politics; and Kevin Phillips, The Emerging Republican Majority.

30. The Suburban Boom after World War II

The response to this phenomenon--the critique of suburbia--is as interesting as the phenomenon itself; either would make a good topic. Most of the following date from the fifties: William H. Whyte, The Organization Man, part VII; A. C. Spectorsky, The Exurbanites; Frederick Lewis Allen, "The Big Change in Suburbia" and "Crisis in the Suburbs," Harper's, June, July 1954; Maurice Stein, "Suburbia: A Walk on the Mild Side," Dissent, summer 1957; John R. Seeley et al., Crestwood Heights; Erich Fromm, The Sane Society; Philip Slater, The Pursuit of Loneliness.

31. The Rise of Personnel Management in American Industry: From Scientific Management to "Human Relations"

Frederick W. Taylor, Scientific Management; Frank B. Gilbreth, Motion Study; Elton Mayo, The Human Problems of an Industrial Civilization and The Social Problems of an Industrial Civilization; R. J. Roethlisberger and W. J. Dickson, Management and the Worker; R. J. Roethlisberger, Management and Morale; Reinhard Bendix, Work and Authority in Industry; Herbert Marcuse, One-Dimensional Man.

32. The Sociology of Work

Hannah Arendt, The Human Condition; Daniel Bell, Work and Its Discontents; Stuart Chase, Men at Work; William Gomberg, A Trade Union Analysis of Time Study; W. Lloyd Warner and J. O. Lowe, The Social System of the Modern Factory; Andriana Tilgher, Work: What It Has Meant to Men through the Ages; C. Wright Mills, White Collar; Charles R. Walker and Robert H. Guest, The Man on the Assembly Line

33. The Corporate Executive

Chester L. Barnard, The Functions of the Executive; editors of Fortune, The Executive Life (1956); C. Wright Mills, The Power Elite; W. H. Whyte, The Organization Man; Reinhard Bendix, Work and Authority in Industry; W. Lloyd Warner, Occupational Mobility in American Business and Industry.

34. Religion in 20th-Century America

Charles Wright Ferguson, Confusion of Tongues; Will Herberg, Protestant, Catholic, Jew; Herbert Schneider, Religion in 20th Century America; "Religion and the Intellectuals," Partisan Review, 1950; Sydney Ahlstrom, "Continental Influences on American Christian Thought since World War I," Church History, XXVII (1958), 256-72.

35. Feminism and Progressivism

According to Aileen Kraditor (The Ideas of the Woman Suffrage Movement), American feminists became increasingly conservative in the period around the turn of the century, narrowed their agitation to the single demand for suffrage, and used more and more reactionary arguments to justify it. William Leach (True Love and Perfect Union) argues, on the contrary, that feminists arrived at a comprehensive program for the reform of sex and society and that this program anticipated much of progressivism. But since Leach's book deals with an earlier period (the 1870s), the links between feminism and progressivism--if his argument is correct--still remain to be spelled out. This might be done--or the whole issue opened to reexamination--by analyzing the works of Charlotte Perkings Gilman, the major feminist spokesman during the progressive period, particularly Women and Economics and The Home.

36. The Social Thought of Thorstein Veblen

Veblen's main works are The Theory of the Leisure Class, The Theory of Business Enterprise, The Engineers and the Price System, and The Higher Learning in America. One way of approaching them would be to ask whether Veblen should be regarded as a spokesman for progressivism or as a critic of progressivism, a fairly typical progressive or a thinker whose ideas go far beyond progressivism.

37. Hofstadter on Progressivism

In several works (notably in The Age of Reform, The Progressive Historians, and the essays on Theodore Roosevelt and Wilson in The American Political Tradition), Richard Hofstadter interpreted progressivism as the revolt of the unorganized, rooted in a secularized version of 19th-century evangelical Protestantism and seeking to restore an outmoded system of competitive individualism. Is this interpretation helpful, or is it fundamentally misleading? You might want to compare it to the very different interpretations offered by Gabriel Kolko (The Triumph of Conservatism), James Weinstein (The Corporate Ideal in the Liberal State), and Robert Wiebe (The Search for Order).

38. Progressivism and Fabian Socialism

Trace the influence of Fabian Socialism on American progressivism and the similarities and differences between the two movements. H.G. Wells' The New Machiavelli and Graham Wallas's The Great Society are of particular importance. See also the excellent study of Fabianism by Norman and Jeanne MacKenzie, The Fabians.

39. Economic Planning versus Competition
The conflict within progressivism over the central issue of monopoly can be traced in such books as Charles Van Hise, Concentration and Control; Louis D. Brandeis, The Curse of Bigness; George Soule, A Planned Society; J. G. Frederick, ed., For and Against Technocracy; Rexford G. Tugwell, The Industrial Discipline and the Governmental Arts; Herbert Agar, Land of the Free; and David C. Coyle, Brass Tacks. See also the excellent historical study by Ellis Hawley, The New Deal and the Problem of Monopoly.

40. The New Left
As might be expected, the New Left has given rise to wildly conflicting assessments by participants, observers, and historians, among them Kenneth Keniston, Young Radicals; Theodore Roszak, The Making of a Counter Culture; Joseph Conlin, The Troubles: A Jaundiced Glance Back at the Movement of the Sixties; Norman Mailer, The Armies of the Night; Sheldon Wolin and John Schaar, The Berkeley Rebellion and Beyond; Tom Wolfe, Radical Chic and Mau-Mauing the Flak Catchers.

CORNELL UNIVERSITY

HISTORY 521

CULTURE AND TRADITION IN AMERICA

Tuesdays 3-5:30
Andrew D. White House #110

Fall Term 1979
Prof. Kammen
Undergrad. Level

Each week different members of the seminar will be responsible for discussing various portions of the assigned reading. All of the reading assignments are on reserve in Uris Library. All paperback books are available at the Triangle and Campus bookstores. A few copies of the hardcover books are also available for purchase.

Sept. 11 CULTURE AND THE PROBLEM OF TRADITION

Harry Levin, "The Tradition of Tradition," in Levin, Contents of Criticism (1958), pp. 55-66.

Raymond Williams, Culture and Society, 1780-1950 (1958), pp. 3-158.

Robert Redfield, The Little Community, the Peasant Society and Culture (Chicago, 1956), Univ. of Chicago Press paperback.

R.W.B. Lewis, The American Adam: Innocence, Tragedy, and Tradition in the Nineteenth Century (1955), Univ. of Chicago Press paperback.

Sept. 18 CULTURE AND PATRIOTISM IN COMPARATIVE PERSPECTIVE

Wallace Davies, Patriotism on Parade: The Story of Veterans' and Hereditary Organizations in America, 1783-1900 (1955), Harvard Univ. Press.

George J. Manson, "A Renaissance of Patriotism," The Independent, LII (July 5, 1900), pp. 1612-1615. (Olin Stacks AP2 I38++)

Charles B. Hosmer, Jr., Presence of the Past: A History of the Preservation Movement in the United States before Williamsburg (1965), G.P. Putnam's Sons.

W. Lloyd Warner, The Living and the Dead: A Study of the Symbolic Life of Americans (1959), Part II, "The Symbols of History," and Part III, "Symbols both Secular and Sacred," pp. 103-320.

John H. Schaar, "The Case for Patriotism," in American Review, XVII (May 1973), pp. 59-99.

Peter Karsten, Patriot-Heroes in England and America: Political Symbolism and Changing Values Over Three Centuries (1978), Univ. of Wisconsin Press.

Johan Huizinga, "Patriotism and Nationalism in European History," in Huizinga, Men and Ideas (New York, 1959), pp. 97-155. (out-of-print)

Sept. 25 CULTURE AND SPACE IN AMERICA, SESSION I

John Higham, *From Boundlessness to Consolidation: The Transformation of American Culture, 1848-1860* (pamphlet, 1969). Bobbs-Merrill reprint # H-414.

Jeannette Mirsky, *Elisha Kent Kane and the Seafaring Frontier* (1954).

William R. Stanton, *The Great U.S. Exploring Expedition of 1838-1842* (1975).

David B. Tyler, *The Wilkes Expedition: The First United States Exploring Expedition (1838-1842)*, (1968).

John D. Unruh, Jr., *The Plains Across: The Overland Emigrants and the Trans-Mississippi West, 1840-1860* (1979).

David C. Huntington, *The Landscapes of Frederic Edwin Church: Vision of an American Era* (1966).

Herman Melville, *Typee* (1846).

Herman Melville, *Mardi* (1849).

James Fenimore Cooper, *The Sea Lions* (1848).

Elton W. Hall, "Panoramic Views of Whaling by Benjamin Russell," in *Art and Commerce: American Prints of the Nineteenth Century* (1978), 25-49.

Ray B. Browne, "Whale Lore and Popular Print in Mid-19th-Century America: Sketches Toward a Profile," *Prospects*, I (1975), pp. 29-40.

Oct. 2 CULTURE AND THE NATIONAL CHARACTER

Henry Nash Smith, *Virgin Land: The American West as Symbol and Myth* (1950), Harvard Univ. Press paperback.

George Fredrickson, *The Black Image in the White Mind: The Debate on Afro-American Character and Destiny, 1817-1914* (1971), Harper & Row paperback.

David Grimsted, *Melodrama Unveiled: American Theater and Culture, 1800-1850* (1968).

Neil Harris, *Humbug: The Art of P.T. Barnum* (1973).

Oct. 9 USES OF THE PAST, SESSION I (IMAGINATIVE)

Nathaniel Hawthorne, *The House of the Seven Gables* (1851), Signet paperback.

Mark Twain, *A Connecticut Yankee in King Arthur's Court* (1889), Signet paperback.

Alan S. Wheelock, "The Burden of the Past," <u>Essex Institute Historical Collections</u>, CX (April 1974), pp. 86-110.

Peter Shaw, "Hawthorne's Ritual Typology of the American Revolution," <u>Prospects</u>, III (1977), pp. 483-98.

Oct. 16 USES OF THE PAST, SESSION II (HISTORY AND NATIONALISM)

David Levin, <u>History as Romantic Art: Bancroft, Prescott, Motley, and Parkman</u> (1959).

Henry Adams, <u>Mont-Saint-Michel and Chartres</u> (1904).

Henry Adams, <u>The Degradation of the Democratic Dogma</u> (1919), pp. 1-263.

Kathryn K. Sklar, "American Women Historians in Context, 1770-1930," <u>Feminist Studies</u>, III (Fall 1975), pp. 171-84. HQ1101 F32

Jan C. Dawson, "The Puritan and the Cavalier: The South's Perception of Contrasting Traditions," <u>The Journal of Southern History</u>, XLIV (Nov. 1978), pp. 507-614.

Frances Fitzgerald, <u>America Revised: History Schoolbooks in the 20th Century</u> (1979), Atlantic-Little, Brown.

Oct. 30 CULTURE AND SPACE IN AMERICA, SESSION II

John B. Jackson, <u>American Space: The Centennial Years, 1865-1876</u> (1972), W.W. Norton paperback.

Gordon B. Dodds, <u>Hiram Martin Chittenden: His Public Career</u> (1973). Chittenden was an officer in the Army Corps of Engineers, a major figure in the reclamation movement and historian of the trans-Mississippi West. See also Gordon B. Dodds, "Hiram Martin Chittenden, Historian," <u>Pacific Historical Review</u>, XXX (Aug. 1961), pp. 257-69. (Olin Stacks F851 P12)

John F. Reiger, <u>American Sportsmen and the Origins of Conservation</u> (1975). They helped to create state and national parks.

Peter J. Schmitt, <u>Back to Nature: The Arcadian Myth in Urban America</u> (1969), Oxford Univ. Press.

R. Richard Wohl, "The 'Country Boy' Myth and Its Place in American Urban Culture: The 19th-Century Contribution," <u>Perspectives in American History</u>, III (1969), pp. 77-158.

Vincent J. Scully, <u>The Shingle Style and the Stick Style</u> (rev. ed.; New Haven, 1971), pp. 1-53, 143-54.

Charles Eliot Norton, "The Lack of Old Homes in America," <u>Scribner's Magazine</u>, V (May 1889), pp. 636-40. (Olin Stacks AP2 S43)

Ronald F. Lee, <u>The Origin and Evolution of the National Military Park Idea</u> (1973). (pamphlet)

Horace M. Albright, Origins of National Park Service Administration of Historic Sites (1971). (pamphlet)

Henry Glassie, "Meaningful Things and Appropriate Myths: The Artifact Place in American Studies," Prospects, III (1977), pp. 1-46.

Nov. 6 CULTURE AND SELF: THREE TRADITIONS

The Education of Henry Adams (1907), edited by Ernest Samuels, Houghton Mifflin Riverside paperback edition.

Abraham Cahan, The Rise of David Levinsky (1917), Harper & Row paperback.

Carl Sandburg, Always the Young Strangers (1953).

Nov. 13 USES OF THE PAST, SESSION III (AMERICAN REGIONALISM & NATIONALISM)

Paul Horgan, Lamy of Santa Fe: His Life and Times (1975).

Willa Cather, Death Comes for the Archbishop (1975).

Edmund Wilson, "Talking United States," (1936) in Wilson, The Shores of Light (1952), pp. 630-39. (On H.L. Mencken's The American Language.)

Jean Lipman, comp., The Collector in America (New York, 1970), pp. 48-61, 74-89, 234-41. (Essays on Garbisch, Hirshhorn, and Levitt.)

Joan Shelley Rubin, "Constance Rourke in Context: The Uses of Myth," American Quarterly, XXVIII (Winter, 1976), 575-88.

L. Moody Simms, "Folk Music in America: John Powell and the 'National Musical Idiom'," Journal of Popular Culture, VII (Winter 1973), 510-17.

Jack Temple Kirby, Media-Made Dixie: The South in the American Imagination (1978).

Patrick Gerster & Nicholas Cords, "The Northern Origins of Southern Mythology," Journal of Southern History, XLIII (Nov. 1977), pp. 567-82.

Nov. 27 CULTURE AND THE NEW DEAL

Jerry Mangione, The Dream and the Deal: The Federal Writers Project, 1935-1943 (1972), Avon paperback.

A.H. Jones, "The Search for a Usable American Past in the New Deal Era," American Quarterly, XXIII (Dec. 1971), pp. 710-24.

Jane D. Mathews, "Arts and the People: The New Deal Quest for a Cultural Democracy," Journal of American History, LXII (Sept. 1975), pp. 316-39.

Norman R. Yetman, "The Background of the Slave Narrative Collection," American Quarterly, XIX (Fall 1967), pp. 534-53.

Karal Ann Marling, "A Note on New Deal Iconography: Futurology and the Historical Myth," Prospects, IV (1979), pp. 421-40.

Maurice R. Stein, The Eclipse of Community: An Interpretation of American Studies (1960; rev. ed. 1972), Princeton Univ. Press paperback.

Robert Dallek, Democrat and Diplomat: The Life of William E. Dodd (1968).

Dec. 4 THE GOVERNMENT AND NATIONAL TRADITION

William F. McDonald, Federal Relief Administration and the Arts (1969), pp. 751-828.

H.G. Jones, The Records of a Nation: Their Management, Preservation, and Use (1969), pp. 3-171.

Donald McCoy, The National Archives: America's Ministry of Documents, 1934-1968 (1978), Univ. of North Carolina Press.

Lester Cappon, "Why Presidential Libraries?" The Yale Review, LXVIII (Autumn 1978), pp. 11-34.

Alan Havig, "Presidential Images, History, and Homage: Memorializing Theodore Roosevelt, 1919-1967," American Quarterly, XXX (Fall 1978), pp. 514-32.

Dec. 11 ESSAY PRESENTATIONS AND DISCUSSION

Johan Huizinga, "The Task of Cultural History," in Huizinga, Men and Ideas (1959), pp. 17-76.

UNIVERSITY OF MICHIGAN

AMERICAN CULTURE 201: AMERICAN VALUES

Fall 1981

Instructor: John King (3638 Haven Hall/764-6380)

Teaching Assistants: (440M Lorch Hall/763-0031)

Martin Burke
Helen Levy
Barney Pace
Richard Parmater
Zaneta Vargas

Required Books (all in paperback as well as on reserve in the Undergraduate Library)

Max Weber, The Protestant Ethic and the Spirit of Capitalism.
Henry David Thoreau, Walden.
Edward Bellamy, Looking Backward.
Charlotte Perkins Gilman, Herland and The Yellow Wallpaper.
Anzia Yezierska, Bread Givers.
Frederick Taylor, The Principles of Scientific Management.
Richard Wright, Native Son.
Ruth Benedict, Patterns of Culture.
James Agee, Let Us Now Praise Famous Men.
B.F. Skinner, Walden Two.
C. Wright Mills, White Collar.
Jack Kerouac, The Dharma Bums.
Mary McCarthy, The Seventeenth Degree.

Course Description:

> Philadelphia, July 4--President Ford came here from Valley Forge to recall that first Fourth of July as "the beginning of a continuing adventure," unfinished, unfulfilled, but still. . . "the most successful realization of humanity's universal hope. The world may or may not follow, but we lead because our whole history says we must."
>
> New York Times, July 5, 1976

> So we beat on, boats against the current, borne ceaselessly into the past.
>
> Fitzgerald, The Great Gatsby (with indebtedness to Sacvan Bercovitch)

This course focuses upon selected values of the American people from 1830 to the present, a period in which Americans became increasingly aware that their nation was undergoing fundamental change. In the face of this change, various men and women from Henry David Thoreau to Mary McCarthy have undertaken an "inquiry into values," examining their nation, often in the terms of a "jeremiad" or a lament that America has fallen from grace. From the European discovery of America to the present, it has been assumed that America was a special land, a land anointed by God (to the Puritan's mind), chosen as the New Jerusalem, the

(OVER)

landscape in which the millennium would occur. From John Winthrop (a Puritan founder) to Jimmy Carter, America was to become "as a city upon the hill," a beacon shining forth its light for the rest of the world. When that light has dimmed, Americans have denounced their land in a peculiar way, mourning its declension. And then they have written of what America--as "America"--is supposed to be, and of how a person should act, what his values should be, if that person is properly to become an American. They have undertaken their inquiry into values, proposing, often in the form of a utopian vision, a reconstruction of their nation, a return to inherent values.

This course will examine these visions: Thoreau's Walden, Bellamy's Boston in the year 2000, Skinner's Walden Two, Mary McCarthy's celebration of North Vietnam as a new America. It will inquire into the lives of the authors. And it will seek to understand the values these men and women have demanded that America should possess. The visions have changed across time, often under the impact of new technologies, but a core has remained that Americans have continued to celebrate and have continued to discuss, lament, and recreate in an ongoing obsession with the meaning of their land.

A few of the themes and the topics to be discussed include the following:

pastoralism, or the search for a "middle landscape," for an America neither too savage, nor too civilized and therefore "European."

agrarianism, or the assumption that the good American is of the soil, that he is, or should be, a farmer standing upon his own land.

the work ethic, or the assumption that work is, in and of itself, necessary for the character of the American.

alienation, or the fear that new industries, technologies, and modes of production have effaced meaningful work, and therefore the character of the American.

identity, or the quest for a personal reference in a land increasingly huge and unintelligible, the search for self and individual distinction in a land that celebrates conformity to singular ideals.

efficiency, or the need for the American to work (and to play) without waste, without the loss of time, for time, as Benjamin Franklin said, is money.

the American as Adam, or the belief that the American is, or should be, a new man, born again without ties to history, for history, as Henry Ford said, is bunk.

the frontier, or the belief that America has been defined by its frontier, and that without a frontier, or a "new frontier," America will lose what the frontier provided: character traits of individualism, equality, inventiveness, ruggedness, tough-mindedness.

pragmatism, or the need to be "practical," to study only those things that "work," to celebrate only those individuals who do "real" things.

anti-intellectualism, or the fear of the "egg-head," of the "theory," of the idea that appears "foreign," impractical, "un-American."

Course Description (continued):

the melting pot, or the belief that America can--and should--forge its varied ethnic populations into a singular commodity, that to be an American all peoples should lose their past, their history, their color, and become American.

the self-made man, and, more recently, the self-made woman, or the belief that if the American only works hard enough, believes enough, he or she can make it, that from out of the rubble a Rocky can indeed emerge to conquer.

the machine, the garden, the Republic, and the individual, or the need to believe that the Republic and the landscape can survive the machine, that no matter how complex the technology, a Han Solo will drive his spacecraft across light warps as singularly as a teenager drives his hot rod, that individualism, in other words, will still count in America, that one man, in the name of the Republic, can still destroy the Death Star.

Course Requirements:

It is expected that students will complete a mid-term and a final examination, and write a short, five to eight-page paper. The purpose of the paper is to analyze selected readings, attempting to present books thematically rather than to summarize their content. Paper topics should be approved by your teaching assistant prior to the week of (to be determined by your teaching assistant). Papers will be due in section during the week of (to be determined by your teaching assistant).

Grading:

The heart of the course lies in the reading and the discussion section. Thus, in addition to the examinations and paper, an individual's commitment to his or her section will be weighed heavily. Though commitment may be determined by the instructor in a variety of ways, individuals should provide some evidence that they have confronted the readings and grappled with the issues involved. Within each section, consistency of attendance and thoughtful participation should outweigh mere verbosity.

Readings:

THE MIDDLE LANDSCAPE (1830-1880)

Sept. 14-18: Thoreau, chapters entitled "Where I Lived, and What I Lived For," "Economy," "Baker Farm," and "Spring" in Walden.

THE PROTESTANT ETHIC

Sept. 21-25: Weber, Protestant Ethic.

THE NEW LANDSCAPE

Sept. 28-Oct. 2: Bellamy, Looking Backward.

THE ASCETIC ECONOMY (1900)

Oct. 5-9: Taylor, Principles of Scientific Management.

(OVER)

LOOKING FORWARD (1900)

Oct. 12-16: Gilman, Herland and The Yellow Wall Paper.

THE FITTING PERSONALITY (1880-1920)

Oct. 19-23: Yezierska, Bread Givers.

Oct. 23: MID-TERM EXAMINATION, in lecture room (Friday)

FOLK AND CULTURE (1930)

Oct. 26-30: Benedict, "The Pueblos of New Mexico," in Patterns of Culture, and other sections as assigned by your teaching assistant.

Nov. 2-6: Agee, Let Us Now Praise Famous Men, pp. 70-77, 105-54, 181-97, 289-315, and other sections as assigned by your teaching assistar

NATIVE SON (1940)

Nov. 9-13: Wright, Native Son.

SCIENCE AND FAITH (1950)

Nov. 16-20: Skinner, Walden Two.

Nov. 20: Paper due.

Nov. 23-25: Kerouac, The Dharma Bums. (Thanksgiving holiday Thursday and Friday)

WAR AND ALIENATION (1960)

Nov. 30-Dec. 4: Mills, White Collar, pp. ix-40, 189-238, 259-265, 282-286.

Dec. 7-11: McCarthy, "Vietnam" and "Hanoi," in The Seventeenth Degree.

Dec. 17: FINAL EXAMINATION, 1:30-3:30 (in lecture room).

UNIVERSITY OF NORTH CAROLINA

History 154
MWF 11, Saunders 212
Spring 1982

Professor John Kasson
Hamilton 473

POPULAR CULTURE AND AMERICAN HISTORY

Outline and Schedule of Classes and Readings:

1. INTRODUCTION

Aims and Expectations: Everything You've Always Wanted to Know About History 154--But Were Afraid to Ask (Jan. 13)
Why Study Popular Culture? (Jan. 15)
A Typology of Folk, Popular, and Elite Art (Jan. 18)
Popular Culture and Antebellum America (Jan. 20)
Discussion: The Character and Function of Popular Arts (Jan. 21-22)

2. POPULAR CULTURE AS RITUAL IN NINETEENTH-CENTURY AMERICA

P. T. Barnum and the Legitimization of Democratic Amusement (Jan. 25)
The Need for Blackface Minstrelsy (Jan. 27)
Discussion: The Significance of P. T. Barnum (Jan. 28-29)
Reading: P. T. Barnum, Struggles and Triumphs: Or, Forty Years' Recollections (1869), selections.

3. WOMANHOOD, HOME, AND FAMILY IN NINETEENTH-CENTURY POPULAR ART

The Domestic Ideal (Feb. 1)
Nudity and Prudery (Feb. 3)
Discussion: The Cult of Domesticity and True Womanhood (Feb. 4-5).
Reading: Barbara Welter, "The Cult of True Womanhood: 1820-1860" (Bobbs-Merrill reprint)

4. THE SIGNIFICANCE OF SENTIMENTALITY

Death and Consolation (Feb. 8)
"Scribbling Women": Women as Professional Writers (Feb. 10).
Discussion: The Deathbed Scene in Nineteenth-Century Popular Literature (Feb. 11-12)
Reading: Mimeographed materials and Harriet Beecher Stowe, Uncle Tom's Cabin (1852).

5. SENTIMENTALITY AND SOCIAL REFORM

"God Wrote It": Harriet Beecher Stowe and Uncle Tom's Cabin (Feb. 15)
Uncle Tom's Cabin as a Domestic Novel (Feb. 17)
Discussion: Uncle Tom's Cabin (Feb. 18-19)

6. MARK TWAIN AND THE AMBIGUOUS POSITION OF THE POPULAR ARTIST

Mark Twain and His Audience (Feb. 22)
Pudd'nhead Wilson as Popular Art (Feb. 24)
Discussion: Mark Twain and Pudd'nhead Wilson (Feb. 25-26)
Reading: Mark Twain, Pudd'nhead Wilson (1894).

7. THE STRENUOUS LIFE: AMERICAN CULTURE AT THE TURN OF THE CENTURY

The Search for Outlets for the Strenuous Life (Mar. 1)
Civilization's Frustrations and the "Savage Virtues": From The Virginian to Tarzan (Mar. 3)

7. cont.

Discussion: The Virginian and Tarzan (Mar. 4-5)
Reading: Edgar Rice Burroughs, Tarzan of the Apes (1914) or Owen Wister, The Virginian (1902).

SPRING VACATION (Mar. 6-14)

8. THE POPULAR ARTS AND THE EMERGENCE OF A NEW MASS CULTURE

Coney Island and Cultural Revolt (Mar. 15)
The Face of the New Mass Culture (Mar. 17)
HOUR EXAMINATION (Mar. 19)
The White Middle Class Discovers Jazz (Mar. 22)
Styles of Jazz (Mar. 24)
Discussion: Popular Arts and Cultural Authority (Mar. 25-26)
Reading: John F. Kasson, Amusing the Million: Coney Island at the Turn of the Century (1978)
Neil Leonard, Jazz and the White Americans, pp. 29-72 (on reserve).

9. AMERICAN FILM COMEDY BETWEEN THE WARS

Rituals of Adjustment and Dreams of Triumph: Chaplin and Keaton (Mar. 29)
The Comedy of Cultural Subversion: The Marx Brothers and Mae West (Mar. 31)
Discussion of film comedy (Apr. 1-2)
Reading: Robert Sklar, Movie-Made America (1975), pp. 3-32, 67-140, 175-94.
Excerpts from students' "Motion Picture Autobiographies," in Robert Sklar, ed., The Plastic Age, pp. 43-55 (on reserve).

10. THE URBANIZATION OF THE DETECTIVE STORY

From Genteel Detectives to "Tough Guys": The Detective Story as a Cultural Document (Apr. 5)
The Maltese Falcon: Game and Ritual in a World of Chance (Apr. 7)
Discussion: The Maltese Falcon and the 1930s (Apr. 8-9)
Reading: Dashiell Hammett, The Maltese Falcon (1930).

11. THE MARTIAN PANIC AND THE POWER OF RADIO

Easter Monday (Apr. 12)
Hopes and Fears for Radio in the 1930s (Apr. 14)
Discussion: Orson Welles's Invasion and the Cantril Study (Apr. 15-16)
Reading: Hadley Cantril, The Invasion from Mars: A Study in the Psychology of Panic (1940) chapters 1, 4, 7, 9 (on reserve)
Listen to recording of radio play in UL

12. POPULAR ARTS AND RECENT AMERICA

Walt Disney's Wonderful World of Fakelore (Apr. 19)
Rock 'n' Roll and a New Youth Culture (Apr. 21)
Discussion: Growing Up in the Mass Media (Apr. 22-23)
"It Don't Worry Me": Robert Altman's America (Apr. 26)
Conclusion (Apr. 28)
Film: Robert Altman, Nashville (1975)
Reading: Geoffrey Stokes, Star-Making Machinery: Inside the Business of Rock and Roll (1976).

COURSE REQUIREMENTS FOR UNDERGRADUATES*

Regular Preparation and Attendance at Both Lectures and Discussion. 5-7 pg. Essay on Uncle Tom's Cabin (due Feb. 25) or Pudd'nhead Wilson (due Mar 5). Hour Examination (Mar. 19) Final Examination (May 7).

*These requirements apply equally to students enrolled on a pass/fail basis. Graduate students should consult with the instructor at the beginning of the course concerning additional requirements.

All Students are asked actively to support the Honor System in this and all their University work.

UNIVERSITY OF NORTH CAROLINA

HISTORY 269

TOPICS IN AMERICAN CULTURAL HISTORY

Spring 1982

Tuesdays, 2 p.m.
423 Hamilton Hall

Professor John Kasson
Office: Hamilton 473
Office hours: Tues. 10:30-12,
Wed. 1:30-3 and by appt.

The general topic of this course will be Class, Culture, Art, Taste, and Leisure in America, 1830-1920. Our coverage will necessarily be selective rather than comprehensive. We will consider the character of American cultural expression on various levels, the ways in which different groups have exercised cultural influence in American life, and the growing challenge of a new mass culture. Throughout, we will aim to penetrate the cultural categories and to examine the symbolic forms by which Americans in the nineteenth and early twentieth centuries understood and participated in their worlds. While our discussion will center upon the lives of white middle-class Protestants, we will also study Afro-American and Yiddish-American cultural experience.

In tandem with these substantive concerns, the course will explore various methodological issues in American cultural history and acquaint students with a variety of modes of cultural analysis. While the subjects of our study will include prominent individuals and groups from "high" culture, we will also be concerned with "popular" and (to a lesser extent) "folk" cultures. Thus we will attempt to move from the more traditional notion of intellectual history as the discourse of intellectuals to a broader conception of the history of mentalities. We will similarly endeavor to transcend the notion that significant issues can be addressed only in certifiably Great Events by examining apparently commonplace materials (as well as unusual ones) for the meanings they may yield. Such a broadening of conceptions necessitates a broader understanding of available "texts" of cultural expression. We will consider how historians have analyzed not only written documents, literary texts, and the like, but also how scholars have enhanced our understanding of cultural history through attention to paintings, photographs, sculpture, architecture, and other material artifacts, through study of rituals as revealed in drama, play, etiquette, and gesture, and through oral traditions such as folktales, songs, and jokes.

Most of the assigned reading in the course has been published in the last few years; it is material that invites argument and demands appraisal. Class discussions will be devoted to discussion of this reading and to questions of cultural interpretation. In addition, each student should prepare a very brief (1-2 page) critical evaluation of each major reading assignment in advance of class, that will help serve as a basis for our discussion. At the end of the semester students will also be asked to submit a longer essay on a major theme of the course.

Schedule of Class Topics and Readings:

1. INTRODUCTION: AIMS AND ASSUMPTIONS (Jan. 19)

2. THE SEMIOTICS OF CULTURE: CULTURAL HISTORY, THE SOCIAL SCIENCES, AND CULTURAL ANTHROPOLOGY (Jan. 26)

2. cont.

Required reading:

Laurence Veysey, "Intellectual History and the New Social History," and Gordon S. Wood, "Intellectual History and the Social Sciences," in John Higham and Paul K. Conkin, eds., New Directions in American Intellectual History (Baltimore: Johns Hopkins University Press, 1979), pp. 3-41.

Clifford Geertz, "Thick Description: Toward an Interpretative Theory of Culture," and "Deep Play: Notes on the Balinese Cockfight," in The Interpretation of Cultures (New York: Basic Books, 1973), pp. 3-30, 412-53.

Ronald G. Walters, "Signs of the Times: Clifford Geertz and Historians," Social Research, 47 (Autumn 1980): 537-56.

Recommended reading:

Clifford Geertz, Negara: The Threatre State in Nineteenth-Century Bali (Princeton: Princeton University Press, 1980).

Clifford Geertz, "Blurred Genres: The Refiguration of Social Thought," The American Scholar, 49 (Spring 1980): 165-79.

Giles Gunn, "The Semiotics of Culture and the Interpretation of Literature: Clifford Geertz and the Moral Imagination," Studies in Literature (1979): 109-28.

Paul Rabinow and William M. Sullivan, ed., Interpretive Social Science: A Reader (Berkeley: University of California Press, 1979).

3. MARXIST REVISIONISM AND CULTURAL THEORY (Feb. 2)

Required reading:

Raymond Williams, Marxism and Literature (Oxford: Oxford University Press, 1977).

Recommended reading:

Marshall Sahlins, Culture and Practical Reason (Univ. of Chicago Press, 1976).

4. DEATH AND SENTIMENTALITY IN NINETEENTH-CENTURY AMERICAN CULTURE: (Feb. 9)

Required reading:

Harriet Beecher Stowe, Uncle Tom's Cabin (1852).

Martha V. Pike and Janice Gray Armstrong, A Time to Mourn: Expressions of Grief in Nineteenth Century America (Stony Brook, N.Y.: The Museum at Stony Brook, 1980).

Ann Douglas, The Feminization of American Culture (New York: Knopf, 1977), introduction, chapter 6.

Recommended reading:

David Stannard, ed., Death in America (Philadelphia: University of Pennsylvania Press, 1975).

David Stannard, The Puritan Way of Death: A Study in Religion, Culture, and Social Change (New York: Oxford, 1977).

James J. Farrell, Inventing the American Way of Death, 1830-1920 (Philadelphia: Temple University Press, 1980).

Philippe Ariès, The Hour of Our Death (New York: Knopf, 1981).

James Van Der Zee, The Harlem Book of the Dead (Dobbs Ferry: Morgan & Morgan, 197

5. THE SIGNIFICANCE OF SENTIMENTALITY (Feb. 16)

Required reading:

Ann Douglas, The Feminization of American Culture.

5. cont.

Barbara Welter, "The Feminization of American Religion," in Dimity Convictions (Athens, O.: Ohio University Press, 1976).

Recommended reading:

Nancy Cott, The Bonds of Womanhood (New Haven: Yale University Press, 1976).
Kathryn Kish Sklar, Catherine Beecher: A Study in American Domesticity (New Haven, Yale University Press, 1973).
Kirk Jeffrey, "The Family as Utopian Retreat from the City," in Sally TeSelle, ed., The Family, Communes and Utopian Communities (New York: Harper & Row, 1972).
Carroll Smith-Rosenberg, "Beauty, the Beast and the Militant Woman: A Case Study in Sex Roles and Social Stress in Jacksonian America," American Quarterly, 23 (1971): 562-84.
____________, "The Female World of Love and Ritual: Relations Between Women in Nineteenth-Century America," Signs, 1 (1975): 1-30.
____________, "The Hysterical Woman: Sex Roles and Role Conflict in Nineteenth-Century America," Social Research, 39 (1972): 652-78.
____________, Sex as Symbol in Victorian America," Prospects, 5 (1980): 51-70.
Mary Kelley, "The Sentimentalists: Promise and Betrayal in the Home," Signs, 4 (1979): 434-46.

6. TASTE AND IDEOLOGY IN ANTEBELLUM ARTISTS AND THEIR AUDIENCE (Feb. 23).

Required reading:

Jules David Prown, "Style as Evidence," Winterthur Portfolio: 15 (Autumn, 1980): 197-210.
Alan Gowans, "Taste and Ideology: Principles for a New Art History," in The Shaping of Art and Architecture in Nineteenth-Century America (New York: Metropolitan Museum of Art, 1972), pp. 156-87.
David C. Huntington, Art and the Excited Spirit: America in the Romantic Period (Ann Arbor: University of Michigan Museum of Art, 1972).
Neil Harris, The Artist in American Society (New York: George Braziller, 1966), chapters 2, 5, 6.

Recommended reading:

Clifford Geertz, "Ideology as a Cultureal System," in The Interpretation of Cultures, pp. 193-233.
Wendell D. Garrett, "John Adams and the Limited Role of the Fine Arts," Winterthur Portfolio, 1 (1964): 243-55. On the ideological limits Adams attempted to set to his own powerful emotional response to the fine arts.
Lillian B. Miller, Patrons and Patriotism: The Encouragement of the Fine Arts in the United States, 1790-1860 (Chicago: University of Chicago Press, 1966).

7. DOMESTIC TASTE AND SMALL TOWN CULTURE IN POST-BELLUM AMERICA: THE PHOTOGRAPHIC RECORD (Mar. 2)

Required reading:

George Talbot, At Home: Domestic Life in the Post-Centennial Era, 1876-1920 (Madison, Wis.: State Historical Society of Wisconsin, 1976).

Judith Mara Gutman, "Reading Pictures" [review essay of Lesy, Wisconsin Death Trip], Reviews in American History, 1 (Dec. 1973): 488-92.

Roland Delattre, "The Rituals of Humanity and the Rhythms of Reality," Prospects, 5 (1980): 35-49.

Marsha Peters and Bernard Mergen, "'Doing the Rest': The Uses of Photographs in American Studies," American Quarterly, 29 (1977): 280-303.

Alan B. Newman, ed., New England Reflections (NY: Pantheon, 1981).

Recommended reading:

Roland Barthes, Camera Lucida: Reflections on Photography (New York: Hill & Wang, 1981).

John Berger, About Looking (New York: Pantheon Books, 1980).

Susan Sontag, On Photography (New York: Farrar, Straus & Giroux, 1977).

Julia Hirsch, Family Photographs: Content, Meaning and Effect (New York: Oxford, 1981).

The Smith and Telfer Photographic Collection of the New York State Historical Association (Cooperstown, N.Y.: New York State Historical Association, 1978).

William Seale, The Tasteful Interlude: American Interiors Through the Camera's Eye, 1860-1917, (New York: Praeger, 1975).

Kenneth L. Ames, "Material Culture as Nonverbal Communication: A Case Study" [19th-century parlor organs], Journal of American Culture, 3 (1980): 619-41.

_______________, "Meaning in Artifacts: Hall Furnishings in Victorian America," Journal of Interdisciplinary History, 9 (1978): 19-48.

David Handlin, The American Home (Boston: Little, Brown, 1981).

Gwendolyn Wright, Building the Dream: A Social History of Housing in America (New York: Pantheon Books, 1981).

Michael Lesy, Wisconsin Death Trip (New York: Pantheon, 1973).

8. RITUAL, SYMBOLIC INVERSION, AND IMPOSTURE IN POPULAR ENTERTAINMENT (Mar. 16)

Required reading:

Re-read Clifford Geertz, "Deep Play: Notes on the Balinese Cockfight."

Neil Harris, Humbug: The Art of P. T. Barnum (Boston: Little, Brown, 1973), pp. 61-89, 207-31.

Robert C. Toll, Blacking Up: The Minstrel Show in Nineteenth-Century America (New York: Oxford, 1974), pp. 25-103.

John W. Smith, "The Quack Doctor: A Negro Farce in One Act and One Scene," in This Grotesque Essence: Plays from the American Minstrel Stage, ed., Gary D. Engle (Baton Rouge: Louisiana State University Press, 1978), pp. 28-40.

Recommended reading:

Alexander Saxton, "Blackface Minstrealsy and Jacksonian Ideology," American Quarterly, 27 (March 1975): 3-28.

James L. Peacock, "Symbolic Reversal and Social History: Transvestites and Clowns of Java," in Barbara A. Babcock, ed., The Reversible World: Symbolic Inversion in Art and Society (Ithaca: Cornell University Press, 1978), pp. 209-34.

9. AFRO-AMERICAN FOLK CULTURE FROM SLAVERY TO FREEDOM (Mar. 23)

Required reading:

Lawrence W. Levine, Black Culture and Black Consciousness (New York: Oxford, 1977).

Recommended reading:

John W. Blassingame, The Slave Community: Plantation Life in the Ante-Bellum South (New York: Oxford, 1972).

Eugene D. Genovese, Roll, Jordan, Roll: The World the Slaves Made (New York: Pantheon, 1974).

John Vlach, The Afro-American Tradition in Decorative Arts (Kent, O.: Kent State University Press, 1978).

10. THE TRANSFORMATION OF YIDDISH CULTURE IN AMERICA (Mar. 30)

Required reading:

Irving Howe, World of Our Fathers (New York: Simon and Schuster, 1976), selections.

John Corbin, "How the Other Half Laughs" (1898), in Neil Harris, ed., The Land of Contrasts, 1880-1901 (New York: George Braziller, 1970), pp. 159-79.

Recommended reading:

Allon Schoener, ed., Portal to America: The Lower East Side, 1870-1925 (New York: Simon and Schuster, 1967). Includes excerpts from both mainstream and Yiddish press and numerous photographs.

John Higham, Send These to Me: Jews and Other Immigrants in Urban America (New York: Atheneum, 1975).

Werner Sollors, "Theory of American Ethnicity . . . ," and John Ibson, "Virgin Land or Virgin Mary? Studying the Ethnicity of White Americans," both in American Quarterly, 33 (1981): 257-83; 284-308.

11. THE CULTURE OF PROFESSIONALISM IN VICTORIAN AMERICA (April 6)

Required reading:

Burton J. Bledstein, The Culture of Professionalism: The Middle Class and the Development of Higher Education in America (New York: W. W. Norton, 1976).

Daniel Walker Howe, "American Victorianism as a Culture," in Victorian America, ed. Howe (Philadelphia: University of Pennsylvania Press, 1977).

Recommended reading:

Magali Sarfatti Larson, The Rise of Professionalism: A Sociological Analysis (Berkeley: University of California Press, 1977).

__________, "Professionalism: Rise and Fall," International Journal of Health Sciences, 9 (1979): 607-27.

__________, "Proletarianization and Educated Labor," Theory and Society, 9 (1980): 89-130.

Laurence Veysey, "The Plural Organized Worlds of the Humanities," in Alexandra Oleson and John Voss, ed., The Organization of Modern Knowledge in America. (Baltimore: Johns Hopkins University Press, 1979), pp. 51-106.

12. CODES OF BOURGEOIS BEHAVIOR: PUBLIC CIVILITY AND PERSONAL RESTRAINT (Apr. 13)

Required reading:

Selections from various nineteenth-century etiquette books.

12. cont.

Keith Thomas, "The Rise of the Fork" [essay review of Norbert Elias, The Civilizing Process], New York Review of Books, 25 (March 9, 1978): 28-31.

Erving Goffman, "Embarrassment and Social Organization," in Interaction Ritual: Essays on Face-to-Face Behavior (Garden City, N.Y.: Anchor Books, 1967), pp. 97-112.

Recommended reading:

Norbert Elias, The Civilizing Process: The History of Manners, trans. by Edmund Jephcott (New York: Urizen Books, 1978).

Richard Sennett, The Fall of Public Man (New York: Knopf, 1976).

John Murray Cuddihy, The Ordeal of Civility: Freud, Marx, Lévi-Strauss, and the Jewish Struggle with Modernity (New York: Basic Books, 1974).

Arthur M. Schlesinger, Learning How to Behave: A Historical Study of American Etiquette Books (New York: Macmillan, 1946).

13. THE EMERGENCE OF A NEW MASS CULTURE AT THE TURN OF THE CENTURY (Apr. 20)

Required reading:

John Higham, "The Reorientation of American Culture in the 1890's." in John Weiss, ed., The Origins of Modern Consciousness (Detroit: Wayne State University Press, 1965), pp. 25-48; also in Higham, Writing American History (Bloomington, Indiana University Press, 1970).

John F. Kasson, Amusing the Million: Conev Island at the Turn of the Century (New York: Hill & Wang, 1978).

Warren I. Susman, "'Personality' and the Making of Twentieth-Century Culture," in Higham and Conkin, eds., New Directions in American Intellectual History, pp. 212-26.

Christopher Lasch, "The Narcissistic Personality of Our Time," Partisan Review, 44 (1977): 9-19.

Recommended reading:

Roger Callois, Man, Play and Games, trans. by Meyer Barash (New York: Free Press, 1961). A speculative and suggestive essay advancing a typology of play with which to examine the characteristic games of a culture.

Robert Sklar, Movie-Made America: A Social History of American Movies (New York: Random House, 1975). Particularly suggestive in its remarks on the movies and cultural revolt in the earlier twentieth century.

Stuart Ewen, Captains of Consciousness: Advertising and the Social Roots of the Consumer Culture (New York: McGraw-Hill, 1976).

Max Horkheimer and Theodor Adorno, "The Culture Industry: Enlightenment as Mass Deception," in Dialectic of Enlightenment, trans. by John Cumming (New York: Herder & Herder, 1972), pp. 120-67.

14. SUMMING UP (Apr. 27)

BROWN UNIVERSITY

HISTORY 173

Fall, 1983 Syllabus W.G. McLoughlin

THE SOCIAL AND INTELLECTUAL HISTORY OF THE UNITED STATES, 1789-1865

A. Aims of the course:

Karl Marx said, "The mode of production of material life determines the social, political, and spiritual life process in general." This course attempts to demonstrate that sometimes the beliefs and values of a culture play an equally important role in determining the course of history. Events need to be interpreted. How they are interpreted is often a result of the particular religious or social beliefs held sacred by a society. People react in terms of what they perceive to be true--in terms of their understanding of nature, human nature, the supernatural "laws" which govern life. This course attempts to study what Americans have perceived as truth and how they have acted on these assumptions even at the risk of their lives or the loss of their property. In this respect history needs to be studied from the top down as well as from the bottom up for its often the intellectuals, lawyers, scientists, writers, artists, reformers, ministers, educators who articulate and define the beliefs and values upon which people act.

Another way to think about this course is as cultural history--the study of the myths which have shaped American thought and behavior and how these have changed from one generation to another to meet new situations and discoveries. We shall be concerned with "the success myth," manifest destiny, "white supremacy," "male supremacy," "free will," "the agrarian myth," "the classless society," "millennialism," "progress" and other concepts or constellations of ideas which have profoundly influenced American behavior. Our definition of a "myth" would include also the religious beliefs of a people. As Richard Hofstadter wrote, "By myth . . . I do not mean an idea that is simply 'false,' but rather one that so effectively embodies men's values that it profoundly influences their way of perceiving reality and hence their behavior. In this sense, myths have varying degress of fiction or reality." (Age of Reform, p. 24) In addition, myths change their form or definition from one age to the next thus providing continuity and yet incorporating changing circumstances or knowledge.

B. Lectures and section meetings:

The lectures on Mondays and Wednesdays (and sometimes on Fridays) will attempt to do the work of a textbook--providing the general framework and background for the reading and dicussion. The readings will be the basis for discussions during the weekly section meetings. Together, the lectures, readings, and discussions will provide the material for the short papers. (See the "Work Sheet" for a discussion of papers, their due dates, and their function.) Active participation in the discussion meetings is essential not only to give the student a chance to interchange ideas with the instructor about the lectures and reading but also to enable the instructor to discover the extent to which the themes of the course are getting across and to clarify misunderstandings. Active, perceptive, and constructive participation (and questioning) in the section meetings will definitely be counted in the final grades awarded in this course.

C. Books to be purchased:

The attached syllabus is divided into thirteen sections, one per week. All of the books on this list are on reserve in the Rockefeller Library, but students are required to purchase at least one of the books for each week which have a single asterisk(*) in front of them. Generally the books are listed in order of preference and usefulness, but any of the single-starred books will be relevant to this course. Try to choose books you have not already encountered in other courses.

A triple asterisk(***) denotes an essay, article or chapter which is also required reading but which is on reserve at the library.

Please note that the readings vary for the various sections. Consult the instructor for your section regarding the preferred books for purchase and alternative reserve readings each week. This syllabus is for sections 1 and 2.

D. Writing Assignments

The course required three short papers (eight typewritten pages, double-spaced) plus a take-home examination paper. Please consult the "Work Sheet" for information concerning the nature and function of these papers and the dates when they are due. The first paper will be concerned with the reading, lectures and discussions of the first four weeks of the course; the second will be concerned with the second four weeks of reading, lectures, and discussions; the third with the third four weeks.

The take-home examination will be based upon your choice among a variety of topics which are designed to unify the course. This paper will be due on December 15, and like the others, will be an eight-page typewritten paper double-spaced.

N.B. There are very strict deadlines for all of these papers and penalties for lateness. No extensions will be granted so plan them accordingly.

There will be no Incompletes given for this course.

E. Background needed for the course:

Experience has shown that students do not do well in this course who do not have considerable background in American political and economic history at the college level. The course is an upper-level course designed specifically for seniors majoring in History or American Civilization. It is not advisable for Freshmen and Sophomores. AP credit or an advanced prep schools course does not provide adequate background for this course.

While History 51-52 is not absolutely required prior to taking this course, it is strongly suggested. Those who are not History or American Civilization concentrators may need to do additional reading in the standard college textbooks which have been placed on reserve for this course. For a list of these books see the "Work Sheet."

Part One: What Was the Revolution For?

I. Week of Sept. 5-9: Revolutionary Principles and Federalist Attitudes

*Linda Kerber, The Federalists in Dissent
*J. Franklin Jameson, The American Revolution Considered as a Social Movement. N.B. Read along with this, Frederick Tolles, "A Re-evaluation of Jameson" in Esmond Wright, ed. Causes and Consequences of the American Revolution.
***John F. Berens, Providence & Patriotism, Chap. 6 "Politics and Providence."
***John Adams, Political Writings, ed. G.A. Peek, Jr., pp. 145-160; 195-209.
***Richard Hofstadter, chap. 1 of The Paranoid Style in American Politics.
***Michael Crèvecoeur, Letters from an American Farmer (1782) Letter 3, "What Is An American?"

II. Week of Sept. 12-16: Deism, Jeffersonianism, Separation of Church and State.

*Daniel Boorstin, The Lost World of Thomas Jefferson
*Henry F. May, The Enlightenment in America
*Adrienne Koch, The Philosophy of Thomas Jefferson

***Gustav A. Koch, Republican Religion (re-issued as Religion of the American Enlightenment) chaps. 2-3.
***A.P. Stokes, Anson P. Stokes on the separation of church and state in Connecticut and Massachusetts in Church and State in the United States, I.
***Thomas Jefferson, Notes on Virginia; read his views on Indians and Africans
***Reginald Horsman, Race and Manifest Destiny, chap. 6, "The Other Americans" pp. 98-115.

III. Week of Sept. 19-23: The Trans-Appalachian Frontier

*James Barnhart, The Valley of Democracy
*George R. Taylor, ed., The Turner Thesis
*Boynton Merrill, Jefferson's Nephews
*Henry Nash Smith, Virgin Land

***A.K. Moore, The Frontier Mind, Chaps. 9-11.
***Frederick Jackson Turner, "The Significance of the Frontier in American History"
***Wilbur J. Cash, The Mind of the South, chaps. 1-2, pp. 2-60.

IV. Week of Sept. 26-30: The Second Great Awakening, Evangelicalism, and the Scottish Philosophy.

*E.D. Bruce, They All Sang Hallelujah
*Paul Johnson, A Shopkeeper's Millennium
*D.H. Meyer, The Instructed Conscience

***Perry Miller, The Life of the Mind in America, pp. 3-98.
***Donald Mathews, "The Second Great Awakening as an Organizing Process" in American Quarterly, XXI (1969)
***Sydney Ahlstrom, "The Scottish Philosophy in America," Church History, XXIV (1955)

[N.B. The first short paper covering sections I-IV due in class, Monday, October 3.]

Part Two: How Romantic Christian Nationalism Emerged

V. Week of Oct. 3-7: Jacksonianism and the New Entrepreneurs

*John W. Ward, Andrew Jackson, Symbol for an Age
*Marvin Meyers, The Jacksonian Persuasion
*A.M. Schlesinger, The Age of Jackson

***Walter Hugins, Jacksonian Democracy and the Working Class, chap. 7
***George Bancroft, "The Office of the People in Art, Government and Religion," in Joseph Blau, ed. Social Theories of Jacksonian Democracy, pp. 263-273.
***Andrew Jackson, "Veto Message Against Re-chartering the National Bank" (1832)

VI. Week of Oct. 10-14: Romanticism, Transcendentalism

*Paul Boller, American Transcendentalism
*Russell Nye, Society and Culture in America
*O.B. Frothingham, Transcendentalism in New England
*George F. Whicher, The Transcendentalist Revolt

***Ralph Waldo Emerson, "The Divinity School Address," (1837) and "The Transcendentalist," (1842)
***Henry David Thoreau, "Civil Disobedience" (1849)

VII. Week of Oct. 17-21: Perfectionism, Ultraism and Utopian Reform

*Whitney Cross, The Burned-Over District
*R.G. Walters, American Reformers
*David B. Davis, ed. Antebellum Reform

***Eleanor Flexner, Century of Struggle, chaps. 5-6, pp. 71-101
***Whitney Cross, The Burned-Over District, chaps. 10-12
***John L. Thomas, "Romantic Reform in America" in D.B. Davis, Antebellum Reform
***Barbara Welter, The Cult of True Womanhood, 1820-1860", pp. 130-143 in The American Past ed. Irwin Unger, et al.

VIII. Week of Oct. 24-28: Nativists, Immigrants, Factory Workers

*Oscar Handlin, Boston's Immigrants
*A.F.C. Wallace, Rockdale

***Merritt Roe Smith, Harper's Ferry Armory, chap. 9, "Politics and Technology", pp. 252-304
***R.A. Billington, The Protestant Crusade, chaps. 13, 15, and 16 on The Know Nothing Party
***Look at the cartoons in L. Perry Curtis, Jr., Apes and Angels
***David B. Davis, "Some Themes of Counter-Subversion: An Analysis of Anti-Masonic, Anti-Catholic and Anti-Mormon Literature," Mississippi Valley Historical Review, XLVII (1960).

/N.B. The second short paper, covering weeks V-VIII, is due in class, Monday, October 31./

Part Three: Sectional Views of National Destiny

IX. Week of Oct. 31-Nov. 4: Millennialism and Manifest Destiny

*E.L. Tuveson, Redeemer Nation: The Idea of America's Millennial Role
*A.K. Weinberg, Manifest Destiny
*Frederick Merk, Manifest Destiny and Mission
*Robert Berkhofer, The White Man's Indian
*R.A. Billington, The Far Western Frontier

***R.F. Berkhofer, The White Man's Indian, pp. 134-166.
***James H, Moorhead, American Apocalypse, Introduction, pp. 1-22.
***Walt Whitman, "Pioneers, O, Pioneers," "Song of the Broad Axe," "To The States."
***Reginald Horsman, Race and Manifest Destiny, chap. 9 "Romantic Racial Nationalism" pp. 158-186.

X. Week of Nov. 7-11: Racism - North, South, West

*George Fredrickson, Black Image in the White World
*Carl Degler, Neither Black Nor White
*Stanley Elkins, Slavery

***Stanley Elkins, Slavery, pp. 27-80

***William Stanton, The Leopard's Spots, pp. 145-161

XI. Week of Nov. 14-18: Abolition, Anti-Slavery and Black Nationalism

*Aileen Kraditor, Means and Ends in American Abolitionism
*J.B. Stewart, Holy Warriors
*Gerda Lerner, The Grimke Sisters

***Sterling Stuckey, The Ideological Origins of Black Nationalism, pp. 1-30
***David B. Davis, "The Emergence of Immediatism in British and American Anti-Slavery Thought" in D.B. Davis, ed. Ante-Bellum Reform

/Nov. 21-24: There will be a lecture on Monday, November 21, but no sections this week because of Thanksgiving Recess/

XII. Week of Nov. 28-Dec. 2: The Antebellum South

*Eugene Genovese, The Political Economy of Slavery
*Eugene Genovese, The World the Slaveholders Made
*Eugene Genovese, Roll, Jordan, Roll
*Roland Osterweis , Romanticism and Nationalism in the Old South
*George Fitzhugh, Cannibals All

***David Potter, "The Historians Use of Nationalism" in The South and Sectional Conflict

/N.B. The third short paper, covering the weeks IX-XII, is due in class, Monday, December 5. Topics for the final paper will be passed out in class, Monday, December 5./

XIII. Week of Dec. 5-9: The Meaning of the Civil War

*George Fredrickson, The Inner Civil War
*Eric Foner, Free Labor, Free Soil, Free Men

***John C. Calhoun, Discourse on the Constitution or Disquisition on Government
***Abraham Lincoln, "First Inaugural," "Second Inaugural," "Gettysburg Address."

/N.B. The final paper (or take-home exam) on a topic summinng up the course is due in the lecture room at one p.m. on Thursday, December 15/

Fall, 1983

HISTORY 173: WORK SHEET

W.G. McLoughlin

The written work will consist of four short papers (6 to 8 double-spaced typewritten pages) on the following topics and related to the following sections of the reading:

1. Due Monday, October 3 in lecture, on "What Was the Revolution For?" This will be based upon reading, lectures, and discussions for weeks I-IV on the syllabus.

2. Due Monday, October 31 in lecture, on "How Romantic Christian Nationalism Emerged." This will be based upon reading, lectures, and discussions for weeks V-VIII.

3. Due Monday, December 5 in lecture, on "Sectional Views of the Civil War". This will be based upon reading, lectures, and discussions for weeks IX-XII.

4. Due Thursday, December 15 at 1 P.M. in the lecture room, on topics to be announced. This will be based on the general themes of the course from 1789 to 1865 and will include the reading in part XIII. Topic choices for this final paper will be distributed in class on Monday, December 5.

NOTE: Although there will be no three-hour sit-down exam in this course, the Reading Period will be used specifically for the purpose of pulling together the themes and concepts of the course from 1789 to 1865.

A. Function and purpose of the papers

These are not to be research papers nor papers on a single topic but are to be general analytical interpretations of the periods assigned. Their purpose is to make you think about periodization in history, to examine social change and cultural continuities. Historians often use the phrase "Zeitgeist" or "Spirit of the Age." There do seem to be definite patterns to certain periods in history, certain tones or tempers of the times. These usually relate directly to fundamental social, political, demographic, and intellectual developments. They produce "movements", reforms, protests, institutional growth or resistance to change. Above all, they compel the intellectual of the era (and its artists) to re-think their basic beliefs and values about human nature, nature, and the supernatural.

The lectures and reading will raise each week the leading social and intellectual issues of the different periods covered by this course (it is assumed that you are already familiar with the leading political and economic issues). The papers become exercises in the writing and interpretation of history. To do this you will have to evolve your own theory or philosophy of history in order to have a viewpoint from which to analyze and interpret the leading ideas, events, movements and writings of each era. What perspective you choose will govern how you analyze the periods achievements, failures, and confusions. It should also help you to sort out the continuities and the novelties of each era.

History 173 Work Sheet -- Cont'd

The function of the papers is to help you think about the discipline of history and to develop the writing and analytical skills needed to interpret history. For this reason the topics are broad and require you to integrate your reading, listening, talking and thinking as the course proceeds. The papers are too short for complete coverage of all that happens and will be graded on the basis of your skill in highlighting or selecting the more important issues and trends. This requires careful attention to writing skills. History is an art not a science and the art of writing clearly and providing carefully reasoned explanations and adequate documentation is basic to a good paper. A mere descriptive narrative is not sufficient. You must learn to think in terms of posing significant questions and then answering them. To describe "what happened" is only the beginning of writing history--a mere chronicle of events. To write history means to ask why cetain things happened the way they did at that particular time. This means a thorough grasp of the basic forces motivating human action in different social classes, different regions, different religious groups, different ethnic or sex groups. The historian also needs to consider why certain things did not happen that might have; why some movements fail and die out; why others grow in importance and cause major changes or eruptions; why some linger on but do not find resolution. In your papers you should look for the major determinants of social and intellectual change (both within and from outside "America") and also the major reasons for conservative resistance to change.

In the lectures and section meetings we will raise the major explanations for social and cultural change which historians have developed over the years. But it is important to remember that each generation of historians views the same events from different perspectives, asks different questions, utilizes different data. Consequently we will need to think about historiography as we read: from what viewpoint does this particular author view the past; what is his philosophy of history; how illuminating is it and where may it fail to do full justice to the situation? Every history book or article is an interpretation not a definitive, final objective answer. Some arguments (and uses of data) are more convincing than others. It is your task in these papers to make the best use of the data and the work of other historians to provide a convincing interpretation of the era as you see it.

In grading the papers serious attention will be paid to writing skills, to the use of adequate documentation, to the selection of significant questions, to the persuasiveness of the interpretation offered in the light of all the evidence. Being an art, history requires imaginative, creative thinking and analysis. These papers are efforts to help you sharpen your historical insight into the past of the United States. Since you are yourselves products of this historical and cultural ambience, it will require some effort to free yourselves from certain beliefs, values, and preconceptions (not to say prejudices or biases) in order to think clearly about the past. History may judge, but it cannot blame past generations for not acting upon knowledge or feelings that were not yet available to them. We need to know how to think about the past in its own terms, its own language and thought-patterns before we judge it for its failures and successes. In the end, the purpose is not to assess blame or praise, but to estimate what alternatives were available at that time and explain why the majority (or the power structure) of each generation made the choices it did.

* * * * * * * * * * * * * * * * *

In order to help you think about the varieties of ways in which people perceive the world they live in and act upon those perceptions, the following list is provided. Not all of these aspects of thought were of equal importance in every period, but they indicate the complexity the historian faces when he comes to analyze and explain how a whole nation acts. The historian must, to be fair and accurate, be not only well-versed in politics and economics but also in sociology, theology, anthropology, psychology, semiotics, art, literature, and popular culture. In studying American cultural history we shall try to make use of all of these methodologies.

B. IMPORTANT TOPICS IN AMERICAN CULTURAL HISTORY: to be considered in writing the papers.

a. Man's relationship to God: deism, evangelicalism, the decline of Calvinism, revivalism, the Scottish philosophy, Christian nurture, Unitarianism, sectarianism, transcendentalism, immanence, pietism, disinterested benevolence.

b. The higher law concept: natural law, the rights of man, the rights of conscience versus the laws of society, man's God-given reason, the right of revolution.

c. Science and technology: conflicts of religion and science, science and pseudo-science in relation to race and reform, influential inventions or discoveries.

d. Democracy: changing definitions of elitism, aristocracy, egalitarianism, in terms of how much power can be trusted to the common man.

e. Power: conflicts between the national government and the states, farmers and industrialists, capitalists and workers; centralization or nationalism versus sectionalism and individualism: laissez-faire and the general welfare.

f. Man's place in Nature: barbarism vs. civilization, the frontier, nature as a manifestation of God, the myth of the Garden, exploiting nature as a means of progress, the noble savage.

g. Human nature: the sinfulness of man, the perfectability of man, optimism and fear about progress, traditionalism vs. innovation, man as essentially dominated by heart or head (i.e. intuition or reason).

h. Anti-intellectualism: as it is manifested in religious enthusiasm, belief in the supernatural, mysticism, romanticism, transcendentalism, the irrational forces of nature and human nature.

i. The paranoid style: xenophobia, anti-Catholicism, anti-Masonry, and other aspects of national hysteria, the belief that the U.S. should be white, Anglo-Saxon, Protestant nation.

j. Slavery: various views of slavery; various views of Blacks; various approaches to ending slavery; the nature of racism in America.

k. The treatment of minorities: Indians, women, the poor, the foreigners, the Mormons, the insane, children, et. al.

l. Changing definitions of conservative, liberal, radical.

m. Materialism vs. idealism: the Protestant ethic and the success myth; the desire for community, communitarian, utopianism; the loss of innocence, the insecurity over status; self-reliance as looking out for yourself first.

n. America's place in the world: ties to Europe, decadence of Europe, isolationism, spread-eaglism, westward expansion, manifest destiny, millennialism.

C. Suggested Supplementary Reading:

For those who want or need to supplement the lectures by more specialized reading or by reference to general political histories which may provide additional background, the following books and articles have also been placed on reserve.

I. General Reference:

Bernard Bailyn, David B. Davis et. al., The Great Republic (D.C. Heath, Lexington, 1977), Vol. 1.

Richard Current, T. Harry Williams, and Frank Freidel, A History of the United States (New York, 1959), Vol. 1.

Richard Hofstadter, William Miller, and Daniel Aaron, The United States: The History of a Republic (Englewood Cliffs, N.J., 1967)

Samuel E. Morison and Henry S. Commager, The Growth of the American Republic (New York, 1962), Vol. 1.

Edwin Rozwenc, The Making of American Society: An Institutional and Intellectual History of the United States (Boston, 1977), Vol. 1.

II. Intellectual and Social History Reference:

Robert Bellah, The Broken Covenant: American Civil Religion in Time of Trial (New York, 1975)

Daniel Boorstin, "The Place of Thought in American Life," American Scholar 25 (L956), 137-150.

Ralph Gabriel, The Course of American Democratic Thought (New York, 1940)

John C. Greene, "Objectives and Methods in Intellectual History," Mississippi Valley Historical Review 44 (1957), 58-74.

Louis Hartz, The Liberal Tradition and America: An Interpretation of American Political Thought Since the Revolution (New York, 1955)

John Higham, "Intellectual History and Its Neighbors," Journal of the History of Ideas 15 (1954), 339-347.

Richard Hofstadter, The American Political Tradition and the Men Who Made It (New York, 1951)

William McLoughlin, "Revivalism" in E.S. Gaustad, The Rise of Adventism: Religion and Society in Mid-Nineteenth Century America (New York, 1974)

Stow Persons, American Minds: A History of Ideas (New York, 1958).

Morton White, Science and Sentiment in America: Philosophical Thought from Jonathan Edwards to John Dewey (New York, 1972)

HISTORY 173

<u>Questions for section meetings</u>: (Each roman numeral corresponds to the weekly assignment on the syllabus.)

I. a. Considered as a whole, was the Revolution a conservative, or a radical movement?
   b. What were the good and bad aspects of the Federalists' ideology and program for the new nation?
   c. Why did the Federalists gradually lose the support of most Americans?
   d. What were the lasting results of their ideology and program?
   e. What did American lose when it turned against the Federalist belief-value system?

II. a. What is the best way to define deism? Is it a theology? a philosophy of life? a revolt against clerical domination? a social theory?
   b. When was deism most popular? among whom? who were its leaders?
   c. How did deism relate to Jeffersonian democracy?
   d. What were the most valuable and the least valuable aspects of deism and why did it fail to win and hold widespread support in America?
   e. How does Jefferson's view of the ideology and program for the new nation differ from the Federalists' and in what ways was it similar?

III. a. What of the various definitions of "the frontier" is most useful for the purposes of this course?
   b. What is the best way to define and distinguish between what we call "East" and "West" in the years 1789-1825? 1825-1860?
   c. To what extent was the "frontier" more egalitarian? more individualistic? more liberal than the "East"?
   d. To what extent was the frontier "barbaric," "wild," "anti-intellectual," "degenerate," or generally "uncivilized"?
   e. What kinds of people went "to the frontier" and why?

IV. a. How did "the Scottish philosophy" relate to the new religious thought of the period?
   b. Why was the course in "moral philosophy" considered the most important course for all college students?
   c. How do you account for "the deline of Calvinism"?
   d. How do you explain "the Second Great Awakening"? was it mass hysteria? was it an organizing process? was it a shift in beliefs and values?
   e. In what respect did the Second Great Awakening stimulate moral reform?

V. a. Was Jacksonian democracy more backward-looking or more forward-looking? Were the Jacksonians really "the party of fear" and the Whigs "the party of hope"?
   b. From what groups did Jacksonian Democrats get their principal support? and why?
   c. To what extent was Jacksonian democracy related to Evangelicalism, to Romanticism, to Transcendentalism, to Reform?
   d. To what extent was Jacksonian democracy related to urban-industrialism or "modernization"?
   e. What were the Whig alternatives to the philosophy, beliefs, values, programs of Jacksonianism?

History 173 -- Cont'd

VI. a. In what sense was Transcendentalism a local movement (Concord, Boston, Roxbury) and in what sense was it part of a large movement in literary, reform and intellectual change?
b. What are the origins of Transcendentalism (foreign or domestic)?
c. How closely did Transcendentalism ideology resemble what can be called Jacksonian ideology and where did it differ?
d. What did Transcendentalism accomplish?
e. In what respects was Transcendentalism introspective (or even escapist) and in what repsects was it a force for social change?

VII. a. Define the various kinds of "Perfectionism" in America? Is is the same as "ultraism"?
b. What were the various purposes of utopian communities?
c. What is "preservationist reform" and why is it helpful to speak of movements like nativism, anti-Catholicism, anti-feminism, etc. as reforms?
d. What made the period 1830-1860 such a fertile period for reform?
e. Explain the negative and positive results of the reform spirit of the era?

VIII. a. Was opposition to the Irish based more upon their race, their religion or the peasant mentality?
b. Apart from mere prejudice, is there an argument that the great influx of immigrants after 1830 seriously threatened the development of previous hopes and policies for the new nation?
c. In what way did Irish, Scandinavian, and German immigrants differ in their acculturation? Did the melting pot idea work in any respect?
d. To what extent was America "a land of opportunity" for the poor of other lands?
e. What were the major contributions of the immigrants in the years 1830-1860?

IX. a. How did the definitions of "manifest destiny," "God's chosen nation," "the idea of mission" or "the covenant ideal" change from 1789 to 1830 and from 1830-1860?
b. Did the North and the South, the East and West have the same concept of manifest destiny?
c. Did the poor and the rich, the native-born and foreign-born have the same idea of manifest destiny?
d. How did manifest destiny conflict with other ideals on the American ideology?
e. What would have been the best solution to what was called "the Indian problem"?

X. a. What, if anything, is the difference between racism and racial prejudice? or between racial pride and racial bias?
b. What were some of the ways in which black slaves dealt with the problem of slavery?
c. What is the difference between "abolitionism" and "anti-slavery"?
d. Was science purposely or unwittingly a contributing factor to racism?
e. What is the meaning of "Volksgeist" and how does it conflict with the concept of ethnic pluralism in an age of nationalism?

XI. a. What particular strategy for ending slavery would you have devoted your time, money or energy to had you lived in the North between 1830 and 1860?
b. What particular strategies for ending slavery were least useful and why did people support them?
c. What was the most important role black people played in the anti-slavery movement?
d. Was Garrison, in your opinion, a help or a hindrance to abolition?
e. Whom do you consider the most significant (in terms of useful) abolitionist?

XII. a. In what ways was Southern Romanticism different from Northern?
b. Was Southern agriculture more or less capitalistic than Northern and why?
c. How did the South's view of nationalism differ from the North's?
d. What were the principle differences between the Southern and the Northern way of life (apart from the institution of slavery itself)?
e. Was the Evangelical religion of the Southern revivalists any different theologically from that of the North? Was it different in its moral ethic?

XIII. a. At what date did the Civil War become "inevitable" if ever?
b. Do you consider the Republic Party a major cause of the Civil War?
c. Did the war alter the ideology of Northern intellectuals in any significant ways?
d. What was "the Lost Cause" as most Southerners understood that term?
e. How did Lincoln's view of America differ from Calhoun's and Fitzhugh's?

XIV. a. In what ways was the Civil War a turning point or watershed in American history?
b. How could you defend the view that the Civil War, apart from ending the institution of slavery, really changed very little in American development?
c. In what ways was Reconstruction a success?
d. In what ways was Reconstruction a failure?
e. What conflicts in values made Reconstruction an almost impossible task?

Discussion questions relating to the course as a whole:

1. What were the major shifts in the American concept ot human nature between 1789 and 1876?

2. What were the major shifts in the American concept of man's relationship to God?

3. What were the major aspects of science and technology which affected the course of events between 1789 and 1876?

4. Was religion, science, or technology a more important force in American development between 1789 and 1876?

5. How did the definition of "liberalism" and "reform" change in these years.

6. What were the most important changes in man's relationship to Nature?

7. Do Americans seem to you to have been motivated more by individualism and materialism or by nationalism and idealism in the years 1789 to 1876?

8. What were the major ideological conflicts in American culture in these years and how did these conflicts influence American policies and behavior?

9. Did the status of women and/or minorities improve or not in these years?

10. Was the frontier, the resources, the expansion and mobility or America more important than its European heritage and the influx of European ideas between 1789 and 1876?

11. Was sectionalism more or less important than nationalism?

12. Name the three or four more important "myths" governing American behavior (individually and collectively) in the years 1789 and 1876?

13. Name the three or four most important dates or events in the years 1789 to 1865?

14. Name the three of four most influential intellectual ideas and their chief exponents in these years.

15. Was American history moved more from the top down or the bottom up? Or, to put it another way, were intellectuals or movements more important in shaping American life from 1789 to 1876?

BROWN UNIVERSITY William G. McLoughl

Social & Intellectual History of the U.S., 1865-Present

History 174 Syllabus Spring, 1981

Note: Each roman numeral represents one week of the course. "Students should purchase and read one of the books with a single asterisk each week."Copies of all books with a single asterisk are on 24-hour reserve in the Rockefeller Library. Students are also required to read those items marked with a triple asterisk. These are also on reserve in the Rock.

Part I: The Gilded Age, 1865-1895

I. Social Darwinism, the Success Myth and Laissez-faire (week of Feb. 2-6):

*Richard Hofstadter, Social Darwinism in American Thought (1944)
*Daniel T. Rodgers, The Work Ethic in Industrial America (1974)
***William Graham Sumner, "The Forgotten Man" (1883); "State Interference" (1887); "The Absurd Attempt to Make the World Over" (1894); "The Conquest of the United States by Spain" (1898).
Andrew Carnegie, "The Gospel of Wealth" published in The North American Review, June-December, 1889), and "The Advantages of Poverty" published in The Nineteenth Century, March, 1891. These are the first two essays in Carnegie's collected essays entitled The Gospel of Wealth and Other Essays (pub. in 1900 and republished in 1962 by the Harvard Press.)

II. The Populist Revolt (week of Feb. 9-13):

*Lawrence Goodwyn, The Populist Moment (1978)
*Norman Pollack, The Populist Response to Industrialism (1962)
***Hamlin Garland, "Up the Coule" in Main-Traveled Roads (1891)
***C. Vann Woodward, Tom Watson (1938) chaps. 9-10.

III. The Social Gospel Movement and the Third Great Awakening (week of Feb. 16-20):

*Henry F. May, The Protestant Churches and Industrial America (1963)
*James Dombrowski, The Early Days of Christian Socialism (1936)
***Dwight L. Moody in The American Evangelicals, ed. W.G. McLoughlin, chap. 10.
***Herbert G. Gutman, "Protestantism and the American Labor Movement," in Work, Culture and Society (1977) pp. 79-113.
***John L. Thomas, introduction to the Harvard Press edition of Edward Bellamy's Looking Backward.

Part II: The Progressive Era, 1895-1919.

IV. Progressivism (week of Feb. 23-27):

*Morton White, Social Thought in America (1967)
*Allen Davies, Spearheads for Reform (1967)
*Edward A. Purcell, The Crisis of Democratic Theory (1973)
***William James, "Pragmatism" (1907)
***John Dewey, The School and Society (1899) chaps. 1-2.
***Eleanor Flexner, A Century of Struggle, pp. 248-293.

History 174 Syllabus Spring, 1981

Note: Each roman numeral represents one week of the course. "Students should purchase and read one of the books with a single asterisk each week."Copies of all books with a single asterisk are on 24-hour reserve in the Rockefeller Library. Students are also required to read those items marked with a triple asterisk. These are also on reserve in the Rock.

Part I: The Gilded Age, 1865-1895

I. Social Darwinism, the Success Myth and Laissez-faire (week of Feb. 2-6):

*Richard Hofstadter, Social Darwinism in American Thought (1944)
*Daniel T. Rodgers, The Work Ethic in Industrial America (1974)
***William Graham Sumner, "The Forgotten Man" (1883); "State Interference" (1887); "The Absurd Attempt to Make the World Over" (1894); "The Conquest of the United States by Spain" (1898).
Andrew Carnegie, "The Gospel of Wealth" published in The North American Review, June-December, 1889), and "The Advantages of Poverty" published in The Nineteenth Century, March, 1891. These are the first two essays in Carnegie's collected essays entitled The Gospel of Wealth and Other Essays (pub. in 1900 and republished in 1962 by the Harvard Press.)

II. The Populist Revolt (week of Feb. 9-13):

*Lawrence Goodwyn, The Populist Moment (1978)
*Norman Pollack, The Populist Response to Industrialism (1962)
***Hamlin Garland, "Up the Coule" in Main-Traveled Roads (1891)
***C. Vann Woodward, Tom Watson (1938) chaps. 9-10.

III. The Social Gospel Movement and the Third Great Awakening (week of Feb. 16-20):

*Henry F. May, The Protestant Churches and Industrial America (1963)
*James Dombrowski, The Early Days of Christian Socialism (1936)
***Dwight L. Moody in The American Evangelicals, ed. W.G. McLoughlin, chap. 10.
***Herbert G. Gutman, "Protestantism and the American Labor Movement," in Work, Culture and Society (1977) pp. 79-113.
***John L. Thomas, introduction to the Harvard Press edition of Edward Bellamy's Looking Backward.

Part II: The Progressive Era, 1895-1919.

IV. Progressivism (week of Feb. 23-27):

*Morton White, Social Thought in America (1967)
*Allen Davies, Spearheads for Reform (1967)
*Edward A. Purcell, The Crisis of Democratic Theory (1973)
***William James, "Pragmatism" (1907)
***John Dewey, The School and Society (1899) chaps. 1-2.
***Eleanor Flexner, A Century of Struggle, pp. 248-293.

History 174--Syllabus

V. Radicalism in the Progressive Era (Week of March 2-6):

*John Diggins, The American Left in the Twentieth Century (1973)
*Ray Ginger, Eugene V. Debs (1949)
*Upton Sinclair, The Jungle (1906)
***Lincoln Steffens, The Shame of the Cities (1904) read any chapter)
***Lincoln Steffens, "Rhode Island, A State for Sale" in McClure's, Feb., 1905.
***Emma Goldman, Living My Life (1931), chaps 23-25.

VI. The New South (week of March 9-13):

*Paul M. Gaston, The New South Creed (1970)
*C. Vann Woodward, The Strange Career of Jim Crow (1966)
*Albert D. Kirwan, The Revolt of the Rednecks (1951)
***Booker T. Washington, "The Atlanta Exposition" in Up From Slavery (1901) chap. 14.
***Wilbur J. Cash, The Mind of the South (1941) Book III, chap.1, pp. 193-244.

VII. Black People in the North, 1900-1930 (week of March 16-20):

*Gilbert Osofsky, Harlem, the Making of a Ghetto (1963)
*Hugh Hawkins, ed. Booker T. Washington and His Critics (1974)
*W. E. B. DuBois, Souls of Black Folk (1903)
***E. David Cronon, Marcus Garvey (1955) chap. 3, pp. 39-72.

Part III: From the Twenties to the Sixties

VIII. Immigration, Anti-Immigration, and the 1920's (week of March 23-27):

*Roderick Nash, The Nervous Generation (1970)
*John Higham, Strangers in the Land (1955)
*Sinclair Lewis, Babbitt (1922)
***F. Scott Fitzgerald, "May Day," "The Vegetable," and "The Diamond as Big as the Ritz."
***John William Ward, "The Meaning of Lindbergh's Flight" in American Quarterly (1958)
***Paula S. Fass, The Damned and the Beautiful (1977) chap. 2, pp. 53-118.

IX. The 1930's and the Great Depression (week of April 6-10):

*Richard H. Pells, Radical Visions and American Dreams (1973)
*Reinhold Niebuhr, Moral Man and Immoral Society (1932)
*John Steinbeck, In Dubious Battle (1936)
***A. M. Schlesinger, Jr. "Reinhold Niebuhr's Role in American Political Thought," in C.W. Kegley and R. W. Bretall, Reinhold Niebuhr (1956)
***Richard Wright, "Writing for the Communist Party" in The God That Failed, ed., Richard Crossman (1949)
***Wallace Stegner, "The Radio Priest: Father Coughlin," in The Aspirin Age, ed., Isabel Leighton, pp. 232-258.

History 174--Syllabus

X. The Cold War and the Eisenhower Years: 1945-1960 (week of April 13-17)

*C. Wright Mills, White Collar (1951)
*William H. Whyte, Jr., The Organization Man (1956)
*David Potter, People of Plenty (1954)
***Ely Chinoy, The Automobile Workers and the American Dream (1955) chaps. 9-10.
***Richard Hofstadter, The Paranoid Style in American Politics, chap. 2, "Pseudo-Conservatism Revisited," pp. 62-92.

Part IV: From the Sixties to the Present

XI. The Counter-Cultural Rebellion of the Sixties (week of April 20-24):

*Theodore Roszak, The Making of a Counter-Culture (1969)
*Michael Harrington, The Other America (1962)
*Irwin Unger, The Movement: The New Left 1959-1972 (1974)
***Kenneth Kenniston, "You Have to Grow Up in Scarsdale to Know How Bad It Is," in Irwin Unger, et al. eds., The American Past (Waltham, 1971) pp. 420-430.
***Paul Goodman, Growing Up Absurd (1960) chaps. 1-2.

XII. Civil Rights, Black Nationalism, Feminism, Cultural Pluralism (week of April 27-May 1)

*Richard Pollenberg, One Nation Divisible (1980)
*Harold Cruse, The Crisis of the Negro Intellectual (1967)
*David Lewis, King (1978)
*Thomas L. Blair, Retreat to the Ghetto (1977)
*William Chafe, The American Woman (1971)
***Robin Morgan, ed. Sisterhood Is Powerful (1972) pp. 1-70.

XIII. The 1970's: (week of May 4-8):

*Christopher Lasch, The Culture of Narcissism (1979)
*Edwin Schur, The Awareness Trap (1976)
*Marge Piercy, Woman on the Edge of Time (1976)
*Wendell Berry, The Unsettling of America (1977)
***Sheldon S. Wolin, "Reagan Country," in New York Review of Books. Dec. 18, 1980.

HISTORY 174

W.G. McLoughlin
Spring 1982

<u>On choosing the books to be purchased</u>:

Because of the broad nature of this survey course, the differing interests of students, and the fact that some of the more useful books are very expensive or are available only in limited quanities, it has been our practice to offer a choice of books to be purchased and read each week. While something might be gained from having every student read the same book each week, much would be lost by such a restriction. Consequently the University Book Store has on hand two or three books for each of the thirteen weeks of the course. It cannot stock all of these books in equal numbers. Some of the books are out of print and available only in a limited supply of old copies.

All the books ordered for this course are valuable for understanding the themes of this course. Account will be taken of the fact that different students read different books, but basically all are relevant to the themes each week or they would not be listed.

In order to provide some indication of the nature of the books which are available in the bookstore, a brief description of each is given below. It does not matter which book you purchase and read each week. Sections meetings and papers will be based upon general questions concerning the subject matter of the course. No matter which book you read, the material will be relevant and important.

Copies of all the books on this list have been out on 24-hour reserve in the Social Studies Reserve Room so that you may, if you wish, sample the books you do not purchase. In addition, a set of questions relevant to each week's subject matter will be provided which will enable you to participate in the section meeting regardless of which book you choose to read.

It is helpful to discussions if you bring to section meetings each week the book you have purchased, however the discussions will be based upon general themes each week and not upon specific books. You will be able to add significantly to the discussion no matter which of the books you read.

N.B. The reserve room has other items which are required reading each week and which supplement the books available at the book store in important ways (see the syllabus).

I. Hofstadter, <u>Social Darwinism</u>: a general survey of the social uses to which Darwinian thought was put in the Gilded Age both by conservatives and (through Lester Ward) reformers.

Adams, _Education_: one of the greatest American autobiographies tracing the impact of scientific thought upon Adams life as he struggled to be a reformer in an era which worshipped business experience.

Frederic, _Theron Ware_: an insightful novel examining the impact of Darwinism, Liberal Protestantism, revivalism, and an exotic Catholic beauty upon an up-state New York Methodist who tries in vain to get with it.

II. **Wiebe,** _Search for Order_: a wide-ranging analysis of the efforts of American businessmen, government officials and reformers to integrate American life on a national scale.

Rodgers, _Work Ethic_: a general treatment of the Calvinist or Protestant work ethic (the success myth) from the Gilded Age to the 1920's and how that ethic generally lost its meaning and power.

III. **Goodwyn,** _Populist Movement_: the latest and most persuasive interpretation of the efforts of the farmers to come to grips with their changing role in urban-industrialism.

Pollack, _Populist Responses_: an effort to prove that the Populist Revolt was a radical proto-Marxian analysis of capitalism and an effort to overthrow capitalism.

Norris, _The Octopus_: one of the most famous of the naturalistic school of novels which explains the complexity of the farmer's revolt against business oppression in both romantic and Darwinian terms.

IV. **May,** _The Protestant Clergy_: a hardcover but good general discussion of the effort to make Christianity relevant to the issues of urban industrialism; a key study of the Third Great Awakening.

Aaron, _Men of Good Hope_: using short biographical studies, Aaron explains the varieties of reformers in the Gilded Age and the religious roots of social reform.

Kolko, _Triumph of Conservatism_: a controversial study by a New Left historian of the con-

Cont'd

servative aspects of Progessive Reform.

V. White, Social Thought: a perceptive discussion of the leading intellectuals of the Progressive Era and how they challenged the prevailing assumptions in our basic institutions.

Davis, Spearheads: a general treatment of Progressive reformers explaining the motives and results of their efforts to cope with urban-industrial problems.

Ginger, Debs: a biography of the most popular radical of the Progressive Era which explains the surprising success of socialism in that period.

VI. Gaston, New South Creed: a study of the attitudes, beliefs, values and myths of "the New South" as it became industrialized.

Cash, Mind of the South: a colorful account of the rise of the New South by a Southerner who was not a professional historian but had a genuine "feel for" his region.

Kirwan, Revolt of the Rednecks: how the red neck dirt farmers rebelled against the "bourbon" landholders and industrialists of the New South

Hawkins, Washington: a series of essays on the role of Booker T. Washington, his efforts to cope with racism and the black critics of his program.

DuBois, Souls of Black Folk: the classic study of "the twoness" of black Americans by one of the great spokesmen for their struggles.

VIII. Nash, Nervous Generation: perceptive new analysis of the social and intellectual trends of the twenties which challenges the stereotypical view of the "Jazz Age."

Allen, Only Yesterday: the classic view of the twenties which generated the stereotype of "The Jazz Age."

Lewis, Babbitt: the famous novel about the attitudes of the small businessman in the days of Harding and Coolidge.

IX. Pells, Radical Visions: a survey of the various intellectuals

Cont'd

and reformers who offered answers to "the Great Depression" and its causes.

Steinbeck, In Dubious Battle: the famous novel about a strike of applepickers led by a Communist in California.

Niebuhr, Moral Man and Immoral Society: the key book by the key intellectual of Christian realism--a Christian Marxist in the thirties.

X. **Potter,** People of Plenty: a leading historian explains the effects of prosperity, consumerism and the advertisers upon post-war America.

Whyte, Organization Man: a Fortune editor studies (rather critically) the role of the white-collar class in post-war America.

Rovere, McCarthy: a major journalist looks at the Senator who led the second great "Red Scare" and tries to explain the paranoia of Americans in the 1950's.

XI. **Lewis,** King: the best biography of the successes and failures of the leader of the Civil Rights movement of the sixties.

Malcolm X: fascinating autobiography of a black Muslim who scared the daylights out of white America in the sixties.

Kerouac, On the Road: a semi-autobiogrpahical journey through America by the leading writer of the Beat Generation when American young people were discovering drugs and rebelling against white-collar suburbia.

XII. **Roszak,** Counter-Culture: the best study of the social and intellectual revolt of the 1960's and the start of the Fourth Great Awakening.

Harrington, Other America: the study of poverty and the failure of the welfare state in affluent America which started Kennedy and Johnson on "the War on Poverty."

Piercy, Woman on the Edge of Time: a double-edged novel about a poor woman struggling to maintain her sanity in a mental hospital and her vision of a better life in the distant future.

XIII. Lasch, Narcissism: a study of "the me-generation" of the seventies.

Sale, Power Shift: what it means for American society to have the economic power center of shift from the old Northeastern establishment to the Southern Rim (or Sunbelt).

Heilbroner, Human Prospect: an apocalyptic view of America's future by an intellectual liberal.

Rothman, Woman's Proper Place: a good recent study of the movement for women's rights which helps to explain why ERA is having such a hard time getting passed.

History 174 W.G. McLoughlin

STUDY QUESTIONS Spring, 1981

The following questions should be kept in mind while doing each week's reading. These questions will form the focus of the section meetings and students should come to section meetings prepared to discuss these questions in a lively way.

I. Social Darwinism (week of Feb. 2-6)

1. What are the strengths and weaknesses of the Social Darwinism of Spencer and Sumner and how wide an influence did this ideology have in the Gilded Age?

2. What are the strengths and weaknesses of the Reform Darwinism of Lester Ward and the Social Gospelers and how influential was it in the Gilded Age?

3. What is "The Gospel of Wealth" and how does it differ from "The Success Myth?"

4. What earlier American ideas did Darwinism confirm or refute? Did the acceptance of Darwinism necessarily require the abandonment of older ideas which conflicted with it?

5. What were the most successful ways in which Darwinism was reconciled with Christianity and what were the least successful?

II. The Populist Revolt (week of Feb. 9-13)

1. In what ways were the Populists backward-looking and in what ways forward-looking?

2. How was Populism similar to and/or different from Jacksonian reform movements?

3. What are some of the varieties of Populism (i.e., in their diagnosis the problems of the farmer; in their solutions; in their regional tactics?)

4. What happened to Populism after 1896? Did it survive in any form? Was it anti-semitic?

5. Why do some people call Jimmy Carter, Sen. Joe McCarthy, George Wallace and Huey Long "populists"? What has the term come to mean?

III. The Social Gospel Movement (week of Feb. 16-20)

1. What were the principal roots of the Social Gospel movement prior to 1865? Was it a reform movement?

2. What role did science, Labor unrest, religious confusion, and millennial reform ideals play in the rise of the Social Gospel movement?

3. What were the principle objections to the movement by Evangelicals, businessmen, labor leaders, and immigrants?

4. What did the movement accomplish socially, intellectually, religiously?

5. What were the failures of the movement?

IV. Progressivism (week of Feb. 23-27)

1. In what ways was Progressivism backward and forward-looking?

2. Historians differ as to the motivations of Progressives. What do you think they were hoping to achieve, and why?

3. What were the principle achievements and failures of Progressivism?

4. Is Kolko right that Progressivism was really "The Triumph of Conservatism"?

5. Who were the main critics of Progressivism at the time, and what was their criticism?

V. Radicalism in the Progressive Era (week of March 2-6)

1. Is it correct to see Debsian Socialism as anti-Marxist? Why did it have more appeal than the socialism of Daniel De Leon?

2. What accounts for the appeal of anarchism in this era?

3. What is the essential aspect of radicalism for Christopher Lasch?

4. How radical were the workers, the intellectuals, the Social Gospelers?

5. What roots did radicalism have in the American past?

VI. The New South (week of March 9-13)

1. How did the creed of "the New South" manage to co-exist with the creed of "the Lost Cause"?

2. Was the New South operating on any different principles from those of the North in this period?

3. To what extent was the New South in the hands of the North and to what extent was it a rival to the North?

4. Were class divisions any different in the New South from the Old South or from those in the North at this period?

5. How did black people fare in the New South as compared to' exploited wage workers and poor farmers in the North?

VII. <u>Black People in the North</u> (Week of 16-20)

1. What did blacks gain by moving North and what did they lose?

2. What made Harlem such an important place for blacks in the North?

3. Why was there such division among black intellectuals in these years and which ones seem to have been more right in the long run?

4. What was the relation of blacks to the Progressive movement?

5. Why were there so few black radicals, socialists, anarchists, etc.?

VIII. <u>Immigration, Anti-Immigration and the 1920's</u> (week of March 23-27)

1. How did the xenophobia of the post-war era differ from that of the early 19th century and what is the significance of the founding of the ACLU in 1922?

2. What impact did World War I and the Russian Revolution have on American labor, American intellectuals, American political thinkers, the American middle class? Which was the more important force?

3. Matching the arguments for disillusion, for optimism, for prosperity, and for frustration in the 1920's, what is the best way to characterize the decade?

4. What did George F. Babbitt, Mencken, Fitzgerald, Lindbergh, Mary Pickford and Coolidge have in common?

5. What were the main achievements and failures of the 1920's?

IX. <u>The 1930's, the New Deal, the Great Depression:</u> (week of April 6-10)

1. Was the Crash a more important watershed for American social and intellectual thought than World War I and why or why not?

2. What accounts for the emergence of "the radical right" in America in the 1930's? or did it start earlier?

3. Why didn't Americans adopt socialism in the 1930's?

4. Were most intellectuals basically more radical than F.D.R.? Why or why not?

5. What were the main schocks to the American ideology in the 1930's?

X. The Cold War and the Eisenhower Years (week of April 13-17)

1. In what ways were the years 1945-1960 similar to those of the post World War I years and in what ways different?

2. Why is this era described as "the Age of Affluence," "the Age of Anxiety," and the age of "the End of Ideology?"

3. What were the differences between the neo-conservatives and the neo-liberals of these years?

4. In what sense is Eisenhower a good symbol for the era and who might you suggest as a more appropriate symbol or spokesperson for it?

5. Did the era sustain the American Dream or mark its final demise?

XI. The Counter-Cultural Rebellion of the Sixties (week of April 20-24)

1. Were the major sources of the counter-culture religious, social, political, philosophical or economic? and how did the New Left relate to the Old Left?

2. When did the counter-culture really begin and what did it signify? What is the significance, for example, of the shift from civil rights to anti-war protest?

3. Did the counter-culture accomplish anything useful or was it essentially a negative movement? Were the "hippies" more important than rural communes?

4. What roles did the intellectuals, writers, politicians, labor leaders take toward this movement (or can it be called "a movement" at all)?

5. Looking back from 1979, who appear now to have been the most important figures and what were the most important books, events, and insights?

XII. Civil Rights, Black Nationalism, and Feminism (week of April 27-May 1)

1. Who were the most important black leaders of the last twenty years and why?

2. Has the civil rights movement been a success or a failure?

3. How far has feminism come and how far has it yet to go? And which of its leaders seems to have been most significant or effective? and why?

4. Why were Native Americans and Asian-Americans so late in

joining the movement for equal rights?

5. Have women's rights and the rights of ethnic minorities much in common? Have these two movements been hindered more by outside opposition or by their own internal conflicts, contradictions, and ambivalences?

XIII. <u>Escapism, Ecological Action and Religious Awakening</u> (week of May 4-8)

1. Has the ecology movement any future as a movement or have the energy crunch and inflation effectively killed it?

2. What makes people see the 1970's as "the me generation" or the era of hedonism and narcissim? Is this a significant aspect of the 1970's?

3. In what sense is there a religious awakening under way and what predictions would you make as to its future? What religious ideas do you think are most important now?

4. What was the reason for the interest in the occult, magic, Satanism, ESP, UFO's, and other non-empirical forces in the years 1965-1975.

5. What is the role of drugs, sex, professional sports, and rock music in contemporary America? Are they essentially "opiates of the masses" or sources of new energies for reform?

W.G. McLoughlin

WORKSHEET

History 174 - Spring 1982

The written work in this course will consist of three short papers and a final-exam paper (to be done during Reading Period). These papers (including the final-exam paper) should be no more than eight double-spaced typewritten pages each. They do not require any reading or research beyond the regular assignments on the syllabus. While footnotes are not necessary in these papers, it is important to identify the source of any quotations and credit should be given to any author whose work you paraphrase.

Dates and subjects of papers:

First paper due in lecture on Monday, March 1: topic, "The Gilded Age, 1865-1895." This paper should be based on the reading lectures, and section meetings for I-III on the syllabus.

Second paper due in lecture on Monday March 29: topic, "The Progressive Era, 1895-1919." This paper should be based on the reading, lectures, and section meetings for IV-VII on the syllabus.

Third paper due in lecture on Monday, May 3: topic, "From the Twenties to the Sixties." This paper should be based on the reading, lectures, and section meetings for VIII-XI on the syllabus.

Final-Exam Paper due one p.m. Monday, May 17 in lecture room; This paper is to be done during the Reading Period. A choice of topics for these papers will be given out prior to Reading Period. There will be some voluntary section meetings during Reading Period to discuss and review the themes of the course in conjunction with writing the Final-Exam Paper.

The function and purpose of the first three papers is described below. The function and purpose of the Final-Exam Paper will be described when the topics for that paper are distributed.

Function and purpose of papers:

These are not to be research papers but, as indicated, should grow out of the regular weekly reading, lectures, and discussions. The function and purpose is to help you integrate your reading, listening, talking and thinking in concrete form.

The topics are purposely broad and undefined. In a survey course such as this, where so much material has to be covered in so short a time, it is more important to grasp the major social and intellectual issues and trends than to concentrate upon any single topic or issue. The papers are to help you integrate, to correlate, to synthesize, and to organize your thinking about each of the three periods. (The final-exam should pull the whole course together.) It is not enough simply to describe what happened in each period; that is a mere chronicle. What is needed is an insightful explanation of why it happened. Papers give you a chance to exercise your wits and imagination in the field of historical explanation--notably in terms of cause and effect, action and reaction. There is no single correct way to write history and historians have no clearly established right or wrong interpretations. But it is important in studying, thinking about, writing about the past to arrive at some usuable method for explaining the shape it took. One purpose of these papers is to give you the opportunity to test your historical insight and analytical ability.

History may be more art than science, but it does have rules about the use and treatment of evidence. Grades will be based not on any "right" or "wrong" answer but on how well you document your analysis with concrete evidence, and how consistent your explanation is with your own criteria for historical development, and how many different but important factors you integrate into your analysis. The aim of the writer of history is to convince the reader that he has correctly understood and interpreted what happened and why.

Suggested Supplementary Reading:

For those who want or need to supplement the lectures by more specialized reading or by reference to general political histories which may provide additional background, the following books and articles have also been placed on reserve.

I. General Reference:

Richard Current, T. Harry Williams, and Frank Freidel, *A History of the United States* (New York, 1959) Vol. I.

Richard Hofstadter, William Miller, and Daniel Aaron, *The United States: The History of a Republic* (Englewood Cliffs, N.J., 1967)

Samuel E. Morrison and Henry S. Commager, *The Growth of the American Republic* (New York, 1962), Vol. I.

Edwin Rozwenc, *The Making of American Society: An Institutional and Intellectual History of the United States* (Boston, 1972), Vol. I.

II. Intellectual and Social History Reference:

Robert Bellah, *The Broken Covenant: American Civil Religion in Time of Trial* (New York, 1975)

Daniel Boorstin, "The Place of Thought in American Life," *American Scholar* 25 (1956), 137-150.

Ralph Gabriel, The Course of American Democratic Thought (New York, 1940)

John C. Greene, "Objectives and Methods in Intellectual History," Mississippi Valley Historical Review 44 (1957), 58-74.

Louis Hartz, The Liberal Tradition and America: An Interpretation of American Political Thought Since the Revolution (New York, 1955)

John Higham, "Intellectual History and Its Neighbors," Journal of the History of Ideas 15 (1954), 339-347.

Richard Hofstadter, The American Political Tradition and the Men Who Made It (New York, 1951)

Stow Persons, American Minds: A History of Ideas (New York, 1958)

Morton White, Science and Sentiment in American Philosophical Thought from Jonathan Edwards to John Dewey (New York, 1972)

UNIVERSITY OF PENNSYLVANIA

HISTORY 200

Junior-Senior Seminar

AMERICAN INTELLECTUAL HISTORY . . . . 308 College Hall
Wednesday 1 - 3

Dr. Bruce Kuklick
Office X 6252

In this course we will be carefully reading a number of texts that I hope are interesting and also illustrate an American intellectual tradition. We will be concerned with the ideas in the texts themselves, the tradition of ideas the texts form, and the social and personal contexts that produced them.

I will conduct the class myself for the first two weeks (on Jonathan Edwards) with informal lectures and discussions. For the rest of the semester I'll be demanding more of you by way of discussion. To achieve this aim each of you, each week, should write a two-page (500 word) paper on the week's reading. It will be due before the class meeting, and won't be accepted thereafter. (Those of you who miss the paper or the class may make up the work by writing a similar paper on another non-assigned text).

With the below list of assignments I've also included a list of questions that might help you focus your papers and ideas.

Grades will depend on papers and class discussion.

Books are available at the Penn Book Center (37th and Walnut); *ones are on reserve in Van Pelt.

Weeks 1 and 2: Jonathan Edwards, Selections edited by Faust and Johnson (Hill and Wang). Read as much of the "Introduction" as you can to give yourself a sense of Edwards; then

Week 1: pp. 46-72, 92-111; 155-172.

Week 2: 206-254, 263-309; 316-339; 349-371.

What kind of person do you think Edwards was? Do you think Edward's ideas glorify god or denigrate humanity? What happens when someone is saved? What is it like to taste the sweetness of holiness? Why do you think people believed ideas like this?

Week 3: Benjamin Franklin, Autobiography (Modern Library)

What are the differences in the ideas of Franklin and Edwards? Which one seems to you to be more "American"? In what sense is Franklin's thought? What social changes may have led to the differences between the ideas of the two men?

Week 4: W. E. Channing, Unitarian Christianity*

How is Channing's religion "rational" in contrast to Edwards? How does Channing defend free will? What prompts him to be so optimistic about humanity? Is his optimism like that of Franklin? Why do you think Emerson described Unitarianism as a "cold corpse" religion?

Week 5: Ralph Waldo Emerson, Emerson's Nature, ed. Sealts and Ferguson (Southern Illinois)

Is Emerson like or unlike Edwards? Why do you think Emerson was so popular in the nineteenth century? How scientific a thinker is Emerson? Do you think Emerson's religion is different from the "corpse cold" Unitarianism? Which religion is most rational: Edward's, Channing's, or Emerson's? Which man is most rational?

Week 6: Herman Melville, Great Short Works (Harper & Row). Read "Billy Budd", "Bartleby", Beneto Cereno" and whatever else strikes your fancy.

or

Hawthorne, Selected Short Stories (Fawcett)

How are the themes of these writers of fiction like those of the other people we've read? What Calvinist ideas survive in Hawthorne and Melville? What Emersonian ideas do they embody? What are their ideas about truth and reality? What do Hawthorne and Melville make of science and technological progress? Why?

Week 7: Harold Frederic, The Damnation of Theron Ware

or

Mark Twain, A Connecticut Yankee

What is the role of religion in these books? How has technology, according to these authors, transformed American life? Is Ware like Edwards? What sort of pessimism is there in Frederic and Melville? What sort of optimism in Twain and Emerson? Are the writers in week 6 or 7 better?

Week 8: William James, Pragmatism (Hackett Publishing Co.)

Compare Franklin and James. Does James mediate the "tough" and "tender" minded? What role does James give to religion? Compare James to Edwards. Is James more or less optimistic than Melville? What role does James give to science? Is pragmatism true?

Week 9: John Dewey, The Child and the Curriculum and the School and Society (one volume)

The Quest for Certainty*, chapter 10.

What do Dewey and James have in common? What sort of connections are there between the religious and scientific interests of the eighteenth and nineteenth century writers we have discussed and the themes you find in Dewey? Do you think Dewey believes in "social control"? What would (or does) it mean to have a scientific politics, ethics, and educational system? Is the world redeemed for Dewey as it is for Edwards? If so, how? Would the Connecticut Yankee be impressed by Dewey?

Week 10: Willa Cather, My Antonia

or

Randolph Bourne, War and the Intellectuals (Harper)

What does Bourne think of James and Dewey? Why? Is Cather a pragmatist? How is her vision of things like or unlike Dewey's? How are Cather and Bourne alike? Why is Bourne so angry and Cather so romantic?

Week 11: Walter Lippman, Drift and Mastery*

or

Walter Lippman, The Good Society*

How has Lippman changed his mind between the earlier and the later book? What was going on in the world that might have led him to change it? Do you see similar changes in Dewey in the same period? How do you think Lippman feels about "drift" in the 1930's? What is his vision of the "Good Society" in the 1910's?

Week 12: Ruth Benedict, Patterns of Culture (Houghton Mifflin)

Does this sort of cultural anthropology have a moral message? If so, what? How does Benedict's work relate to James, Dewey, Lippman? The book is about "primitive" societies; if you consider when it was written, is it also about contemporary society? How does Benedict fit into the sorts of ideas about social science that we have been discussing?

Week 13: Walt Whitman Rostow, The Stages of Economic Growth

or

Arthur Miller, Death of a Salesman

Compare Rostow to Dewey and Benedict. What role does religion play in his thought? How are his ideas like (or unlike) those of the Connecticut Yankee? What would Melville say about Rostow? What would Rostow say about Willy Loman? How is Willy like Franklin? What is the American dream for Willy? What does Miller think is wrong with that dream?

UNIVERSITY OF VIRGINIA

HIUS 753, Graduate Colloquium

Basic Traditions of American Thought — Professor Ross

1. Introduction

Part I: Puritanism

2. Perry Miller, The New England Mind: The Seventeenth Century.

   Report: How have historians since Miller revised his account of the Puritan mind?

3. Sacvan Bercovitch, The Puritan Origins of the American Self. Read the text of Cotton Mather's Nehemias Americanus, pp. 187-205 before, and again after, you read the body of the book.

   Report: How does one "explicate" a text in American intellectual history?

4. Wm. McLoughlin, Revivals, Awakenings and Reform.

   Report: In what ways have historians related the Puritan tradition to later American culture?

Part II: Republicanism

5. J.G.A. Pocock, The Machiavellian Moment, Introduction, pp. 3-87, 156-218, 329-333. The pages assigned purposely overrun chapters so as to provide summaries of the material skipped.
   J.H. Hexter, Review of The Machiavellian Moment, History and Theory, XVI (1977), 306-36.

   Report: What assumptions does Pocock make about the nature of ideas and their function in history?

6. Pocock, Machiavellian Moment, pp. 333-552.

   Report: Precisely in what ways, according to Pocock, does the civic humanist tradition remain at the foundation of American politics after the Revolution?

7. Marvin Meyers, The Jacksonian Persuasion; Daniel Howe, The Political Culture of the American Whigs.

   Report: Can Pocock's analysis of republicanism support a synthetic view of American politics?

Part III: Romanticism

8. M.H. Abrams, Natural Supernaturalism, ch. 1, 3 to p. 172, 4 to p. 225, 6-8.
   Perry Miller, The Transcendentalists, Introduction
   R.W. Emerson, "Nature."

   Report: Can romanticism, as Abrams defines it, be related to the variety of liberal/evangelical/perfectionist heirs of Puritanism?

9. **Leo Marx, The Machine in the Garden**

   Report: What is the historiographical status of American studies analyses of myth and symbol, like those of Marx and Bercovitch?

10. **Henry Adams, The Education of Henry Adams**

    Report: Does Adams emerge from this text as a late Puritan, a late Republican, or a late Romantic?

Part IV: Scientism

11. **Donald Fleming, John Wm. Draper and the Religion of Science**

    Report: What are the historical sources of nineteenth century scientism?

12. **Morton White, Social Thought in America**

    Report: How have historians defined the change in American thought which occured between 1880 and 1920?

13. **Thomas Haskell, The Emergence of Professional Social Science**

    Report: What cultural implications have historians drawn from the triumph of scientism in the twentieth century?

Conclusion: On Intellectual History

14. John Higham and Paul Conkin (eds.), New Directions in American Intellectual History, Essays by Veysey, Wood, Hollinger, Welter and Murphy.
    Newsletter, Intellectual History Group, Exchange between Diggins, Haskell, Ross and Veysey
    Dominick La Capra, "Rethinking Intellectual History and Reading Texts," History and Theory, XIX, no. 3, 245-76.

<u>Readings</u>: All required books are available in low cost editions at Newcomb Hall bookstore. All required books and articles are on reserve in the Reserve Reading Room of Alderman Library.

<u>Requirements</u>: Besides the required reading for each week, there are the following requirements for the colloquium:

1. All students must hand in a typewritten <u>precis</u> of Pocock's <u>Machiavellian Moment</u>, in two parts, about four pages each, due in class.

2. Each week, one student will present a paper of at least ten pages in length, on the question labelled "Report" for the week. In some cases the question is historiographic and based largely on additional reading; in some cases the question is analytical and relies heavily on a close reading of the required texts; in almost all cases the question requires both analysis and additional reading. Once report topics are assigned, students should see me as soon as possible to get suggestions for additional reading. The papers must be given to the department secretaries by 9 a.m. on the Friday preceeding the colloquium. The secretaries will then xerox a number of copies and leave them on the mantel in Room 101 for all students to read prior to the colloquium meeting.

3. For all students, the question posed each week should be one focus of your thinking about the reading. On the basis of your own analysis, additional reading and prior knowledge, you should be prepared each week to discuss and criticize the student paper.

UNIVERSITY OF WISCONSIN
Department of History
Fall 1983

History 302 — Professor Paul Boyer
History of American Thought 1859 to the Present

This course examines the shifting currents of American social thought from the Age of Darwin to the Age of Reagan. We will explore how successive generations of novelists, philosophers, theologians, sociologists, and activists responded to the dramatic changes in the social and technological framework of American life in these eventful decades.

This is primarily a lecture course, but several classes have been set aside for discussion. For undergraduates, the work of the course consists of a midterm, a final, a paper (see below), and participation in the scheduled discussions. Grading is as follows: Midterm: 25%, Paper and discussion: 25%, Final: 50%. For graduate students and those wishing Honors credit, several additional discussion sections will be scheduled, supplementary readings will be suggested, and the paper will be longer (ca. 15-18 pages), with the topic to be worked out in consultation with the instructor.

Assigned Books. The following are all in paperback, and should be available in the University Bookstore. In addition, they have been placed on Reserve in Helen C. White:

Horatio Alger, Ragged Dick
Edward Bellamy, Looking Backward
Charlotte Perkins Gilman, Herland
William James, Pragmatism and Other Essays (Ed., J. L. Blau)
John Dewey: The Essential Writings (Ed., David Sidorsky)
The Social Thought of Jame Addams (Ed., Christopher Lasch)
Sinclair Lewis, Arrowsmith
Nathaniel West, A Cool Million
Daniel Bell, The End of Ideology
John P. Diggins, The American Left in the Twentieth Century
Walter Miller Jr., A Canticle for Liebowitz
Jacques Ellul, The Technological Society

Paper: Undergraduates will write a 7-8 page paper on one of the assigned books in the course. This paper should not merely summarize the work, but critically discuss its ideas, with particular attention to the author's underlying assumptions, values, ideology, or beliefs. In the case of collections of essays (i.e., James, Addams, Dewey, Bell) specific essays may be selected as the focus of the paper, in consultation with the instructor. Papers will be welcome at any time during the semester up to the final due date: Monday, November 28. IMPORTANT: University penalties for plagiarism can be severe. All quoted or closely paraphrased material in a paper must be clearly attributed to the original source.

Office Hours: Mon., 1:30-2:30; Wed., 4-5; Fri. 11-12; or by appointment (263-1829). Office: Humanities 4131.

Lecture, Discussion, and Reading Schedule:

I. THE GILDED AGE

M 8/29 Course Introduction

W 8/31 The Meaning of the Civil War

F 9/2 The Darwinian Revolution

M 9/5 University Holiday

W 9/7 William Graham Sumner: Social Darwinist

F 9/9 Andrew Carnegie: The Tycoon as Social Philosopher

M 9/12 DISCUSSION: Horatio Alger, Ragged Dick (]867)

W 9/14 Booker T. Washington: Variations on the Alger Theme

F 9/16 Panaceas, Utopias, and Revolutionary Nightmares
(Reading: Edward Bellamy, Looking Backward [1888]).

M 9/19 Lester Ward and Thorstein Veblen: Critics of Laissez Faire Ideology and Gilded-Age Culture

W 9/21 Charlotte Perkins Gilman: The Darwinian as Feminist
(Reading: Gilman, Herland [1915]).

F 9/23 "Why Is There No Socialism in the United States?"
(Reading: Daniel Bell, The End of Ideology, Chap. 13, "The Failure of American Socialism.")

M 9/26 William James: Psychologist of the Soul

W 9/28 William James and the Origins of Pragmatism
(Reading: James, "What Pragmatism Means" [1907]).

F 9/30 Darwinism and American Fiction: Norris, Dreiser, London

M 10/3 HOUR EXAM

II. THE EARLY 20TH CENTURY

W 10/5 From Self to Society: The Social Thought of John Dewey
(Reading: Dewey, "The Significance of the Problem of Knowledge" [1897]; "The Influence of Darwinism on Philosophy" [1909]; "The Democratic Conception in Education" [1916] in Sidorsky [Ed.,], John Dewey: The Essential Writings, 53-69, 13-22, 219-225.)

F 10/7 Theorists of Social Control in an Urban-Industrial Age

M 10/10 Herbert Croly: Political Theory in the Age of TR and Wilson

W 10/12 Walter Lippmann and the Crisis of Authority

F 10/14 "Scientific" Racism: The Worlds of Charles B. Davenport and Madison Grant

M 10/17 W. E. B. DuBois and the Dilemma of the Black Intellectual

W 10/21 DISCUSSION: The Social Thought of Jane Addams

(Reading: Addams, "The Subjective Necessity for Social Settlements" [1892]; excerpt from Democracy and Social Ethics [1902]; excerpt from Twenty Years at Hull House [1910]; "Why Women Should Vote" [1910]; and "The Larger Aspects of the Woman's Movement" [1914]. Lasch, pp. 1-43, 62-84, 143-162. Also xiii-xxxi.)

M 10/24 Multiplicity and Unity: Henry Adams' Search for Meaning

W 10/26 Freud Comes to America

F 10/28 Randolph Bourne and the Watershed of World War I

(Reading: John Dewey, except from Creative Intelligence [1917], in Sidorsky, pp. 86-95; Jane Addams, excerpt from Peace and Bread in Time of War [1922], Lasch, 231-246.)

III. THE ERA BETWEEN THE WARS

M 10/31 The 1920s: Defection of the Intellectuals

W 11/2 Views of Science and Technology in the 1920s: Hope and Promise

F 11/4 Views of Science and Technology in the 1920s: A Darker Side

M 11/7 DISCUSSION: Sinclair Lewis, Arrowsmith (1925)

W 11/9 When Harlem Was in Vogue: White Fantasies and Black Realities in the 1920s

F 11/11 Social Thought in the 1930s: Niebuhr, Dewey, and the New Deal

M 11/14 Literature and Society in the Early Depression Years

W 11/16 The Era of the Popular Front: Literature and Politics, 1935-40

F 11/18 DISCUSSION: Nathaniel West, A Cool Million (1934)

IV. SINCE WORLD WAR II

M 11/21 Scientists and Public Policy, 1939-1947

W 11/23 The End of Ideology? Social Thought in the 1950s

(Reading: Daniel Bell, The End of Ideology [1960],
Chaps. 3 "Is There a Ruling Class in America?"
6 "Status Politics and New Anxieties"
14 "The Mood of Three Generations"
Epilogue: "The End of Ideology in the West"

F 11/25 University Holiday

M 11/28 Nuclear Weapons in American Thought and Culture. Paper due today.

W 11/30 Nuclear Weapons in American Thought and Culture

(Reading: Walter Miller Jr., A Canticle for Liebowitz [1954]).

F 12/2 DISCUSSION: Growing Up With the Bomb - The Class as a Research Source

M 12/5 Rise and Fall of the New Left

W 12/7 Paradoxes and Contradictions on the Right

F 12/9 Technology, Consciousness, and Culture

(Reading: Jacques Ellul, The Technological Society [first French edn., 1954; English translation, 1964], Foreword by Robert K. Merton; Translator's Introduction; Ellul's "Note to the Reader," and "Foreword to the Revised American Edition;" 3-22, 319-436.

UNIVERSITY OF CONNECTICUT

History 337
R.D. Brown, 1983

American Social History, 1600-1865

January 26 — Introductory Remarks: The Idea of Social History

February 2 — French and English Models

J.H. Hexter, "Fernand Braudel and the Monde Braudellien..." J. of Mod. Hist., 44 (1972), pp. 480-539. RESERVE
Fernand Braudel, The Mediterranean, New York, Harper 1975, I, part one, ch. 4 (Climate and History), pp. 231-275. RESERVE
Emmanuel LeRoy Ladurie, Montaillou: The Promised Land of Error, New York 1978, Introduction (vii-xvii) and chs. 15, 16, 17, pp. 231-287. RESERVE
E.P. Thompson, "Time, Work-Discipline, and Industrial Capitalism," Past and Present, No. 38, Dec. 1967, pp. 56-97. RESERVE
Douglas Hay, "Property, Authority and the Criminal Law," in Hay, et al., Albion's Fatal Tree, New York, Pantheon, 1975, pp. 17-63. RESERVE

February 9 — Community: Seventeenth-Century Settlements

David Grayson Allen, In English Ways: The Movement of Societies and the Transferral of English Local Law and Custom to Massachusetts in the Seventeenth Century, New York, Norton 1972, entire.
Karen O. Kupperman, "Apathy and Death in Early Jamestown," J. of Amer. Hist. , 66, 1979, pp. 24-40. RESERVE
Edmund S. Morgan, American Slavery, American Freedom, New York, Norton 1975, chs. 4-7, pp. 71-157.

February 16 — Community: The Revolutionary Era

Robert A. Gross, The Minutemen and their World, New York Hill & Wang 1976, entire.
Charles S. Sydnor, American Revolutionaries in the Making, New York, Free Press 1965, entire.
Rhys Isaac, The Transformation of Virginia, 1740-1790, Chapel Hill: U. of North Carolina Press 1982, Ch. 6 (Textures of Community), pp. 115-138. RESERVE

February 23 — Community: Urbanization and Industrialization in the Nineteenth Century

Anthony F.C. Wallace, Rockdale: The Growth of an American Village in the Early Industrial Revolution, New York Knopf 1978, Chs. 1, 2 (pp. 3-69) and Chs. 7, 8 (pp. 296-397).

Alan Dawley, *Class and Community: The Industrial Revolution in Lynn*, Cambridge, Harvard Univ. Press 1976, Chs. 2, 3, 4 (pp. 42-128). RESERVE

Thomas Dublin, *Women at Work: The Transformation of Work and Community in Lowell, Massachusetts*, 1826-1860, New York, Columbia Univ. Press 1979, chs. 2-6, pp. 14-107. RESERVE

March 2 Slavery, Eighteenth Century

Edmund S. Morgan, *American Slavery, American Freedom*, chs. 8-18, pp. 158-387.

Peter H. Wood, *Black Majority: Negroes in Colonial South Carolina from 1670 through the Stone Rebellion*, New York 1974, part 4, pp. 271-327. RESERVE

March 9 Slavery, Nineteenth Century

Eugene Genovese, *Roll, Jordan Roll*, New York, Pantheon 1974, Book One, pp. 1-158; Book Two, Part 2, pp. 285-324; Book Four, pp. 587-659.

March 23 Family I, Sex and Marriage

Nancy F. Cott, "Divorce and the Changing Status of Women in Eighteenth-Century Massachusetts," in Michael Gordon, ed., *The American Family in Social-Historical Perspective*, 2nd ed., New York, St. Martin's 1978, ch. 7, pp. 115-139. RESERVE

Julie Roy Jeffrey, *Frontier Women: The Trans-Mississippi West, 1840-1880*, New York 1979, entire (204 p.)

T.J. Barker-Benfield, "The Spermatic Economy: A Nineteenth-Century View of Sexuality, " in Gordon, ed., *American Family*, ch. 18, pp. 374-402. RESERVE

March 30 Family II, Stages of Life and Sex Roles

Joseph F. Kett, "The Stages of Life," in Gordon, ed., *American Family*, ch. 10, pp. 166-191. RESERVE

Barbara Welter, "The Cult of True Womanhood: 1820-1860," in Gordon, ed., *American Family*, ch. 15, pp. 313-333. RESERVE

David Hackett Fischer, *Growing Old in America*, expanded edition, New York, Oxford 1978, chs. Intro, 1-4, pp. 3-195.

April 6 Work and Leisure, I

Paul Faler, "Cultural Aspects of the Industrial Revolution: Lynn, Massachusetts, Shoemakers and Industrial Morality, 1820-1860," *Labor History*, 15 (1974), pp. 367-394. RESERVE

Paul E. Johnson, *A Shopkeeper's Millenium: Society and Revivals in Rochester,* New York, 1815-1837, New York 1978, enitre (204 p.)

Herbert G. Gutman, "Work, Culture, and Society in Industrializing America, 1815-1919," in Work, Culture, pp. 3-78. RESERVE

April 13 Work and Leisure, II

T.H. Breen, "Horses and Gentlemen: The Cultural Significance of Gambling among the Gentry of Virginia," Wm. and Mary Qtly. , 3rd ser., 34 (April 1977), pp. 239-257. RESERVE

W.J. Rorabaugh, The Alcoholic Republic: An American Tradition, New York, Oxford 1979, complete (250 p.)

April 20 Modernization

Richard D. Brown, Modernization: The Transformation of American Life, 1600-1865, New York, Hill & Wang 1976, entire

April 27 Evaluating Social History Scholarship

May 4 FINAL EXAM

All students are expected to do the readings promptly each week. Since the success of the course rests heavily on the quality of discussion, students should take their responsibility to read carefully and thoughtfully very seriously. As an aid to discussion, you will be required to hand in a 2-3 page typed comment on the week's readings by noon on Wednesdays. Your comments will be reflected in your grade, though no grade will be assigned to individual comments. Of the eleven dates when such comments will be due, you are permitted two misses without penalty.

You are required to present one brief essay (7-9 pages) in which you identify the best and worst reading assignments of the semester explaining and defending your choices. During the term you are expected to meet with me at least once to discuss your candidates for inclusion. You should make a final decision by April 22 so as to allow time to draft your essay. It must be in by April 27.

There will be a written final exam consisting of two-hour essays. You must hand in two suitable questions in advance of the exam by May 2.

Office hours: Wood Hall 234, MWF 2-3:30 p.m., and by appointment.

UNIVERSITY OF WISCONSIN
Department of History

History 901 — Carl Kaestle
Proseminar in American History — Fall, 1983

VARIETIES OF SOCIAL HISTORY: AMERICA IN THE NINETEENTH CENTURY

Introduction

Scope of the course: This proseminar is designed as an introduction to nineteenth-century American social history. Within that broad topic, the emphasis is on recent works dealing with the daily lives and careers of non-elite whites in the Northeast. No previous reading in social history is assumed, so some earlier innovative works, such as Rothman's Discovery of the Asylum, are included, along with recent books like Dublin's Women at Work and Johnson's Shopkeeper's Millennium. Students who have read some of these works may broaden their reading from the supplementary list.

Methodological emphasis: Although this is not a course in methodology, there will be continual attention to methodological problems encountered in studying ordinary people in the past. Current knowledge about American social history is so rudimentary and so precarious that methodological problems are central. No previous knowledge of statistics is required or expected, and most of the statistical techniques used in the quantitative studies assigned are elementary.

Assignments: In addition to reading the assigned works and contributing to the general discussion, each student will prepare three papers. One of these papers will report on work done and insights gained during an independent reading period in the middle of the semester.

Paperback books to purchase:

- Alan Dawley, Class and Community
- Thomas Dublin, Women at Work
- Paul Johnson, A Shopkeeper's Millenium
- Joseph Kett, Rites of Passage
- Lawrence Levine, Black Culture and Black Consciousness
- Leon Litwack, Been in the Storm So Long
- David Rothman, The Discovery of the Asylum
- Kathryn Kish Sklar, Catharine Beecher: A Study in American Domesticity

Two books assigned as required reading are available only in hard-bound editions. Copies will be placed on reserve, so purchase is optional:

- Kathleen Conzen, Immigrant Milwaukee
- Mary Ryan, Cradle of the Middle Class

WEEK 1
August 30
Introduction to the Course

WEEK 2
September 7
Introduction, continued

A. What is social history?

Read:
James Henretta, "Social History as Lived and Written," American Historical Review 84 (December, 1979), 1293-1333.
Peter Stearns, "Trends in Social History," in Michael Kammen, ed., The Past Before Us (Ithaca, Cornell University Press, 1980), pp. 205-230.
Robert Berkhofer, "The Difficulty of Studying Man in Past Time," in his Behavioral Approach to History (New York, Free Press, 1969), Chapter 1.

B. Eighteenth-Century Background

Read:
James Henretta, "Families and Farms: Mentalite in Pre-Industrial America," William and Mary Quarterly (January, 1978), 3-32.
Christopher Clark, "The Household Economy, Market Exchange and the Rise of Capitalism in the Connecticut Valley, 1800-1860," Journal of Social History 13 (Winter, 1979), 169-189.
Gary B. Nash, "The Disordered Urban Economies," in his The Urban Crucible (Cambridge, Harvard University Press, 1979), Chapter 12, pp. 312-338.

UNIT ONE: SOCIAL STRUCTURE, SOCIAL CHANGE, SOCIAL GROUPS

WEEK 3
September 14
Industrialization and the Male Worker

Read:
Alan Dawley, Class and Community: The Industrial Revolution in Lynn (Cambridge, Harvard University Press, 1976, pb.).

WEEK 4
September 21
Industrialization and the Female Worker

Read:
Thomas Dublin, Women at Work: The Transformation of Work and comunity in Lowell, Massachusetts, 1826-1850 (New York, Columbia University Press, 1979, pb.).

<u>WEEK 5</u>
September 28 — <u>Immigration</u>

<u>Read</u>:

Kathleen Neils Conzen, <u>Immigrant Milwaukee, 1836-1860</u> (Cambridge, Harvard University Press, 1976).

<u>WEEK 6</u>
October 5 — <u>Emmancipation</u>

<u>Read</u>:

Leon F. Litwack, <u>Been in the Storm So Long: The Aftermath of Slavery</u> (New York, Random House, 1974, Vintage pb.).

<u>WEEK 7</u>
October 12 — <u>Emancipation, continued</u>

<u>Read</u>:

Lawrence Levine, <u>Black Culture and Black Consciousness: Afro-American Folk Thought from Slavery to Freedom</u> (New York, Oxford University Press, 1977, pb.).

UNIT TWO: THE FAMILY AND SOCIALIZATION

<u>WEEK 8</u>
October 19 — <u>Domesticity</u>

<u>Read</u>:

Kathryn Kish Sklar, <u>Catherine Beecher: A Study in American Domesticity</u> (New Haven, Yale University Press, 1973, pb.).

<u>WEEK 9</u>
October 26 — <u>Adolescence</u>

<u>Read</u>:

Joseph Kett, <u>Rites of Passage: Adolescence in America, 1790 to the Present</u> (New York, Basic Books, 1977, pb.).

UNIT THREE: INDEPENDENT PROJECTS ON 19-CENTURY SOCIAL HISTORY

There will be individual conferences with me during Week 10, a social gathering at my home during Week 11, and double seminar sessions during Week 12 to report on independent reading projects.

UNIT FOUR: REFORM AND INSTITUTIONS

WEEK 13
November 23

Religion and Class Formation

Read:

Paul E. Johnson, A Shopkeeper's Millennium: Society and Revivals in Rochester, New York, 1815-1837 (New York, Hill & Wang, 1978, pb.).

WEEK 14
November 30

Religion and Class Formation, continued

Read:

Mary Ryan, Cradle of the Middle Class: The Family in Oneida County, New York, 1790-1865 (Cambridge, Cambridge University Press, 1981).

WEEK 15
December 7

Institutions for Deviants

Read:

David Rothman, The Discovery of the Asylum: Social Order and Disorder in the New Republic (Boston, Little, Brown & Co., 1971, pb.).

HISTORY 901: Proseminar in American History
Fall, 1983

Carl Kaestle, University of Wisconsin

Approaches to Nineteenth-Century American Social History

SUPPLEMENTARY READING

1. Eighteenth-century background: preindustrial America:

James Henretta, The Evolution of American Society (Lexington, Mass., Heath, 1974, pb).

Jackson T. Main, The Social Structure of Revolutionary America (Princeton, 1966, pb).

James T. Lemon and Gary B. Nash, "The Distribution of Wealth in Eighteenth-Century America: A Century of Change in Chester County, Pennsylvania, 1693-1802," Journal of Social History 2 (Fall, 1968), 1-24.

Alan Kulikoff, "The Progress of Inequality in Revolutionary Boston," William and Mary Quarterly 28 (June, 1971), 375-412.

Richard D. Brown, Modernization: The Transformation of American Life, 1600-1865 (New York, Hill and Wang, pb, 1976).

Gary B. Nash, The Urban Crucible: Social Change, Political Consciousness, and the Origins of the American Revolution (Cambridge, Harvard University Press, 1979).

Philip Greven, The Protestant Temperament: Patterns of Child-Reading, Religious Experience, and the Self in Early America (New York, Alfred Knopf, 1977).

2. Industrialization and the male worker:

Paul Faler, Mechanics and Manufacturers in the Early Industrial Revolution: Lynn, Massachusetts, 1780-1860 (Albany, State University of New York Press, pb., 1981)

Daniel Rodgers, The Work Ethic in Industrial America 1850-1920 (Chicago University of Chicago Press, 1978).

Herbert Gutman, "Work, Culture, and Society in Industrializing America, 1815-1919," American Historical Review (June, 1973), and reprinted in Herbert Gutman, Work Culture and Society in Industrializing America (New York, Vintage pb., 1977).

Daniel Rodgers, "'Tradition,' 'Modernity,' and the American Industrial Worker: Reflections and Critique," Journal of Interdisciplinary History 7 (1977).

Tamara K. Hareven and Randolph Langenback, Amoskeag: Life and Work in an American Factory City (New York, Pantheon, 1978 pb).

Tamara K. Hareven, Family Time and Industrial Time (Cambridge, Cambridge University Press, 1982).

John T. Cumbler, Working-Class Community in Industrial Cities, 1880-1930 (Westport, Conn., Greenwood Press, 1979).

Daniel Walkowitz, Worker City, Company Town: Iron and Cotton-Worker Protest in Troy and Cohoes, New York, 1855-1884 (Urban, University of Illinois Press, 1978).

3. Industrialization and the female worker:

Milton Cantor and Bruce Laurie, eds., Class, Sex, and the Woman Worker (Westport, Conn., Greenwood Press, 1977).

Maris Vinovskis and Richard Bernard, "The Female School Teacher in Antebellum America," Journal of Social History, 10 (Spring, 1977), 322-345.

Keith Melder, "Woman's High Calling: The Teaching Profession in America, 1830-1860," American Studies 13 (Fall, 1972), 19-32.

Susan Kleinberg, "Technology and Women's Work: The Lives of Working-Class Women in Pittsburgh, 1870-1900," Labor History 17 (Winter, 1976).

David M. Katzman, Seven Days a Week: Women and Domestic Service in Industrializing America (New York, Oxford University Press, 1978).

Marjorie Davies, "Woman's Place Is At the Typewriter: The Feminization of the Clerical Labor Force," Radical America 8 (July-August, 1974), 1-28.

Karen Oppenheim Mason, Maris A. Vinovskis, and Tamara Hareven, "Women's Work and the Life Course in Essex County, Massachusetts," in Tamara Hareven, ed., Transitions: The Family and the Life Course in Historical Perspective (New York, Academic Press, 1978), pp. 187-216.

4. Immigration and ethnicity

John Higham, Strangers in the Land: Patterns of American Nativism 1860-1925 (New Brunswick, Rutgers University Press, 1955, Atheneum pb.).

David Ward, Cities and Immigrants: A Geography of Change in Nineteenth Century America (New York, Oxford University Press, 1971 pb.).

Robert Ernst, Immigrant Life in New York City, 1825-1863 (New York, 1949).

Moses Rischin, The Promised City: New York's Jews, 1870-1914 (Cambridge, 1962, Harper Torchbook pb.).

David Cole, Immigrant City: Lawrence, Massachusetts, 1845-1921 (Chapel Hill, 1963).

Oscar Handlin, The Uprooted (Boston, 1951, pb.).

Oscar Handlin, Boston's Immigrants (Cambridge, rev. ed., 1959, Beacon pb.).

Virginia Yans-McLaughlin, Family and Community: Italian Immigrants in Buffalo, 1880-1930 (Ithaca, Cornell University Press, 1977, pb.).

John Bodnar, Immigration and Industrialization: Ethnicity in an American Mill Town, 1870-1940 (Pittsburgh, University of Pittsburg Press, 1977).

Thomas Archdeacon, Becoming American: An Ethnic History (New York, MacMillan Free Press, 1983).

5. Slavery and freedom

Herbert Gutman, The Black Family in Slavery and Freedom, 1750-1925 (New York, Pantheon pb., 1976).

Eugene D. Genovese, Roll, Jordan, Roll: The World the Slaves Made (New York, Vintage pb., 1972).

John W. Blassingame, The Slave Community: Plantation Life in the Antebellum South (New York, Oxford University Press pb., rev. ed., 1979).

Thomas Webber, Deep Like the Rivers: Education in the Slave Quarter Community, 1831-1865 (New York, Norton pb., 1978).

Leon F. Litwack, Been in the Storm So Long: The Aftermath of Slavery (New York, Random House, 1979, Vintage pb.).

Roger Ransom and Richard Sutch, One Kind of Freedom: The Economic Consequences of Emancipation (Cambridge, Cambridge University Press, 1977).

6. History of the family

Tamara K. Hareven, "The Dynamics of Kin in an Industrial Family," in John Demos and Sarane Spence Boocock, eds., Turning Points: Historical and Sociological Essays on the Family (Chicago, Supplement to the American Journal of Sociology, volume 84, 1978), pp. 151-182.

John Modell and Tamara Hareven, "Urbanization and the Malleable Household: An Examination of Boarding and Lodging in American Families," Journal of Marriage and the Family 35 (August, 1973), 467-479.

Robert V. Wells, "Family History and Demographic Transition," Journal of Social History 9 (Fall, 1975), 1-20.

John Modell, Frank F. Furstenberg, and Theordore Hershberg, "Social Change and Life Course Development in Historical Perspective," Journal of Family History 1 (September, 1976).

Michael Gordon, ed., The American Family in Social-Historical Perspective (New York, St. Martin's Press pb., 3rd ed., 1983).

Tamara K. Hareven and Maris A. Vinovskis, eds., Family and Population in Nineteenth-Century America (Princeton, Princeton University Press, 1978, pb.).

Tamara K. Hareven, ed., Transitions: The Family and the Life Course in Historical Perspective (New York, Academic Press, 1978).

Tamara K. Hareven, ed., Family and Kin in Urban Communities, 1700-1930 (New York, New Viewpoints pb., 1977).

Maris A. Vinovskis, Demographic Changes in America from the Revolution to the Civil War: An Analysis of the Socio-Economic Determinants of Fertility Differentials and Trends in Massachusetts from 1765-1860 (New York, Academic Press, 1982).

7. Women in the family and society

Carl Degler, At Odds: Women and the Family in America from the Revolution to the Present (New York, Oxford University Press, 1980).

Mary Beth Norton, Liberty's Daughters" The Revolutionary Experience of American Women, 1750-1800 (Boston, Little-Brown, 1980).

Linda K. Kerber, Women of the Republic: Intellect and Ideology in Revolutionary America (Chapel Hill, University of North Carolina Press, pb., 1980).

Gerda Lerner, The Majority Finds Its Past: Placing Women in History (New York, Oxford University Press, 1979, pb.).

Keith E. Melder, Beginnings of Sisterhood: The American Women's Rights Movement, 1800-1850 (New York, Schocken pb., 1977).

Barbara Welter, "The Feminization of American Religion, 1800-1860" in her Dimity Convictions: The American Woman in the Nineteenth Century (Athens, Ohio University Press, pb., 1976), pp. 83-102.

Nancy F. Cott, The Bonds of Womanhood: "Women's Sphere" in New England (New Haven, Yale University Press, 1977, pb.).

Ann Douglas, The Feminization of American Culture (New York, Alfred Knopf, 1977).

Barbara Welter, "The Cult of True Womanhood: 1820-1860," American Quarterly 18 (1966), 151-174.

Ellen DuBois, Feminism and Suffrage: The Emergence of an Independence Woman's Movement in America, 1848-1869 (Ithaca, Cornell University Press pb., 1978).

Carroll Smith-Rosenberg, "The Female World of Love and Ritual: Relations Between Women in Nineteenth-Century America," Signs 1 (Autumn, 1975), 1-29.

Ann Douglas Wood, "'The Fasionable Diseases': Women's Complaints and Their Treatment in Nineteenth-Century America," Journal of Interdisciplinary History 4 (Summer, 1973), 25-52.

Regina Morantz, "The Lady and her Physician," in Mary Hartmann and Lois Banner, Clio's Consciousness Raised, (New York, Harper Torchbook, 1974, pb.), pp. 38-52.

Susan Strasser, Never Done: A History of American Housework (New York, Pantheon, 1982, pb.).

Anne Firor Scott, The Southern Lady: From Pedestal to Politics, 1830-1930 (Chicago, University of Chicago Press, 1970, pb.).

8. **Adolescence and youth**

John and Virginia Demos, "Adolescence in Historical Perspective," Journal of Marriage and the Family 31 (November, 1969), 632-638.

Steven L. Schlossman, Love and the American Delinquent: The Theory and Practice of "Progressive" Juvenile Justice, 1825-1920 (Chicago University of Chicago Press, 1977).

Michael B. Katz and Ian F. Davey, "Youth and Early Industrialization in a Candian City," in Demos and Boocock, Turning Points, pp. 81-119.

Carl F. Kaestle and Maris A. Vinovskis, "From Fireside to Factory: School Entry and School Leaving in Nineteenth-Century Massachusetts," in Hareven, ed., Transitions, pp. 135-186.

John Modell, Frank F. Furstenberg, and Theodore Hersberg, "Social Change and Life Course Development in Historical Perspective," Journal of Family History 1 (September, 1976).

Barbara Cross, Horace Bushnell: Minister to a Changing America (Chicago, University of Chicago Press, 1958).

Dorothy Ross, G. Stanley Hall: The Psychologist as Prophet (Chicago, University of Chicago Press, 1972).

9. **Antebellum reform and religion**

Ronald G. Walters, American Reformers, 1815-1860 (New York, Hill and Wang pb., 1978).

Alice Felt Tyler, Freedom's Ferment: Phases of American Social History from the Colonial Period to the Outbreak of the Civil War (Minneapolis, University of Minnesota Press, 1944, Harper Torchbook pb.).

Carroll Smith Rosenberg, Religion and the Rise of the American City: The New York City Mission Movement, 1812-1870 (Ithaca, Cornell University Press, 1971).

Timothy L. Smith, Revivalism and Social Reform: American Protestantism on the Eve of the Civil War (Abington Press, 1957, Harper Torchbook pb.).

Whitney R. Cross, The Burned-Over District: Social and Intellectual History of Enthusiastic Religion in Western New York, 1800-1850 (New York, Harper Torchbook pb., 1950).

William G. McLaughlin, Revivals, Awakenings and Reform: An Essay on Religion and Social Change in America, 1607-1977 (Chicago, University of Chicago Press, 1978, pb.), chapter four.

Charles I. Foster, An Errand of Mercy: The Evangelical United Front, 1790-1837 (Chapel Hill, 1960).

Paul Boyer, Urban Masses and Moral Order in America, 1820-1920 (Cambridge, Harvard University Press, 1978).

Richard H. Sewell, Ballots for Freedom: Antislavery Politics in the United States, 1837-1860 (New York, Oxford University Press, 1976).

James M. McPherson, The Struggle for Equality: Abolitionists and the Negro in the Civil War and Reconstruction (Princeton, Princeton University Press, 1964).

James B. Stewart, Holy Warriors: The Abolitionists and American Slavery (New York, Hill and Wang, 1976, pb.).

Donald G. Mathews, Religion in the Old South (Chicago, University of Chicago Press, 1977).

10. Schooling

Michael B. Katz, The Irony of Early School Reform: Educational Innovation in Mid-Nineteenth Century Massachusetts (Cambridge, Harvard University Press, 1968, Beacon pb.).

Michael B. Katz, "The Origins of Public Education: A Reassessment," History of Education Quarterly 16 (Winter, 1976), 381-407.

Carl F. Kaestle, The Evolution of an Urban School System: New York City, 1750-1850 (Cambridge, Harvard University Press, 1973).

Stanley K. Schultz, The Culture Factory: Boston Public Schools, 1789-1860 (New York, Oxford University Press, 1973).

David B. Tyack, The One Best System: A History of American Urban Education (Cambridge, Harvard University Press, 1974 pb.).

Carl F. Kaestle and Maris A. Vinovskis, Education and Social Change in Nineteenth-Century Massachusetts (New York, Cambridge University Press, 1980).

Rush Walter, Popular Education and Democratic Thought in America (New York, Columbia University Press, 1962, pb.).

Selwyn, K. Troen, The Public and the Schools: Shaping the St. Louis System, 1838-1920 (Columbia, University of Missouri Press, 1975).

James W. Saunders, The Education of an Urban Minority: Catholics in Chicago, 1833-1965 (New York, Oxford University Press, 1977).

David B. Tyack and Elizabeth Hansot, Managers of Virtue: Public School Leadership in America, 1820-1980 (New York, Basic Books, 1982).

Carl F. Kaestle, Pillars of the Republic: Common Schools and American Society, 1780-1860 (New York, Hill and Wang, 1983).

11. Institutions for deviants

Gerald Grob, The State and the Mentally Ill: A History of the Worcester State Hospital in Massachusetts, 1830-1920 (Chapel Hill, 1966).

W. David Lewis, From Newgate to Dannemora: The Rise of the Penitentiary in New York, 1796-1848 (Ithaca, 1965).

Gerald Grob, Mental Institutions in America: Social Policy to 1875 (New York, Free Press, 1973).

Raymond Mohl, Poverty in New York, 1783-1825 (New York, Oxford University Press, 1971).

Barbara G. Rosenkrantz and Maris A. Vinovskis, "The Invisible Lunatics: Old Age and Insanity in Mid-Nineteenth-Century Massachusetts," in Spicker, Woodward, and VanTassel, eds., Aging and the Elderly (Humanities Press, 1978), pp. 95-125.

David J. Rothman, Conscience and Convenience: The Asylum and Its Alternatives in Progressive America (Boston, Little, Brown, 1980).

Blake McKelvey, American Prisons (Montclair, New Jersey, 1977).

UNIVERSITY OF PENNSYLVANIA

HISTORY 163/URBAN STUDIES 25/WOMEN'S STUDIES 163

AMERICAN SOCIAL HISTORY

Fall 1982 Tues. and Thurs. 9-10:30
Instructor: Michael Katz

Syllabus

This course concentrates on American social history in the nineteenth century. It is concerned, first, with the way in which industrialization, urbanization, and immigration altered American social life. Particular attention will be paid to work, class, family structure, the role of women, ethnicity, social reform, and social institutions.

The requirements are: (1) reading one book per week and participation in class discussion; (2) three short papers (explained below); (3) a final examination. All work must be handed in on time. Extensions will not be given.

Short papers: each of these papers should be based on a different primary source. One should be a nineteenth or early twentieth century newspaper; a second should be a statistical source (not the Historical Abstracts of Statistics); the third should be either government reports or a collection of letters and/or diaries.

Students should select and study a source -- several issues of the newspaper; several tables of statistics; several issues of the report of the same board, agency, or institution; a number of letters. They should ask, and report on, the following questions about each source:

What source did you use?
How was it compiled?
What kinds of problems or questions can be answered with it?
What are its strengths?
What are its limitations?
What is one problem, theme, or issue in the source you studied, and what hypotheses or conclusions can you draw from it?

Although the papers should address the preceding questions, they should be written in essay form. That is, they should have a clear thesis and a coherent structure.

The papers should be 5-10 pp. in length and will be due on dates to be established early in the semester.

READING LIST
(All books are available in paperback)

I. Class, Social Structure, and Social Mobility

1. Daniel Rodgers, THE WORK ETHIC IN INDUSTRIAL AMERICA (Chicago)

2. Stephan Thernstrom, POVERTY AND PROGRESS (Harvard)

3. Thomas Dublin, WOMEN AT WORK (Columbia)

II. Ethnicity and Race

4. George Rawick, FROM SUNDOWN TO SUNUP (Greenwood)

5. Philip Taylor, DISTANT MAGNET (Harper and Row)

6. Kenneth Kusmer, A GHETTO TAKES SHAPE (Illinois)

III. Women and Family

7. Nancy Cott, BONDS OF WOMANHOOD (Yale)

8. John Mack Faragher, WOMEN AND MEN ON THE OVERLAND TRAIL (Yale)

9. James Mohr, ABORTION IN AMERICA (Oxford)

IV. Social Institutions and Social Reform

10. David Rothman, THE DISCOVERY OF THE ASYLUM (Little Brown)

11. Joseph Kett, RITES OF PASSAGE (Basic)

12. Alan Trachtenberg, THE INCORPORATION OF AMERICA (Hill and Wang)

BOSTON UNIVERSITY

An Example of a Present Problems and Policy Background Course

Sam Bass Warner, Jr.

HI 535M: AMERICAN URBAN HISTORY

Professor Warner
Fall 1978

Tuesday Evenings, 6-9 pm
CLA 211

The goals of this course are twofold: it offers an introduction to the history of the American city for any who are curious, and it provides a medium for more advanced explorations by those who are so inclined.

You may take this course in either of two ways; the credit is the same for both. Course A is the introduction. No previous background or knowledge is assumed and it is specifically designed for undergraduate upperclassmen and for those in professional programs whose principal concerns are not historical. Course B is appropriate for undergraduate majors and those in graduate programs to whom urban history is an important concern. You may select either course regardless of your university enrollment.

Course A. The lectures and readings cover the most important aspects of urbanization and survey the basic changes which have taken place over the past 200 years. To get credit for this course you should attend the lectures, do the reading, look at the different districts of Boston, and take the hour examination (Oct. 31) and the final (Dec. 19). Examination questions will be handed out in class a week in advance for the purposes of review, and the exams will consist of essay questions selected from the advance lists.

Course B. Students in this course will do all the reading assigned for Course A and will in addition select one of the topics from the course bibliography in which to do further reading. You will not take the hour exam or the final but will instead keep a reading log. The first logs are to be handed in Oct. 31; the entire log must be handed in Dec. 12.

The purpose of the log is to enable the student to read widely and to pick out of the reading issues and themes of particular interest to the student's own knowledge and goals. Log entries should vary from one to five pages per book depending upon its salience to the student's own goals. Logs should not be mini-book reports, but rather discuss some question of significance raised by the reading. A good log in time develops several themes and relates learning from later readings to earlier ones. A bad log fails to find or develop connections. Logs must be typed. After the logs are handed in, you should see the instructor, who will discuss your readingss with you.

There is no other way to learn history than by reading and by looking. Since we live in an old American city, all the sequences of urbanization can be observed here by looking at the various sections of metropolitan Boston. But looking, no matter how thoroughly, will not suffice because the built city is at all times a blend of many eras [Kevin Lynch, *What Time Is This Place?* (Cambridge, 1972)]. The assignments are designed to take you quickly into the periodization of American urban development so that you can find clues to the past in city journeys after the first two weeks of class.

HI 535M (2)

Please be advised that NO INCOMPLETES ARE GIVEN in this course. Ken Kesey's rule prevails--"You are either on the bus, or off the bus." If as you consider enrolling in this course you feel an incomplete coming on, please find another course.

BOOKS TO PURCHASE:

Boston Society of Architects, Joseph L. Eldredge, ed., Architecture Boston (1976)
Oscar Handlin, Boston's Immigrants (1941)
Andrew Levinson, The Working Class Majority (1974)
Wyndham Mortimer, Organize! (1971)
K. H. Schaeffer & Elliot Sclar, Access for All (1975)
Clarence Stein, Toward New Towns for America (1957)
John F. C. Turner, Housing by People (1976)
Sam Bass Warner, Jr., The Private City (1968)
______, The Urban Wilderness (1972)

Mugar Library Reserve:

Thostein Veblen, The Theory of Business Enterprise (New York, 1904), Chs. 9-10.

SCHEDULE OF LECTURES, PRESENTATIONS, AND DISCUSSIONS

Date	Lecture Topic	Visual Presentation and Discussion
Sept. 12	Introduction Access for All, ch. 1-6	
Sept. 19	The Sequences of Urbanization; Urban Wilderness, Part II	Urban Periodization
Sept. 26	Work & Labor Before 1860 Private City, ch. 1-4	The North End's Time Layers Architecture Boston, ch. 2
Oct. 3	The Rural Contribution Boston's Immigrants	Charlestown, Handlin's Boston, & Whitman's New York Architecture Boston, ch. 8
Oct. 10	Transportation Access for All, ch. 7, 9-10 Urban Wilderness, pp. 37-52	Downtown & Waterfront and Shoppint Strips and Centers Architecture Boston, ch. 1,3
Oct. 17	Municipal Politics Private City, ch. 5-7	Beacon Hill & the Search for Urban Order Architecture Boston, ch. 4
Oct. 24	Institutions and the City	South Cove & South End, Howell's Boston & New York Architecture Boston, ch. 7

HI 535M (3)

Oct. 31	HOUR EXAMINATION, COURSE A FIRST READING LOGS, COURSE B	
Nov. 7	The Family Urban Wilderness, ch. 6 Working Class Majority	Back Bay, Fifth Ave. vs. Newport Architecture Boston, ch. 5
Nov. 14	Work & Labor Since 1870 Organize! Theory of Business Enterprise, ch. 9-10	Roxbury and to Newton and Beyond Architecture Boston, ch. 9
Nov. 21	Urban Man & Urban Nature	The Fenway, A Community of Art and Nature Architecture Boston, ch. 6
Nov. 28	Housing Reform Urban Wilderness, ch. 7-9 Toward New Towns for America	From Tenement Regulation to Housing Projects
Dec. 5	Planning Housing by People	New Towns & Regional Design
Dec. 12	Reading Period; No Class COMPLETED LOGS, COURSE B	
Dec. 19	FINAL EXAMINATION	

THE SEQUENCES OF URBANIZATION

All manner of events influence the historical course of human settlements: the movement and habits of populations, the shifting relations of trade, changes in the modes of technology, the development of new land and resources, innovations in manufactures, alterations in the diet of human symbols, changes in political institutions, and wars. These events do not come singly towards urbanization, but in a web of interactions, some pressing change in one direction, some in other, even contrary, directions. Viewed over long time spans, however, these myriad events appear to make recognizable sequences.

In the American case there seem to have been rather distinct urban eras. During the years prior to 1820, or thereabouts, Americans lived in isolated farmsteads or in small villages. Ninety per cent of the population dwelt in settlements smaller than 2,500 inhabitants. There followed during the next fifty years a time of intense urbanization, a pace never again duplicated. The rural population fell to 75% of the nation's inhabitants, and cities (places of 25,000 - 249,999) and metropolises (places of 250,000 and more) sprang up on the landscape. The ensuing fifty years continued these trends with towns, cities, and metropolises all growing rapidly, albeit not so fast as before. The continued vigorous growth of the largest human settlements (metropolises 8.2% of the U.S. population in 1870; 19.6% in 1920) seemed at the time, and even more so today, to be the characteristic feature of the era. In our own time, since 1920, the rural population has fallen to 27% of all U.S. inhabitants, but metropolitan growth has slowed to almost the average national rate of increase. Instead towns and cities multiply, either in a scattered form in underdeveloped areas like the Sunbelt, or in a new form of continuous urban settlement like the northeast megalopolis (Boston-Washington).

Even such a simple listing of aggregate population groupings according to their political boundaries suggests that the conditions of human life have undergone extraordinary alteration during the past 150 yeats. Such a review urges caution in predicting what the future may hold.

If you come to this course from some exposure to urban economics, urban geography, or urban sociology, you will have brought with you a particular approach to accounting for these historical changes: the equilibrium model. Equilibrium models are not incorrect: indeed they are currently the modes of analysis employed by both physical and economic planners throughout the world, and within their own special terms they work. The approach of such planning and social science, however, does not explain the historical course of urbanization. Rather equilibrium models interpret and predict adjustments which human activities will make within the confines of the major historical changes themselves.

Modern urban economics, urban geography, and urban sociology are intellectual specialties which depend to varying degrees for their analysis upon the basic thinking of classical economics and its assumptions of cost minimization and market pricing. All their urban reasoning begins after the important issues of urban history are defined. All, whether capitalist or Marxist in outlook, depend on equilibrium models to explain alterations in human settlement patterns. To make these models work, social scientists in economics, geography, and sociology begin by specifying a rate of population growth, a rate of per capita income change, some rate of technological change which alters transportation costs, and some rate of technological change which alters production cost schedules.

Armed with these assumptions they see the shifting patterns of human settlement as moves towards an equilibrium of the classical economic elements of land, labor, and capital. In the Marxian case each equilibrium generates a polar situation among the classes which drives society to a new equilibrium and a new polarity. The geographers employ equilibrium models and hypotheses of economics for their central place theory and assumptions of a hierarchical ordering of cities [Brian J.L. Berry and Frank E. Horton, Geographic Perspectives on Urban Systems (Englewood, 1970)]; the economists use a paradigm of international trade to arrive at similar results [Wilbur Thompson, Preface to Urban Economics (Baltimore, 1965)].

Current dissatisfaction with equilibrium models of all kinds stems from their inability to explore aspects of human life which are now inescapable; population change, income distribution, changes in technology, and the composition of the symbolic climate. These are the issues which the equilibrium models made their prior assumptions about. They are the central issues of urban history.

An alternative mode of thinking is the evolutionary model. These hypotheses assume that population, income, technology, and symbols move together in such a way that both the human and the natural environment are simultaneously altered by decisions made by the human population. From this evolutionary point of view the future is unknown. Cities are viewed as partially order collectivities which at some times spin off populations, and at other times draw them so that the different configurations of urban settlements represent both the perpetuation of advantages of past environments and a realization of new opportunities.

To the evolutionary view that which separates life in a town from life in New York today is only incidentally a matter of scale per se (as equilibrium models would have it). Over time as the nation's human settlements get larger, more cities become larger, while even more settlements become cities. There are thus a whole series of thresholds which change in intensity as the densities of people, organizations, activities, and artifacts change. These thresholds are moving thresholds, not set relationships which work according to the fixed relationships of the market or cost minimization. The thresholds are a series of simultaneous relationships between people and their urban environment, between each city and the area it serves, and between the possibilities of the present and the legacy of past urban decisions [John B. Sharpless and Sam Bass Warner, Jr., "Urban History," American Behavioral Scientist, 21 (Nov.-Dec. 1977), 221-244.]

Evolutionary models are enjoying a renewed vogue because of the current bankruptcy of economic thinking in the face of unanticipated conditions in both the "advanced" and the "underdeveloped" countries. During the early twentieth century evolutionary models were immensely popular, but contemporaries set them to racist and imperialistic fantasies and thereby discredited their use for generations. The enduring pioneer works of urban history, however, rest upon an evolutionary view: Patrick Geddes, Cities in Evolution (London, 1915) and Lewis Mumford, The Culture of Cities (New York, 1938). A most persuasive modern restatement of the history of urbanization according to an evolutionary model is Eric E. Lampard, "The Urbanizing World," in H. J. Dyos and Michael Wolff, The Victorian City, v. a (London, 1973), 3-57.

To give some sense of the sequence of changes which have taken place in the American urban environment since the eighteenth century we will begin this course with a slide lecture of views of cities and metropolises in the past. To organize this survey we will employ the periodization of the technological fiction of Geddes and Mumford.

According to the technological fiction, social change is propelled by technological change, and each period in history is chacterized by a dominant technology. Thus, the years prior to 1820 were a time of wind, water, horse, and human power, and hand tools. In the decades from 1820 through 1870 the dominant technology employed water and steam power, complex iron and wooden tools, the iron railroad, and horsedrawn agricultural machinery. From 1870 through 1920 the dominants were electric power and light, steel rails and machinery, the telephone, the mechanized factory, and steam-powered agricultural machiner. In our own era petroleum and atomic power, the automobile, automated machines and computers, scientific agriculture, and the beginnings of human sciences have emerged as the new modes. This periodization of American history is equivalent to the Geddes-Mumford labelling of: the Eotechnic, the Paleotechnic, the Neotechnic, and the Biotechnic. These periods also roughly conform to major alterations in the nature and distribution of the nation's population [Sam Bass Warner, Jr., and Sylvia Fleisch, "The Past of Today's Present, A Social History of America's Metropolises, 1960-1860," Journal of Urban History, 3 (November, 1976), 3-65].

Although the technological fiction is a very convenient way for ordering up a great variety of data, it is well to remember that it is only a fiction, or convention. It is well, too, to remember that the writing of technological determinism employs both equilibrium and ecological models, depending upon the scholarly training of the author. However, the course of technology does not adequately explain why cities are the way they are, nor does it predict the behavior of cities in the past. Consider for a moment the wide variety of choices which a society can make with any given technology. The difference between Europe and the United States is not a different kit of tools. Contrast the BBC and Post Office organization of television and telephones in England to America's national networks and national monopolies. Compare the American public trade school to the German or Scandinavian trade systems. Recall that Philadelphia and Baltimore long continued building row houses when the rest of the nation had switched to apartments and detached housing. Think of America's fascination with bombs when all our reports since World War II show mass bombing to be about as effective as Eotechnic Hannibal's elephants. If you are French or English, contemplate the Concorde; if you are An American taxpayer, meditate on the moon rockets.

After the lecture you can review the material by looking at the picture essays in The Urban Wilderness. You can follow the sequences of urban environments in greater detail in John A. Kouwenhoven, Columbia Historical Portrait of New York (New York, 1953) and Richard C. Wade and Harold M. Mayer, Chicago: Growth of a Metropolis (Chicago, 1969). A Boston review can be constructed from Walter Muir Whitehill, A Topographical History of Boston (Cambridge, 2nd ed., 1968) and Boston Society of Architects, Joseph L. Eldridge, ed., Architecture in Boston, etc. Useful guide books to walking tours of Boston besides Eldridge are: Boston: The Official Bicentennial Guidebook (Boston, 1975) and Paul Hogarth, Walking Tours of Old Boston (Boston, 1978). You might also find William F. Robinson, Abandoned New England (Boston, 1976) helpful for a sense of nineteenth-century technology. A standard reference for technology is: Melvin Kranzberg and Carroll Pursell, Technology in Western Civilization, 2 vol. (New York, 1967).

WORK AND LABOR BEFORE 1870

Compared to the massive building and elaborate technology of later periods, the first era of industrialization went forward with relatively modest alterations in the built environment of human settlements. There were, to be sure, some new elements: factories, bridges, dams, canals, railroad stations, and telegraph poles. But the first era of urbanization and industrialization most radically altered the relationships among people, not their physical setting.

In general, a myriad of small inventions, plus basic changes in the manner of doing business and the scale of markets, transformed the society. The shifts in marketing and the meaning of those shifts for commonplace life from the consumer's and the manufacturer's point of view can be gathered from a very readable and informative article by Dorothy S. Brady which bears the horrendous title of "Relative Prices in the Nineteenth Century," Journal of Economic History, 24 (June, 1964), 145-203. The most unusual urban marketing innovation, Harry E. Resseguie, "Alexander Tuney Stewart and the Development of the Department Store, 1823-1876," Business History Review, 39 (Autumn, 1965), 301-322. The slow rise of large business organizations is chronicled in Alfred Chandler's article, "The Beginning of Big Business in American Industry," Business History Review, 33 (Spring, 1959), 1-31.

The interactions between urbanization and industrialization took two different forms. One was the industrialized region of water-powered mill towns of which New England is characteristic. The other was the big city complex of craftsmen of which New York, Philadelphia, Cincinnati, and St. Louis were examples. In the lecture we will contrast Lowell, Mass., with Newark, N.J., as cases of each type. John Coolidge, Mill and Mansion (Cambridge, 1942) and Susan E. Hirsch, Roots of the American Working Class, The Industrialization of Newark 1800-1860 (Philadelphia, 1978).

The wage and hour changes for workers in the period are estimated in Stanley Lebergott, Manpower and Economic Growth: The American Record Since 1800 (Princeton, 1964). In general, industrialization and the enlargement of capitalist markets meant the abolition of unfree white labor for apprentices and debtors, and the abolition of black slavery. In both big city and mill town shops machines made possible the substitution of girls and children for men while the flood of overseas immigrants worked in a contrary direction. It freed native children for schooling.

The response of workers to the disruption of their traditional ways of working was imaginative and often explosive. All the ideas of the later labor movement were tried out. A general account can be found in Foster R. Dulles, Labor in America (3rd ed., New York, 1966), and in greater detail in the first volume of John R. Commons et al., History of Labor in the United States (New York, 1918); Norman Ware, The Industrial Worker, 1840-60 (Boston, 1924) and Alan Dawley, Class and Community: The Industrial Revolution in Lynn (Cambridge, 1976) are useful for New England. The best single book on artisans, shopkeepers, and social mobility in this early industrial era is Clyde and Sally Griffen, Natives and Newcomers, The Ordering of Opportunity in Mid-Nineteenth Century Poughkeepsie (Cambridge, 1979). Anthony F.C. Wallace has written an extremely evocative study of Philadelphia cotton mill families and villages, 1820-1865, Rockdale, The Growth of an American Village in the Early Industrial Revolution (New York, 1978). Articles are big city labor are: Leonard Bernstein, "The Working People of Philadelphia from Colonial Times to the General Strike of 1835," Penna. Magazine of History and Biogrpahy, 74 (July, 1950), 332-339; and David Montgomery, "The Working Classes of the Pre-Industrial American City, 1780-1830," Labor History, 9 (Winter, 1968), 3-22.

For changes in black life, Richard C. Wade, Slavery in the Cities (New York, 1964), and Leon F. Litwack, North of Slavery: the Negro in the Free States, 1790-1860 (Chicago, 1961). The experience of women, Susan Reverby et al., America's Working Women (New York, 1976), and Barbara Berg, The Remembered Gate: Origins of American Feminism -- The Woman and the City (New York, 1978). Radical alternatives to the directions society was taking, alternatives we associate with the 1960's, see Dolores Hayden, Seven American Utopias: The Architecture of Communitarian Socialism, 1790-1975.

THE RURAL CONTRIBUTION

Since the history of the United States, like the history of all modern peoples, consists of the process of urbanization of a formerly rural population, rural traditions and rural people strongly influenced the choice of paths which the nation's urbanization took. We will touch upon only two lines of rural influence: the traditions of land management, and the traditions rural immigrants brought to cities.

Some aspects of our land traditions are taken up in The Urban Wilderness. For further detail the history of land plans themselves can be followed in John W. Reps, The Making of Urban America (Princeton, 1965). The unfolding of New England land divisions is best understood by consulting Anthony N.B. Garvan, Architecture and Town Planning in Colonial Connecticut (New Haven, 1951), and Richard L. Bushman, From Puritan to Yankee (Cambridge, 1967). The changing meanings of rural land are wonderfully sketched by John B. Jackson in his book of essays, Landscapes (Ervin H. Zube, ed., Amherst, 1970), especially his "The Westward-Moving House" and "The Almost Perfect Town." His survey of both rural and townscape in the mid-nineteenth century is also very suggestive, American Space (New York, 1972).

During the nineteenth century cities were such lethal environments that they could not maintain themselves by natural reproduction, so both their continuance and growth depended upon the inflow of rural migrants. The classic treatment of the conflict and accommodations between immigrants and residents is Oscar Handlin's Boston's Immigrants. You may want to follow this Boston story down to the present racial controversies in Elizabeth H. Pleck, Black Migration and Poverty, Boston 1865-1900 (New York, 1979); and Alan Lupo, Liberty's Chosen Home (Boston, 1977).

Immigrant literature is vast, but one might best begin with some recent scholarship which has the additional merit of summarizing the historical arguments to date. Jo Ellen Vinyard, The Irish on the Urban Frontier: Nineteenth Century Detroit (New York, 1976), shows the Irish to have had a very different experience in that city than in Boston or New York. Prof. Vinyard explores the possibility that the difference was caused by rapid economic growth in the mid-western city. Joseph Barton's Peasants and Strangers (Cambridge, 1975) is the story of the varying strategies for coping taken by Rumanians, Slavs, and Italians in Cleveland. It is a fine study and a good antidote for one's immigrant stereotypes. There are two excellent recent studies of New York. The first is a complete statistical estimate, Ira Rosenwaike, Population History of New York City (Syracuse, 1972). The other is a modern mobility study, Thomas Kessner, The Golden Door: Italian and Jewish Immigrant Mobility -- 1880-1915 (New York, 1977). It is also a help to one's thinking to compare this overseas immigrant literature to the experience of white rural natives. A good literary path would be Hamlin Garland, Main-Travelled Roads (1891) for the rural Wisconsin background, Harvey W. Zorbaugh, The Gold Coast and the Slum (Chicago, 1929) for the native and immigrant settlements in Chicago after World War I, and John Dos Passos, Manhatten Transfer (1925) for a portrait and feeling of New York from the outside view of a young man come to the metropolis.

In the section of the syllabus on the Family there are further suggestions of novels and autobiographies of migrants to the city.

TRANSPORTATION

Shifts in the nature and supply of transportation so patently alter both the relationships among cities and their internal structure that the subject has long been dealt with by urbanists. Indeed, since transportation cost analysis fits so easily into our habits of economic thinking, the subject is often pursued to the neglect of other facets of urbanization.

A brief sequence which would carry the reader from the early nineteenth century to the present would be the following: George R. Taylor, The Transportation Revolution, 1815-1860 (New York, 1951) and his "Beginning of Mass Transportation in Urban America," Smithsonian Journal of History, 1 (Summer and Autumn 1966), 35-50, 31-54; David Ward, Cities and Immigrants (New York, 1971); and Sam Bass Warner, Jr., Streetcar Suburbs (Cambridge, 1962) and Charles W. Cheape, Moving the Masses (Cambridge, 1980), a transit history of Boston, New York, and Philadelphia. For the automobile era, James J. Flink, The Car Culture (Cambridge, 1975); Wilfred Owen, The Metropolitan Transportation Problem (Washington, 1966); Mark A. Rose, Interstate: Express Highway Politics, 1941-56 (Lawrence, 1977), and Gary T. Scwartz, "Urban Freeways and the Interstate System," Southern California Law Review, 49 (March, 1976), 406-513; Alan Altschuler, "The Decision-Making Environment of Urban Transportation," Public Policy (Spring, 1977). Boston has been the site of much transportation conflict and attempts to integrate many voices in the metropolis into the planning process, Allan K. Sloan, Citizen Participation in Transportation Planning (Cambridge, 1974), and Ralph Gakenheimer, Transportation Planning as Response to Controversy (Cambridge, 1976).

One might also find it useful to compare the experience of Europe with the same technology. John P. McKay, Tramways and Trolleys: The Rise of Urban Mass Transport in Europe (Princeton, 1976), and Donald L. Foley, "The Rising Use of Cars in Britain and France," Institute of Urban and Regional Development Working Paper #268 (University of Calif., Berkeley, July, 1976). Also a useful reference work is the contractors' official history: American Public Works Association, The History of Public Works in the United States, 1776-1976 (Chicago, 1976).

MUNICIPAL POLITICS

Municipal governments in America have two major functions which do not always work in tandem. One function is representation, both symbolic and actual. Much of the business of the polling place, the city council, the mayor's office, and the law courts, and most of the action reported in the daily newspapers consist of the clashes of representation. The action centers around cultural conflict, the pulling and hauling for representation and dominance. Here people struggle to have "their people" and "their culture" placed in positions of power so that their turf is protected and their view of what a city should be becomes the official view. The outcomes of this competition are often only changes in personnel and slight changes in emphasis in the choice of municipal programs, but these representational conflicts are deeply felt and turn out more voters than service squabbles.

The other major function of municipal government is the provision of services to city dwellers who may or may not be adequately included in the representational system. In American history the services to land grew first and have year in and year out until very recently received the largest part of city budgets: streets, water, sewers, police, and fire. During the nineteenth century human services gradually took their place beside the services to land, first in education, then in health, and periodically in relief for the poor. Much of the reform and policy literature of the American City has dealt with the problems of teaming the representational and service functions.

The best single historical model which approximates the sequences of municipal representation is Dahl's, in which he proposes a succession of elites. The first elite, that of the early nineteenth century, was a fused elite of business and politics in which elected officials embodied the contemporary union of mercantile and social status. This elite was replaced by a manufacturing elite, who in turn gave way to ethnic elites, who gave way in our time to leaders who rose through coalitions of fragmented ethnic and interest groups.

The generality of this model, first developed to summarize the history of New Haven, is open to some question. For instance, Banfield and Wilson in their studies of the late fifties and early sixties found considerable variety in the composition and organization of municipal elites. Edward E. Banfield and James Q. Wilson, City Politics (Cambridge, 1963), especially chapters 17-19 on the power structure, and the role of business and labor. A recent article summarizes all the dabate: David C. Hammack, "Problems in the Historical Study of Power in the Cities and Towns of the United States, 1800-1960," American Historical Review, 83 (April, 1978), 323-349. Of course, when one shifts one's concern from a single town or municipality to a metropolitan region, the complexities of analysis multiply exponentially. The place to start with this literature is Robert C. Wood, 1400 Governments: The Political Economy of the New York Metropolitan Region (Cambridge, 1961), and Robert A. Caro, The Power Broker: Robert Moses and the Fall of New York (New York, 1974).

The major events of American municipal history are set forth in Ernest S. Griffeth, A History of American City Government, 4 vols. (1938, 1972, 1976). For the peculiarity of Boston's municipal origins, as opposed to the normal American patterns, Jon C. Teaford, The Municipal Revolution in America, 1650-1825 (Chicago, 1975), and Sylvia D. Fries, The Urban Idea in Colonial America (Philadelphia, 1977). This early municipal literature is best understood if put in the context of the conflicts of artisans, journeymen, merchants and landowners prior to the Revolution. A fine synthesis of the new scholarship is Gary B. Nash, The Urban Crucible, Social Change, Political Consciousness, and the Origins of the American Revolution (Cambridge, 1979).

The classic of our reform literature is Lincoln Steffens, The Shame of the Cities (New York, 1904). His discovery of the business corruption of local government still has relevance if freely interpreted. The important heritage of Steffens' Progressive reform era is sympathetically covered in Martin J. Schiesl, The Politics of Efficiency, Municipal Administration and Reform in America 1880-1920 (Berkeley, 1977). Two studies show the links between crime and municipal politics: Lloyd Wendt and Herman Kogan, Bosses of Lusty Chicago (1943, reprint, Bloomington, 1967), the story of "Bathhouse John" Couglin and "Hinky Dink" Kenna; and Humbert S. Nelli, The Business of Crime: Italians and Syndicate Crime in the U.S. (New York, 1976). These last books should be read in conjunction with Mike Royko, Boss Richard J. Daley of Chicago (New York, 1971). Sally M. Miller's Victor Berger and the Promise of Constructive Socialism, 1910-1920 (Westport, 1973), introduces the alternative of municipal Socialism, and Henry F. Bedford's Trouble Downtown (New York, 1978), is a quick overview of a few local urban crises which have had national political impact during the twentieth century.

INSTITUTIONS AND THE CITY

Because our sociologists have concentrated upon the census characteristics of urban populations, while our economists have fixed upon the location of manufacturing and retail activities, and our planners and architects have embraced these special findings as background to their own interests in buildings and land use, and our political scientists and historians have been fascinated by the politics and policies of reform, one of the most significant aspects of city life has suffered neglect -- the growth of institutions in cities and their impact on urban living.

Consider the Boston area for a moment. Boston is what it is today because it is a regional and national center for higher education. Its population (an extraordinarily high percentage in the 19-29 age group), its economy (heavy exports of educational and research services), its physical form (campuses and buildings of every academic fashion since the eighteenth century), and its politics (intense conflict between academic reform and local ethnic representation), all reflect this institutional configuration.

A history of the growth of higher education in Boston would not serve to increase our general understanding of American cities, but one can use the development of public education to seek insights into the interaction between institutional growth and urban cultural change.

The nineteenth century was a time of extraordinary institutional innovation. The private corporation, hospitals, universities, public schools, even municipal government, as we know it, were all inventions of that century. The Private City touches upon some of this material. A Marxist perspective is provided by David M. Gordon, ed., Problems in Political Economy: An Urban Approach (Lexington, 1977). For the lecture we will concentrate on the history of public education. Today public schools are the largest single public employee group and have the greatest number of clients of any government institutions. Their changing structure and impact upon cities raise most of the issues of urban institutional history.

When considering the school material, it would be well to reflect on the peculiar state of our society, in which cultural conflict is an allowed activity for schools, but not for private business corporations. It is legitimate to make cultural demands upon schools, but our society has agreed to allow giant business corporations to operate under the fiction that their only accountable task is making products and providing work. The question of what work and what products is by convention (and in comparison to schools) a very narrowly circumscribed subject. Yet, except for the most dilatory graduate students, Americans spend more of their lives at work than in school.

The single best survey of public educational institutional history is David B. Tyack, The One Best System: A History of American Urban Education (Cambridge, 1974), and the best case study is Diane Ravitch, The Great School Wars, New York City, 1805-1973 (New York, 1974). For a sophisticated contemporary discussion of the culture of schools and the transactions between teacher and student, James Herndon, How to Survive in Your Native Land (New York, 1971). An important new evaluation of the relationship between urban schools and their teaching of the poor and the children of color, see Ronald Edmonds and John Frederiksen, "Search for Effective Schools," June, 1977, MS. for forthcoming article [in library reserve]. For mid-nineteenth-century Massachusetts there is Michael B. Katz's over-argued The Irony of Early School Reform (Cambridge, 1968); and for Boston a slow but informative survey, Stanley K. Schultz, The Culture Factory: Boston Public Schools, 1789-1860 (New York, 1973). A thoughtful and imaginative approach to the foregoing can be nourished by consulting a study of recent programs, Ivar Berg, Education and Jobs: the Great Training Robbery (Boston, 1971).

Schools were, of course, only the largest of the urban public institutions for socialization, there were many others. The unfolding of moral reform beginnings into the modern range of urban institutions, and especially urban planning is told in Paul Boyer, Urban Masses and Moral Order in America 1820-1920 (Cambridge, 1978). The police: Roger Lane, Policing the City of Boston, 1822-1885 (Cambridge, 1967); or James F. Richardson, The New York

Police: Colonial Times to 1901 (New York, 1970); David R. Johnson, Policing the Urban Underworld: The Impact of Crime on the Development of the American Police 1800-1887 (Philadelphia, 1979); and Robert M. Fogelson, Big-City Police (Cambridge, 1977). See also David J. Rothman, The Discovery of Asylum: Social Order and Disorder in the New Republic (Boston, 1971).

THE FAMILY

The Family is both a product of the constraints and possibilities of changing urban environments and an important actor who determines the course of urbanization itself. Decisions to move or not to move, to marry sooner or later, to have more children, or less, have not been uniform over time nor the same among all regions, classes, and races. Such demographic variations create strong differences in rate of urbanization and in conditions within cities and regions. In the Atlantic world the shift from populations with high mobility, low fertility, and low mortality is a little-understood but crucial determinant in the history of our urbanization. This change, known to demographers as the "demographic transition," is best described in Eric E. Lampard, "The Urbanizing World," in H.J. Dyos and Michael Wolff, The Victorian City, vol. 1 (London and Boston, 1973), 3-57. The facts of this case can be brought down to the present with George Sternlieb and James W. Hughes, Current Population Trends in the U.S. (New Brunswick, 1978).

The implications of this long trend for urban life and institutions and for the family itself can be grasped by reading Michael Young and Peter Willmott, The Symmetrical Family (London, 1972: New York, 1974), especially the historical chapters, 1-3. Young and Willmott is an English book, based on metropolitan London data; to make the translation to America, consult Peter G. Filene, Him/Her Self: Sex Roles in Modern America (New York, 1974), and John P. Robinson and Philip E. Converse, "Social Change Reflected in the Use of Time," in Angus Campbell and Philip E. Converse, The Human Meaning of Social Change (New York, 1972), and Joseph F. Kett, Rites of Passage: Adolescence in America, 1790 to the Present (New York, 1977); and Roger Lane's speculations on the long-term social trends in urban industrialism in his Violent Death in the City, Suicide, Accident, and Murder in Nineteenth Century Philadelphia (Cambridge, 1979). There is also a useful article literature: Tamara K. Hareven, Family and Kin in Urban Communities, 1700-1930 (New York, 1977), John G. Clark et al., Three Generations in Twentieth Century America (Homewood, 1977), and Winifred D.W. Bolin, "The Economics of Middle-Income Family Life: Working Women During the Great Depression," Journal of American History, 65 (June, 1978), 60-74; and a recent summary volume of essays on the changing history of age and family sequences, John Demos and Sarone S. Boocock, Turning Points (American Journal of Sociology, v. 84 Supplement, 1978).

Novels and autobiographies are perhaps the best way to acquire a sense of the texture and meanings of past family living styles. Some classics are: Edith Wharton, Age of Innocence (1920), a story of wealthy New York families in the years after the Civil War. It should be contrasted with Henry Seidel Canby, The Age of Confidence (1934), reminiscences of life among the wealthy in a small city (Wilmington, Delaware) during the 1880's and 1890's. Irish working class and lower middle class life in Chicago from before the Great War to the Great Depression, James T. Farrell, Studs Lonigan (1932-35). This should be compared to a New York Irish autobiography, William Gleason, A Mass for the Dead (1968). The Jewish experience during the same years, Abraham Cahan, The Rise of David Levinsky (1917) and Henry Roth, Call It Sleep (1934). Two very different paths in the black "Great Migration" to northern cities in the early twentieth century, William Attaway, Blood on the Forge (1941), Kentucky to Pittsburgh, and a success story autobiography, James Weldon Johnson, Along This Way (1933), Florida to Harlem. Harriette Arnow, The Dollmaker (1954) tells the story of poor whites coming from Kentucky to Detroit during World War II; resident white poor who are struggling in the city and having a bad time of it are characterized in Joyce Carol Oates, Them (1970). For the suburbanites of the fifties, Richard Yates, Revolutionary Road (1961).

WORK AND LABOR SINCE 1870

The source of much of the cultural and political change which has taken place during the past century lies in the interactions between urbanization and industrialization. Put in skeletal terms, the rise of a national network of cities brought with it the opportunities of national and metropolitan markets. These new economic possibilities in turn encouraged mechanized production of manufactured goods, national and metropolitan communications and sales, and the bureaucratization of manufacturing, services, and government. Although much research needs to be done which would investigate the specific ties among national and metropolitan markets, private corporations, public institutions, and the bureaucratization of work, some of the bold threads can be discerned by reading Norman Scott Brien Gras' classic essay on the metropolitanization of society in his An Introduction to Economic History (New York, 1922). The complexities of the change come out in Michael P. Conzen's study of shifting banking territories, "The Maturing Urban System in the U.S., 1840-1910," Annals of the Association of American Geographers, 67 (March, 1977), 88-108. The classic study on the rise of the giant twentieth-century American corporation is Alfred D. Chandler, Jr., Strategy and Structure (Cambridge, 1962), and his The Visible Hand: The Managerial Revolution in American Business (Cambridge, 1977). There is also a beginning literature on the multinational corporation and the city. Robert B. Cohen, The Impact of Foreign Direct Investment in U.S. Cities and Regions (Atlantic Sciences Corp., Arlington, Virginia, HUD Contract 5193-79, 1979).

The consequences for society of the new organization of business have been extraordinarily far-reaching. Since 1920 millions of farmers have been driven off the land and into cities. This rural population, both native and foreign, still constitutes a major pool of cheap labor. The other labor pool has been women, who now constitute about forty per cent of the monetized work force -- twice their proportion a century ago. Susan Reverby et al., America's Working Women (New York, 1976).

The major institutional response to the large scale corporate organization has been the ruse of the labor union. A fine study of the nineteenth century community-based unions in John T. Cumbler, Working Class Community in Industrial America (Westport, 1979), a study of Lyn and Fall River, Mass. 1880-1930. It has its parallel in Daniel Walkowitz's history of the iron workers of Troy, N.Y., Worker City, Company Town (Urbana, 1979). These cases should be read with Herbert G. Gutman's essays on nineteenth century workers culture, Work, Culture, and Society (New York, 1966-73). Wyndham Mortimer's Organize! is a fine account of the rise of the United Auto Workers and gives an excellent sense of the coming of the new national, industrial unions. To update Mortimer's experience one should consult the latest book on UAW-GM relations, William Serrin, The Company and the Union (New York, 1966-73). The defeat of alternatives, democratic socialism, and syndiacalism, is movingly told in Ray Ginger, Eugene V. Debs (1949, reprint, New York, 1962), and William D. Haywood, Bill Haywood's Book (New York, 1929). The standard labor history for the post-World War I era is Irving Bernstein, The Lean Years (Boston, 1966), and his The Turbulent Years (Boston, 1970). Bernstein's cautious assessments are modified by the enthusiastic Richard O. Boyer and Herbert M. Morais, Labor's Untold Story (New York, 1955).

The interpretations of the effects upon commonplace urban life caused by these orgainizational changes in the work setting are various. The predominant American school argues that most workers became bureaucrats on the job and sought relief from the tensions of the workplace in heightened concentration upon family and consumer escapes. The pioneer in this thinking is Thorstein Veblen. The best followers of his lead are, besides Lewis Mumford, C. Wright Mills, White Collar (New York, 1951); William H. Whyte, Jr., The Organization Man (New York, 1956); and Jules Henry, Culture Against Man (New York, 1963). Karl Marx explored these tendencies of large-scale production and proposed the concept of alienation. His speculations have been tested in modern American contexts by Robert Blauner. Alienation and Freedom: the Factory Worker and His Industry (Chicago, 1964). A Marxist interpretation is Harry Braverman, Labor and Monopoly Capital: The Degradation of Work in the 20th Century (New York, 1974).

The mechanisms whereby the economic pleasures and pains of this society are allocated are still imperfectly understood. The income shares of fractions of the population have remained quite stable since 1914, Herman P. Miller, Rich Man, Poor Man (New York, 1971). The vexed issue of wealth, as opposed to income, is discussed in Lester C. Thurow, Generating Inequality: Mechanisms of Distribution in the U. S. Economy (New York, 1975). Speculation about the relative steadiness of inter-generational shifts in occupational titles can be found in Stephen Thernstrom, The Other Bostonians: Poverty and Progress in the American Metropolis, 1880-1970 (Cambridge, 1973). A review of the literature of the history of American social mobility is Edward Pessen, Three Centuries of Social Mobility in America (Lexington, 1974). Current Marxist debates on the modes of allocation of the fruits of the society can be found in David M. Gordon, Problems in Economy: An Urban Perspective (Lexington, 1975), and David Harvey, Social Justice and the City (Baltimore, 1973).

URBAN MAN AND URBAN NATURE

Man as a species has become so numerous, and his built environment and activities have become so predominant that thoughtful people are now concerned that in order for both man and the rest of nature to continue to flourish, humans must consciously order their behavior so as to maintain and nourish urban, regional, and global ecologies. To this new consciousness the earth has suddenly become not a world apart which we can rely upon, but something, like a field, which we must actively tend.

As Americans we bring to this new task very inappropriate habits of feeling and understanding. Our tradition considers man and the works of man as one category, the balance of nature another. Yet, if we must now regard all environments as matters for our concern, urban man is as much a part of nature as the beasts of the field or the creatures of the forest and oceans.

The best single work which traces the intellectual background to our current concerns is Donald Fleming, "Roots of the New Conservative Movement," in Perspectives in American History, 6 (1972), 7-91. An excellent new book covers the same ground in a broader and more sympathetic way, Donald Worster, Nature's Economy (San Francisco, 1977). There is a marvelous English book which traces the changing perception of what constitutes the country and what the city since the seventeenth century, Raymond Williams, The Country and the City (New York, 1973). For the United States there exists a partial opposite, Leo Marx, The Machine and The Garden (New York, 1967). For a tentative metropolitan explication of these issues see Sam Bass Warner Jr., The Way We Really Live: Social Change in Metropolitan Boston Since 1920 (Boston Public Library, 1977).

Because of our habit of seeing man and nature as opposites, our interventions into the built environment of cities take two distinct forms -- the public health movement and the park movement. The first deals directly with a few of man's physical and economic behaviors, the second dealt largely with our religious feelings about non-human nature.

The history of the public health movement can be sketched by consulting Nelson Blake, Water for the Cities (Syracuse, 1956): John Duffy, A History of Public Health in New York City, 1625-1866 (New York, 1968); Odin W. Anderson, The Uneasy Equilibrium: Private and Public Financing of Health Service in the U.S., 1875-1965 (New Haven, 1968); and Peter De Vise et al., Slum Medicine: Chicago's Apartheid Health System (Univ. of Chicago Interuniversity Social Research Committee, Report #6, Chicago, 1969). A brief historical review and an excellent analysis of the current meaning of our urban health systems is nicely set forth in Amasa B. Ford, Urban Health in America (New York, 1976).

For the park movement it might be best to start with an Anglo-American overview, Goerge F. Chadwick, The Park and the Town (New York, 1966), and then to consult Olmsted's plans, which are published in Albert Fein, Frederick Law Olmsted and the American Environmental Tradition (New York, 1972), and Julius Gy Fabos et al., Frederick Law Olmsted Sr. (Amherst, 1968). A fascinating biography of America's pioneer landscape architect, which clearly shows the blend of evangelical religion and Yankee practicality, is Laura Wood Roper, FLO: A Biography of Frederick Law Olmsted (Baltimore, 1973). During the twenties the religious impulse and the urban park movement became separated and the city component of park activity died. Leonard K. Eaton, Landscape Artist in America, Jens Jensen (Chicago, 1964). The religious inspiration, however, moved out to larger visions, Benton MacKaye, The New Exploration: A Philosohy of Regional Planning (1928, reprint Urbana, 1962).

Recently there have been new attempts to redefine the relationships between natural man and the rest of nature in secular ecological terms. Ian L. McHarg, Design with Nature (New York, 1969) and Kevin Lynch, Managing the Sense of a Region (Cambridge, 1976). To pursue this new approach a new way of thinking is required. The new style in its research manifestation could best be termed urban natural history. The first beginnings of this work are suggested by Don Gill and Penelope Bonnett, Nature in the Urban Landscape: A Study of City Ecosystems (Baltimore, 1973); John Kieran, A Natural History of New York City (Boston, 1959);

and a wonderful Boston guidebook, Nancy M. Page and Richard E. Weaver, Jr., Wild Plants in the City (New York, 1975). Also useful summaries of the present state of thought appear in Thomas R. Detwyler and Melvin G. Marcus, Urbanization and the Environment (Scituate, 1972).

HOUSING REFORM

Industrialized urbanization manufactured the social problem of housing. It created the problem in actuality by crowding millions of people into structures and streets which violated their traditional ways of living, and it created the problem as a construct of political reform. The later aspect of the housing problem had its roots in a rising concern for urban public health and urban public order.

To say that the housing problem as we know it was a creation of the nineteenth century is not to say that prior to that time all humans were well housed. Before the rapid growth of cities one might guess that the traditions and resources of rural society and town life built shelters in which many were adequately housed, many poorly housed, and a few elegantly housed, and a few dangerously housed. Industrial urbanization by altering both the power and resource relationships between people and their houses created the chronic urban housing problem as it is now experienced--an inability of a modern city to house all its residents according to its contemporary norms for a decent standard. The concern for urban health and order in turn gave this social and economic stratification its special political meanings. John F. C. Turner's book, Housing by People, discusses the current situation after a century of efforts to cope with the obdurate stratification.

To capture a sense of a metropolis prior to industrialization, one should consult M. Dorothy George, London Life in the Eighteenth Century (1925, reprint, New York, 1965), and a poor American's experience with the city, Anon., The Life and Remarkable Adventures of Israel R. Potter (1824, reprint, New York, 1962).

Our reform literature has a progress from health to real estate. It begins with a public health inquiry instigated by cholera epidemics and draft riots, Citizens' Association of New York, Report of the Council of Hygiene and Public Health upon the Sanitary Condition of the City (New York, 1865). There followed a series of works which defined the housing problem as the problem of the inner city immigrant slum. Charles Loring Brace, The Dangerous Classes of New York, and Twenty Years' Work Among Them (New York, 1872); Jacob Riis, How the Other Half Lives (1890, many reprints). The thinking and the building and fire codes of this era became the framework within which we have worked since. The era is nicely summarized in Roy Lubove, The Progressives and the Slums (Pittsburgh, 1962). Lubove's tale is brought down to the present by Anthony Jackson, A Place Called Home: A History of Low-Cost Housing in Manhattan (Cambridge, 1976).

During World War I the federal government momentarily entered the field by providing standard housing for skilled war workers. A thoughtful review of the implications of that effort was written by Frederick Law Olmsted, Jr.,

"Lessons from the Housing Development of the U.S. Housing Corporation," U.S. Department of Labor, Monthly Labor Review, 8 (April, 1919), 27-38. The necessity for federal construction as a consequence of the failure of all previous philanthropic and regulatory efforts is argued in two books. One is a very intelligent history of Chicago's regulation and housing reform campaigns by Edith Abbott and Sophonsiba Breckinridge, The Tenements of Chicago, 1908-1935 (Chicago, 1936); the other an illustrated review of the nation's work, including the new federal programs, James Ford, Slums and Housing, 2 vols. (Cambridge, 1936). A recent book surveys the design of American domestic architecture from Downing to World War I. It is useful as a history of landscaping, plumbing and heating, and plans, and also because it unfolds the general trends of middle class expectations for a decent house. David P. Handlin, The American Home, Architecture and Society 1815-1915 (Boston, 1979).

The New Deal not only built urban public housing projects but also experimented with suburban and rural community construction, Paul K. Conkin, Tomorrow a New World: the New Deal Community Program (Ithaca, 1959); and Joseph L. Arnold, The New Deal in the Suburbs: A History of the Greenbelt Town Program, 1935-1954 (Columbus, 1971). The most intelligent architectural review of the lessons and possibilities of this experience appears in Clarence Stein's influential book, Toward New Towns for America (New York, 1957). A chatty update is Carlos C. Campbell, New Towns: Another Way to Live (Reston, 1976).

The post-World War II urban renewal and public housing mix is best analyzed by Charles Abrams, The City Is the Frontier (New York, 1965), and the Douglas Commission survey, National Commission on Urban Problems, Building the American City, House Document No. 19-34 (91st Congress, 1st Session, Washington, 1969), and Mark I. Gelfand's excellent survey of federal urban policy, A Nation of Cities, The Federal Government and Urban America 1933-1965 (New York, 1975).

Reformers' dissatisfaction with the outcomes of this public and private construction surfaced prominently with Jane Jacobs, Death and Life of Great American Cities (New York, 1961). This release of reform pressure, when combined with conservative displeasure, drastically reduced federal construction and construction aid and produced a new literature of modest goals, Bernard J. Frieden, The Politics of Neglect: Urban Aid for Model Cities and Revenue Sharing (Cambridge, 1975), and Rolf Goetze, Building Neighborhood Confidence (Cambridge, 1976).

PLANNING

Surely one of the expectations in studying urban history is the hope that a review of long trends will help to form an intelligent opinion about what directions contemporary urban policy might take. The past is, to be sure, not often a clear and easy guide to the future, but it is the only guide we possess. Therefore, however ambiguous its directions, it pays attending.

To put the case for history in a modest form, we ought to note that even in the brief span of this course we have been able to point continuously to ways in which the changing patterns of human settlement have influenced the institutions politics, and modes of living in the United States. This way of looking at our existence, a focus which says urban patterns are essential determinants of life, is not one common to contemporary thinking. Our political debate about the regulation of business, energy, transport, communications, education, health care, employment, race, and sex is not organized in such terms. Rather debate centers around the institutional conflicts generated by particular programs, particular agencies of government, and the power positions of the three levels of government (federal, state, and local). There is thus a constant separation between our thinking about plans and the reality of our society. This gap between the actuality of life and the structure of our political institutions is in part the cause of the shortcomings of many of our past plans and policies.

At the outset one might begin by reviewing the very specialized confines of those in the profession called urban planning. An official and complete history of city planning is Mel Scott, American City Planning Since 1890 (Berkeley, 1969), and historical articles on planning appear from time to time in the Journal of the American Institute of Planners. Such a survey should be accompanied by more general reviews of American planning; Jonathan R.T. Hughes, The Governmental Habit: Economic Controls from Colonial Time to the Present (New York, 1977), and Otis L. Graham, Toward A Planned Society: From Roosevelt to Nixon (New York, 1976).

In using the course of American urban history as a measure for current planning and policy, I have found it useful to consider the response of government to urbanization through a series of overlapping themes.

1. It is possible to view the history of public intervention into urban affairs as part of a broad trend of expanding democratic thought which has moved in an ever-widening course since the Revolution. By this reasoning the Revolution became a time when equalitarian demands were legitimized, and ever since then these demands pressed against the class, sex, and racial stratifications of the society. Thus, the nineteenth century institutional innovations of public schools, public libraries, city hospitals, parks, and even the health and safety measures can be seen as an extension of services to offset the stratifications of wealth and income which prevailed in the private society. In this respect one might note that in campaigning for the enlargement of public services and projects, equalitarian rhetoric is always used in generous quantities. Thus even the campaigns themselves can be regarded as additions to the nation's democratic tradition.

This point of view is employed by either conservatives or radicals when advocating a new direction for planning. Anthony Downs, Opening Up the Suburbs: an Urban Strategy for America (New Haven, 1973), Bennett Harrison, Urban Economic Development: Suburbanization, Minority Opportunity, and the Condition of the Central City (Washington, 1974). But today this long democratic trend seems stalled politically on the obdurate issues of race and poverty. Gary A. Tobin, ed., The Changing Structure of the City, What Happened to the Urban Crisis? (Urban Affairs Annual Review, v. 16, 1979).

2. An alternative view of our public policy is to view governments as stumbling after ever-new public demands. In this case a panting and tired government is besieged by both the poor and the affluent, some making demands for help with misfortune, others with demands for the popularization of luxuries. The sudden and massive migration of foreigners to cities in the nine-

teenth century and of blacks from the South in the twentieth thus are the cause of demands for housing and social services: the drastic devaluation of urban property isnce 1929 can be seen as giving rise to the demand for urban renewal; the obsolescence of regional economies produced demands for aid to farmers and to depressed areas. On the luxury side the marketing of mass luxuries by the private sector produces demands for high-speed auto highways everywhere, or the addition of marina or airports for small planes, or the extension of higher education to all children, or the the raising of water quality and air standards. Lloyd Rodwin, Nations and Cities: A Comparison of Strategies for Urban Growth (Boston, 1970); Conference on Environmental Quality and Social Justice, Woodstock, Illinois, 1972, Environmental Quality and Social Justice in Urban America (James Noel Smith, ed., Washington, 1974), and Ann L. Strong, Land Banking. European Reality and American Prospect (Baltimore, 1979).

3. Another way of looking over our unfolding urban plans and policies is to observe that as a political body the United States has not been able to deal head-on with the conflict between our equalitarian ideals and the stratification of our income and wealth distribution. Instead of income redistribution, therefore, we have instituted categorical relief for particular problems -- building and fire codes and public housing for urban slums, unemployment and old-age insurance for the swings of business and the absense of private savings and pensions, model cities and school busing for blacks, urban renewal for inner city property owners, etc.

Although it is a very new intellectual phenomenon, on both the conservative and radical poles of such thinking today the categorical view carries with it the observation of bureaucratization. Thus each program is seen as giving rise to a particular bureaucracy and in time each bureaucracy becomes tied to its own set of supplying and receiving institutions so that as conditions change, federal, state, and local governments are left saddled with expensive and inappropriate undertakings. The seminal analytic study of this process in planning is Philip Selznick, T.V.A. and the Grass Roots (1949, reprint, New York, 1966). The case was continued by Donald N. Rothblatt, Regional Planning: An Appalachian Experience (Lexington, 1971); the issue brought home to roost, George Sternlieb and James W. Hughes, Revitalizing the Northeast (New Brunswick, 1978).

This point of view now dominates our current thinking about urban design. It is most forcibly argued by Peter Blake, Form Follows Fiasco: Why Modern Architecture Hasn't Worked (Boston, 1977); and Stephen R. Seidel, Housing Costs and Government Regulation: Confronting the Regulatory Maze (New Brunswick, 1978). An attempt to find a way out by enlarging the "neutral" services of municipal government to the construction of structures which the users adapt for themselves has been put forward by N.J. Habraken, Supports: An Alternative to Mass Housing (New York, 1962). A more modest and familiar set of proposals for architecture and transportation is Wolf von Eckardt, Back to the Drawing Board (Washington, 1978).

4. Still another alternative view is to follow the path of the Fabians and the Marxists. This school of thought notes that as industrialized urbanization unfolds, more and more of the "necessities" of life leave the private sector and are either provided publicly or heavily subsidized. Education, water, police, fire protection, housing, rail, auto, and air transport, now health and food have all become subjects for direct government supply or heavy government intervention

and subsidy.

If one is of a revolutionary turn of mind, then one sees in this trend long-term rising costs and the inevitable bankruptcy of the capitalist state and the ultimate arrival of the socialist or fascist revolution.

If one is of a more pacific turn of mind, one might observe that the same sequence has been accompanied by an interaction of rising popular income and rising demands for society to universalize ever more elaborate goods and services. Because of the new metropolitan settlement patterns these goods and services can be provided relatively efficiently only through the use of public capital and often large-scale public production as well. In other words, as the Fabians argued years ago, industrialized urbanization inevitably brings with it some kinds of socialism. George Bernard Shaw, The Intelligent Women's Guide to Socialism and Capitalism (New York, 1928); Manuel Castells, The Urban Question: A Marxist Approach (London, 1977). Robert Heilbroner, Business Civilization in Decline (New York, 1975), is a deeply pessimistic book predicting totalitarianism as an inevitable consequence of modern large-scale society.

A lively alternative group says that small-scale community actions are a viable alternative to big business and big government: E.F. Schumacher, Small is Beautiful: Economics as if People Mattered (New York, 1973), and Scott Burns, The Household Economy (Boston, 1975), and an interesting Boston case to contemplate, Stewart E. Perry, Building a Model Black Community: the Roxbury Action Program (Cambridge, 1978).

UNIVERSITY OF PENNSYLVANIA

History 350: Spring, 1983

Class Hours: Tuesday and Thursday, 1:30-3:00

Seymour J. Mandelbaum
123 Fine Arts, x 6492

Office Hours: Tuesday, 3-5
Thursday, 11-1

U.S. URBAN HISTORY

1. Introduction

None of you would be surprised if I started this course by announcing that cities are real things -- rather like a painting or a person -- but that they are (as all such things) subject to varied and conflicting interpretations of their current state and their history. We could then spend the semester studying rival points of view, noting their strengths and weaknessess and repeatedly reminding ourselves that they are partial and biased. In that discussion, cities would remain as complex and elusive but, nevertheless, tangible entities. Historians may recount their past, (hence this course in urban history), while planners and policy-makers guide their future -- all confidently assuming that beyond the darkened glass lies a single palpable reality. If our tastes are theological, we may envy God's holistic view of cities and attempt to approximate it. More simply, we may talk about liking or not liking cities as if we were assessing Beethoven's symphonies. Each is different but they have all been generated by a coherent set of principles (in one case, conventionally called, _the city_; in the other, _Beethoven_.)

This course starts on a very different tack. The words "city" and "urban" seem to me to be very general (and often deliberately obscuring) rubrics spread over a disparate set of mental constructs. Even the most overtly palpable of these constructs -- cities as peculiarly dense concentrations of physical artifacts and people -- is only an idea, a creature of our purposes and our imaginations I'll elaborate on this nominalist view of cities in the first few class sessions. The purpose of the course is not, however, to explicate all of the constructs which have been squeezed under the capacious urban mantle. Instead, I have chosen two topics which interest me and devoted the course to them. They are:

1. the ways in which the spatial distribution of people and activities influence the articulation of future distributive choices.

2. the forms and political dynamics of social control and integration within settlements.

Beyond all the specific things I'd like you to understand about these topics, I'm concerned that you be able to _think historically_ about them. I'll spend some time in the early sessions on the meaning of that goal because it is often confused with a close mate: _explaining historically_ or _understanding historical_ origins.

The topics -- as you will quickly see -- overlap and complement one another. You'll learn more about the first as we do the second. The unavoidable cost of this complementarity is that you will suffer at the beginning for not knowing the end. We must, however, start somewhere. In order to help fill-in contextual gaps, I'd like all of you to read Charles N. Glaab and A. Theodore Brown, A History of Urban America (New York: Macmillan, 3rd edition, 1983). I've assigned particular chapters throughout the syllabus but you might wisely read through the entire text in the first few weeks.

My pedagogical method requires that you prepare for each class session by reading the assignment and thinking about its place in the flow of the course. (I'll often suggest questions which you might keep in mind as you read.) All the materials are on reserve in Rosengarten and many have been stocked by the Bookstore.

The students in this course usually have very diverse backgrounds and it is very difficult for me to know in advance all the different ways either the readings or class sessions may confuse you. Please ask questions aggressively in class and come to see me in my office. There is a sign-up sheet for my office hours on my door so you may be reasonably assured of a fixed time.

2. Writing Assignments

Everyone is to write two papers of approximately 1500 words in length during the course of the semester. The first paper is due on February 25 at noon in Room 127 FA. It will be discussed at a special evening session on March 2 from 7-9 in the 4th Floor Center in the Graduate School of Fine Arts. The second paper is due on April 15 at noon and will be discussed at an evening session on April 20, from 7-9 in the 4th Floor Center.

The first paper requires that you select three sections in a large U.S. metropolitan area:

a. a section first developed in the 1880's.

b. a section first developed in the 1920's.

c. the Central Business District.

Describe the changes in each area over extended periods:

a. the 1830's section in 1930 and 1980.

b. the 1920's section in 1980.

c. the CBD in 1880, 1930 and 1980.

You may use pictures, maps, tables or verbal accounts to characterize the changes. You should justify your choice of descriptive dimensions and your use of particular measures.

The second paper requires that you manipulate the past. Every major U.S. city has experienced brief periods during which the sources of in-migration changed sharply. Select such a period and imagine that you were the major in the prior decade. You anticipate the coming shift, don't believe that it can or should be stopped but would like to prepare your city for it. Sketch your program and then compare it critically with what was done.

The final examination will include two sections. In the first, I'll pose one or more questions which test your mastery of the readings; in the second, I'd like you to sketch how you would revise Our Cities (1937) if given the chance. The background of that volume is described in Glaab and Brown.

3. Grading

The two papers and the final examination each count for 100 points. I may also occasionally ask you to respond to questions about the assigned reading.

I. SYLLABUS

1. 1/18 Introduction

2. 1/20 Population Distribution in an Agricultural Nation

   Glaab and Brown, chapters 1-2.
   David Ward, Cities and Immigrants (1971), 3-38.

3. 1/25 Manufacturing and the New Urban Hierarchy of the Nineteenth Century

   Glaab and Brown, chapters 4 and 6.
   David Ward, 39-49.

4. 1/27 Regional Redistribution and Resources in the 20th Century

   Advisory Commission on Intergovernmental Relations, Regional Growth: Historic Perspective (1980), 1-48, 39-91.

5. 2/1 Reflections on the Dynamics of Redistribution

   Alfred J. Watkins and David C. Perry, "Regional Change and the Impact of Uneven Urban Development," in David C. Perry and Alfred J. Watkins, eds., The Rise of the Sunbelt Cities (1977), 19-54.

6. 2/3 Reflections on the Dynamics of Redistribution

   David M. Gordon, "Class Struggle and the Stages of American Urban Development," and Walt W. Rostow, "Regional Changes in the Fifth Kondratieff Upswing," in Perry and Watkins, 55-103.

II. The Pattern Within Urban Areas

7. 2/8 The Dense City of the 19th Century

   Glaab and Brown, chapter 7
   Ward, 51-101.

8. 2/10 The Dense City of the 19th Century

   Ward, 105-150.

9. 2/15 The Dispersed City of the 20th Century

   Glaab and Brown, chapter 13.
   Peter O. Muller, Contemporary Suburban America (1981) chapters 1-2.

10. 2/17 The Dispersed City of the 20th Century

    Glaab and Brown, Chapters 15-16.
    Peter O. Muller, chapters 3-4.

11. 2/22 Reflections on the Urban Transformation

    Thomas Bender, Toward an Urban Vision (1975), chapters 1-4

12. 2/24 Reflections on Urban Landscape

    Bender, chapters 5- epilogue

FIRST PAPER DUE ON FEBRUARY 25.

13. 3/1 Reflections on the Pattern of Cities: Macro and Micro

    President's Commission for a National Agenda, Urban America in the Eighties (1982)

14. SPECIAL EVENING SESSION, MARCH 2, TO DISCUSS THE FIRST PAPER

II. Social Control and Integration: The Inventor of Problems

15. 3/8 The Problem of Moral Order

    Glaab and Brown, chapter 5
    Paul Boyer, Urban Masses and Moral Order in America (1978), Parts 1-2.

16. 3/10 The Problem of Moral Order

    Glaab and Brown, chapter 11
    Boyer, Parts 3-4.

17. 3/22 The Problem of Physical Order

    Glaab and Brown, chapter 12
    Martin V. Melosi, "Environmental Crisis in the City: The Relationship between Industrialization and Urban Pollution and Joel A. Tarr, James McGurley and Terry F. Yosie, "The Development and Impact of Urban Wastewater Technology: Changing Concepts of Water Quality Control, 1850-1930," in Martin V. Melosi, ed., Pollution and Reform in American Cities, 1870-1930 (1980), 3-31, 59-82.

III. The Federal Framework of Social Control and Integration

18. 3/24 The Federal System

Glaab and Brown, chapter 9.

Daniel J. Elazar, "Federal-State Collaboration in the Nineteenth Century United States," Political Science Quarterly, 79 (1964), 248-281

NO CLASS ON MARCH 29

19. 3/31 The Federal System

John W. Burgess, "The American Commonwealth: Changes in its Relation to the Nation," Political Science Quarterly, 1 (1886), 9-35.

Frank Goodnow, Municipal Government (1909), chapters VI-IX.

NO CLASS ON APRIL 5

20. 4/7 The Federal System

Kenneth T. Jackson, "Metropolitan Government Versus Suburban Autonomy: Politics on the Crabgrass Frontier" in Kenneth T. Jackson and Stanley K. Schultz, eds., Cities in American History (1972), 442-462.

Arnold Fleischmann, "Sunbelt Boosterism: The Politics of Postwar Growth and Annexation in San Antonio," in Perry and Watkins, 151-168.

21. 4/12 The Federal System

Glaab and Brown, chapter 14.

Theodore J. Lowi, "The State of Cities in the Second Republic," in John P. Blair and David Nachmias, eds., Fiscal Retrenchment and Urban Policy (1979), 43-54.

IV. Politics and the Social Order

22. 4/14 The Urban Political Hierarchy

J. Rogers Hollingsworth and Ellen Jane Hollingsworth Dimensions in Urban History: Historical and Social Science Perspectives on Middle-Size American Cities (1979), chapter I.

SECOND PAPER DUE ON APRIL 15

23. 4/19 Elites and Politics

Glaab and Brown, chapter 10

David C. Hammack, Power and Society: Greater New York at the Turn of the Century (1982), Part II.

24. 4/21 Elites and Politics
Hammack, Part III

25. 4/26 The Social Order in Local Boundaries
Ira Katznelson, <u>City Trenches</u> (1981), chapters 1-4.

26. 4/28 The Social Order in Local Boundaries
Katznelson, chapters 5-8.

YALE UNIVERSITY

HISTORY 426a

FALL 1983

THE URBANIZATION OF AMERICA TO 1870

INSTRUCTOR: Bill Cronon, 409 Calhoun.
Phones: 436-0738 (office); 432-0439 (home). Please, no calls to either of these numbers after 8:00 P.M.
Office Hours: 2:00-4:00 Thursdays. I would prefer to see you at these times, but will always be glad to meet with you at other times if this is necessary. Please don't just stop by my office if you need to see me at times other than my office hours; call first and make an appointment.

DESCRIPTION

This seminar constitutes the first half of a two-semester course surveying the history of American cities from colonial times to the present, the break between semesters falling at about 1870. It has two distinct goals: 1) to introduce the themes of urban history both as an academic discipline and as a way of gaining a longer perspective on the problems of modern cities; and 2) to practice doing history in the context of individual and collective research.

Our major task in the course will be to examine the complex social phenomenon called "urbanization" and determine how it changed life in America between 1620 and 1870. What did it mean for more and more people to be living in cities, and what did this fact imply both for cities and for the nation? How did new cities come to be created and how did urbanization change the relationship between city and country? In what ways did the experience of urban life at various times during this period differ for people of different classes, sexes, races, and ethnic groups? What was the role of cities in the westward movement of the American population and in the proliferation of American capitalism? How did people who experienced these changes try to understand what was going on around them? Perhaps most importantly, how did the rise of urban America change American definitions of community, and American notions of the good or the just society?

We will read about and discuss these various themes as they apply to many American cities, but we will practice "doing" them, as historians, in terms of a single city: New Haven. A junior seminar such as this one should accomplish more than a mere introduction to its special topic. Much more important is that it introduce the tools that historians use in doing research. This means learning how to use a wide range of bibliographical aids and becoming aware of the breadth of sources available for doing historical research. It means digging up a wide variety of primary sources, constructing them into a solid analysis of a research problem, and presenting that analysis in lucid and interesting English prose. Equally importantly, it means learning to work together as a group. The ideal research seminar is a collective creation in which individuals coordinate their work together, share their discoveries, and criticize one another constructively and gently. By doing various aspects of our research into New Haven's history jointly as a group, we should learn a great deal not only about how the themes of the course apply to the town in which we live, but also about what it means for historians (and other people) to work together.

WORK

Assignments in the course fall into two distinct groups: readings and discussions on U.S. urban history generally, and research and written work on New Haven. Students will be expected to keep a weekly journal recording their thoughts not only on course readings, but on discussions, research work, and any other material relevant to the broad themes of urban history. In particular, one section of the journal each week in the early part of the course will be devoted to the examination of a particular type of historical document, in order to assess how one should use it in doing history. Journal entries will be collected each week, but will not be graded; they should be regarded as working papers rather than formal prose exercises.

Reading assignments are fairly extensive, averaging about 225 pages per week, but are generally not difficult and have been chosen for their readability. Required readings are listed in the weekly outline that follows. A number of central texts are available at the Yale Co-op:

Charles Glaab & Theodore Brown, A History of Urban America
Paul Boyer & Stephen Nissenbaum, Salem Possessed
Gary Nash, The Urban Crucible
Jon C. Teaford, The Municipal Revolution in America
Benjamin Franklin, The Autobiography
Thomas Dublin, Women at Work
Friedrich Engels, The Condition of the Working Class in England
Thomas Bender, Toward an Urban Vision
Charles Rosenberg, The Cholera Years
Charles Brace, The Dangerous Classes of New York
Horatio Alger, Ragged Dick
Stephan Thernstrom, Poverty and Progress.
William Strunk & E. B. White, The Elements of Style

Don't let the length of this list intimidate you. Many of these books you will not be reading in their entirety. Books are expensive these days, and there's no reason for you to buy copies of all of these unless you want to. Use your discretion; all are available on reserve at Cross Campus Library, and some could easily be shared if you worked out an arrangement with someone else in class. In addition to the books listed above, we will be reading a number of documents and articles (marked "R" on the weekly outline below), all of which will be available on Shelf #1 in the Andrews Study (Room 214) on the second floor of Sterling Library. PLEASE DO NOT REMOVE THE ANDREWS STUDY XEROXES UNLESS YOU ARE MAKING A COPY FOR YOURSELF. If you find that an individual reading is missing from the shelf, contact me and go to the original citation provided in the outline below.

Written work and research will evolve as we go along, but their general outlines are as follows. In the early part of the course, there will be several homework assignments designed to introduce you to a variety of historical documents typically used in urban research; most will be related to some aspect of New Haven. These assignments will not be formal exercises, but will be written up as part of your weekly journal. In addition to dealing with different types of documents, this homework will be designed to show you different ways of ng finding them and different places in which to find them.

In the fifth week of class, you will turn in a brief (5-7 page) paper in which you will do a comparative analysis/synthesis of the arguments contained in two of the books on the syllabus, Gary Nash's The Urban Crucible and Jon C. Teaford's The

Municipal Revolution in America, books which bring radically different perspectives to roughly similar periods of American urban history. The paper will be graded, but its main purposes are to give you a formal writing exercise early in the class and to make you think about the ways in which historians' different theoretical perspectives shape the kind of history they write. Before you write the paper, you will be expected to have read Strunk and White's classic The Elements of Style as a way of encouraging yourself to think critically about your own writing.

About midway through the course, seminar members will divide into research groups, each of which will begin work on what will become the final paper. Because the reading load in this course is so heavy, the final paper is not meant to be a full-scale research project; rather, it is to be an exercise in using and writing about the contents of historical documents similar to the ones you will be looking at in the homework. Each research group will take on the task of writing a short social geography of New Haven during a given decade of the nineteenth century. Using published and manuscript censuses, city directories, travelers' accounts, diaries, maps, newspapers, and other sources, research group members will write up, in papers of about 12 to 18 pages, what New Haven was like in the decade following 1790 or 1810 or 1840 or 1860. Each member of the group will ultimately write a separate paper, but the group as a whole will decide how to gather the evidence and divide up the topics that will go into that paper. We'll spend some time later in the semester discussing how this should best be done.

GRADING

It is impossible to be rigid about grading in a course for which so much of the work is participatory. Your two papers, especially the final one, will obviously play a very important role in the final grade you receive, but your role in class and your journal writing will also be counted heavily.

SYLLABUS, READNGS, AND HOMEWORK

(Note: The number in parentheses after each week's title is the total number of pages assigned for that week. The sections marked HOMEWORK indicate what will be due in class during that week's session.)

September 7: Introductory Slide Lecture
HOMEWORK: Note that sometime in the next three weeks, before you turn in the first paper, you should read Strunk and White, The Elements of Style.

September 14: New World, New Towns (233pp)
Thomas More, Utopia, (R)
Anonymous, "Essay on the Ordering of Towns" (R)
Boyer & Nissenbaum, Salem Possessed (entire)
HOMEWORK: Visiting Cemetaries.

September 21: Eighteenth-Century Transformations (226pp)
Glaab & Brown, A History of Urban America, pp 1-25
Nash, The Urban Crucible, pp 1-157
Teaford, The Municipal Revolution in America, pp 1-44
HOMEWORK: Nash's Tables.

September 28: Franklin's (and Others') Philadelphia (212pp)
Peter Kalm, Travels in North America, pp 16-34 (R)
Benjamin Franklin, Autobiography, (Signet Edition), pp 15-82, 90-121, 133-40, 185-7, 197-216
Eric Foner, Tom Paine and Revolutionary America, pp 19-69
Sam Bass Warner, The Private City, pp 3-21
HOMEWORK: Reading memoirs and travellers' accounts.

October 5: Revolutions (219pp)
Nash, The Urban Crucible, pp 233-384
Teaford, The Municipal Revolution in America, pp 47-115
HOMEWORK: FIRST PAPER DUE.

October 12: New West, New Towns (142pp)
Glaab & Brown, A History of Urban America, pp 26-31, 67-73
Julius Rubin, "Urban Growth and Regional Development," in David T. Gilchrist, ed., The Growth of Seaport Cities, pp 3-21 (R)
Jessup W. Scott, "Internal Trade of the United States," Hunts Merchants Magazine, 9(1843), pp 31-47 (R)
Alfred Andreas, History of Cook County, Illinois, pp 133-8 (R)
James Fenimore Cooper, Home as Found, pp 99-109 (R)
Jacqueline Peterson, "'Wild' Chicago: The Formation and Destruction of a Multiracial Community on the Midwestern Frontier, 1816-1837," in Melvin Holli & Peter Jones, eds., The Ethnic Frontier, pp 25-71 (R)
HOMEWORK: Reading maps.

October 19: Factories and the City (224pp)
Allan Pred, "Manufacturing in the American City, 1800-1840," Annals of the Assocation of American Geographers, 56(1966), pp 307-25 (R)
Engels, The Condition of the Working Class in England, pp 57-107
Henry A. Miles, Lowell As It Was and As It Is, pp 61-84, 116-46, 211-16 (R)
Dublin, Women at Work, pp 1-85
HOMEWORK: City Directories.

October 26: Darkening Visions (182pp)
Glaab & Brown, A History of Urban America, pp 52-67
Bender, Toward an Urban Vision, pp 1-93
Thomas Jefferson, Notes on the State of Virginia, pp 279-81 (R)
Edgar Allan Poe, "The Man of the Crowd," (R)
Nathaniel Hawthorne, "The Hotel," from The Blithedale Romance, (R)
George G. Foster, New York by Gas-Light, pp 5-11, 25-36 (in Sterling microfilm room, FILM B765 F-4).
Herman Melville, "Bartleby the Scrivener," (R)
HOMEWORK: Reading fiction.

November 2: Dangerous Cities, I (247pp)
1850 Sanitary Commission of Massachusetts, Report, pp 149-63 (R)
Rosenberg, The Cholera Years, (entire)
HOMEWORK: Manuscript censuses.

November 9: Dangerous Cities, II (212pp)
Bender, Toward and Urban Vision, pp 95-128
Dublin, Women at Work, pp 86-207
Eisler, The Lowell Offering, pp 44-63 (R)
Foner, The Factory Girls, pp 57-96 (R)
HOMEWORK: For the rest of the semester, you will be working on the final paper.

November 16: Dangerous Classes (249pp)
Glaab & Brown, A History of Urban America, pp 74-111
Edward Pessen, "The Lifestyle of the Antebellum Urban Elite," Mid-America, 55(1973), pp 163-83 (R)
Bender, Toward an Urban Vision, pp 129-57
Brace, The Dangerous Classes of New York, pp 13-131, 223-45, 446-8
Carol Smith-Rosenberg, "Beauty, The Beast, and the Militant Woman," American Qtly, 23(1971), pp 562-84 (R)

(THANKSGIVING BREAK)

November 30: Mobility and Ideology (224pp)
Thernstrom, Poverty and Progress, (entire)
Strongly Recommended: Skim Horatio Alger, Ragged Dick

December 7: The Urban Revolution (108pp)
William Cronon, "To Be the Central City," Chicago History, Fall 1981, pp 130-40 (R)
Bender, Toward an Urban Vision, pp 159-94
Frederick Law Olmsted, "Public Parks and the Enlargement of Towns," (R)
Michael Frisch, "American Urban History as an Example of Recent Historiography," (R)

HARVARD UNIVERSITY / UNIVERSITY OF TEXAS

THE HISTORY OF MEDICINE

Stanley J. Reiser

SYLLABUS

Week I

Lecture 1: *Introduction*

Lecture 2: *The Medical Traditions of Ancient Greece*

Readings: from the Genuine Works of Hippocrates, translated by Francis Adams, New York, William Wood & Company, 1891: "Aphorisms" (pp. 183-186, 192-200), "The Oath" (pp. 276, 278-280), "The Law (pp. 283-285).

Week II *Conceptual Changes in the Analysis of Illness*

Lecture 1: *The Displacement of Humoral Pathology, and the Enclosure of Disease in the Anatomical Lesion.*

Readings: Stanley Joel Reiser, Medicine and the Reign of Technology (New York: Cambridge University Press, 1978), "Examination of the Patient in the Seventeenth and Eighteenth Centuries," pp. 1-22.

Lecture 2: *The Transformation of Medical Diagnosis*

Readings: Reiser, "The Stethoscope and the Detection of Pathology by Sound," pp. 23-44;

Reiser, "Visual Technology and the Anatomization of the Living," pp. 45-68.

Week III *Microscopic, Physiological and Chemical Perceptions of Disease*

Lecture 1: *Microscopy and Physiology*

Readings: Reiser, "The Microscope and the Revelation of a Cellular Universe," pp. 69-90.

Reiser: "The Translation of Physiological Actions into the Language of Machines," pp. 91-121.

Lecture 2: *Chemistry*

Readings: Reiser, "Chemical Signposts of Disease and the Birth of the Diagnostic Laboratory," pp. 122-143.

Week IV *The Rebellion Against Therapeutic Extremism*

Lecture 1: *Homeopathy as a Therapeutic Alternative*

Readings: Hahnemann, S. The Homoeopathic Medical Doctrine, or, "Organon of the Healing Art;" a New System of Physic, translated by Charles H. Devrient, Dublin, W.F. Wakeman, 1833, pp. 103-162,214-220, 283-296.

Lecture 2: *Numerical Analysis and the "Self-Limited Disease"*

Readings: Louis, P.Ch.A., Researches on the Effects of Bloodletting in Some Inflammatory Diseases, trans. C.G. Putnam, Boston, Hilliard, Gray & Company, 1836, pp. 1-23, 55-70; Bigelow, Jacob, A Discourse on Self-Limited Diseases (Boston: Nathan Hale, 1835), pp. 1-35.

Week V *Critical Events in the Development of Modern Surgery*

Lecture 1: *The Discovery of Ether Anaesthesia*
(Note: This lecture will be held in the Ether Dome at the Massachusetts General Hospital, the site of the first public operation using ether.)

Readings: Bigelow, Henry Jacob, "Insensibility During Surgical Operations Produced by Inhalation," Boston Medical and Surgical Journal, vol. 35 (1846), pp. 309-317.

Editorial, "Etherization in Surgical Operations," Lancet (1847), pp. 74-75.

Leach, J., (cartoon) "Wonderful Effects of Ether in a Case of Scolding Wife, Punch, London. vol. 12 (1847), p. 60.

Minutes of Meeting, November 2, 1847, College of Physicians, Transactions College of Physicians (Phil.) 2, 1846-9, pp. 152-176.

Lecture 2: *Surgical Practice in the Nineteenth Century*

Readings: "Amputation of the Hip-Joint as Performed at Edinburgh," Lancet (1824), pp. 291-292.

Lister, Joseph, "On the Antiseptic Principle in the Practice of Surgery," Lancet (1867), pp. 353-56.

"Listerism," Canada Medical and Surgical Journal, vol. 10 (1881-2), pp. 755-56.

"University College: Mr. Erichsen's Introductory Address," Lancet (1873), pp. 489-90.

Marshall, J., "Address in Surgery," British Medical Journal (1885), pp. 235-9.

Week V Lecture 2 (continued)

Tait, Lawson, "An Address on the Development of Surgery and The Germ Theory," British Medical Journal (1887), pp. 166-70.

Dunn, J.T., "Diagnostic Value of X-rays," International Journal of Surgery, vol. 11 (1898), pp. 294-96.

"Death of President McKinley," JAMA (1901), pp. 779-83.

Week VI *The Hospital as a Medical and Social Institution*

Lecture 1: *Hospitals Prior to the Mid-Nineteenth Century*

Readings: Aikin, John, Thoughts on Hospitals, (London), Printed for Joseph Johnson (1771), pp. 5-82.

Jackson, James, and Warren, John C., "Circular Letter" concerning the founding of Massachusetts General Hospital, in A History of the Massachusetts General Hospital (Boston: John Wilson and Son, (1851), pp. 3-9.

Lecture 2: *The Modern Hospital and the Development of the Medical Clinic*

Readings: Nightingale, Florence, Notes on Hospitals (London: Longman, Green, Longman, Roberts, and Green, 1863), pp. 1-24, 56-64, 159-76.

Rowe, George H.M., "The President's Address before the American Hospital Superintendents' Association," Boston Medical and Surgical Journal, vol. 153 (1905), pp. 511-515.

Davis, Michael M., and Warner, Andrew R., Dispensaries: Their Management and Development (New York: Macmillan, 1918), pp. 25-41, 59-70.

Week VII *Therapeutics in the Twentieth Century*

Lecture 1: *Syphilis and Salvarsan "606"*

Readings: Morrow, Prince A., Social Diseases and Marriage: Social Prophylaxis (New York and Philadelphia, 1904), pp. 19-35.

" '606' in the Treatment of Syphilis," Lancet (1910), pp. 740-1.

" '606' ", British Medical Journal, (1910), pp. 798-9.

Week VII Lecture 1 (continued)

Emery, E., "The Preparation '606'," Lancet (1910), pp. 1543-8.

Ehrlich, Paul, and McDonagh, J.E.R., "606" in Theory and Practice (London: Oxford University Press, 1911), Preface and pp. 1-17.

Lecture 2: *Penicillin and the Antibiotic Era*

Readings: Fleming, Alexander, "On the Antibacterial Action of Cultures of a Penicillum, with Special Reference to Their Use in the Isolation of B. *Influenzae*," British Journal of Experimental Pathology, vol. 10 (1929), pp. 226-36.

Fleming, Alexander, "The Discovery of Penicillin," British Medical Bulletin, vol. 2 (1944), pp. 4-5.

Florey, H.W., et al, "Penicillin as a Chemotherapeutic Agent," Lancet (1940), pp. 226-8.

Florey, H.W., "Penicillin: A Survey," British Medical Journal (1944), pp. 169-71.

"Penicillin: Unexcelled and Now Obtainable," New England Journal of Medicine, vol. 232 (1944), p. 411.

"Abuse of Penicillin," New England Journal of Medicine, vol. 233 (1945), pp. 830-32.

Week VIII *The Education of the Physician and the Nurse*

Lecture 1: *The Physician*

Readings: Flexner, Abraham, Medical Education in the United States and Canada, with an introduction by Henry S. Pritchett (New York: The Carnegie Foundation, 1950), pp. 4-51, 143-181.

Lecture 2: *The Nurse*

Readings: Nightingale, Florence, Notes on Nursing: What It Is, and What It Is Not (London: Harrison, 1860), pp. 4-9, 54-79.

"Female Nurses in Military Hospitals," American Medical Times, 1861, pp. 25-26.

"Duties of the Army Surgeon--Females Not Suitable for Nurses," American Medical Times, 1861, p. 30.

Nightingale, Florence, Florence Nightingale to Her Nurses (London: Macmillan and Co., Ltd., 1915), pp. 112-131.

Osler, William, "Nurse and Patient," from Aequanimitas and Other Addresses, (P. Blakiston's Son & Co., 1904), pp. 154-166.

Week IX *An Understanding of the Patient as Person*

Lecture 1: *The Introduction of Freudian Psychotherapy and Social Work into Medicine*

Readings: Freud, Sigmund, "The Origin and Development of Psychoanalysis," from Lectures and Addresses Delivered before the Departments of Psychology and Pedagogy in Celebration of the Twentieth Anniversary of the Opening of Clark University, Sept. 1909, pp. 1-38.

Taylor, E.W., "The Attitude of the Medical Profession Toward the Psychotherapeutic Movement," Boston Medical and Surgical Journal, vol. 157 (1907), pp. 843-849.

Southard, E.E., "Contributions from the Psychopathic Hospital, Boston Massachusetts: Introductory Note," Boston Medical and Surgical Journal, vol. 169 (1913), pp. 109-112.

Cannon, W.B., "The Role of Emotion in Disease," Annals of Internal Medicine, vol. 9 (1936), pp. 1453-1465.

Fremont-Smith, Maurice, "Relationships Between Emotional States and Organic States," New England Journal of Medicine, vol. 208 (1933), pp. 69-71.

Cabot, Richard C., "Suggestions for the Reorganization of Hospital Out-Patient Departments, with Special Reference to the Improvement of Treatment," Maryland Medical Journal, vol 50 (1907), pp. 81-91.

Lecture 2: *The Nature of the Doctor-Patient Relationship*

(Note: The class will meet for this lecture at the Massachusetts General Hospital. Videotapes of interviews between physicians and patients will be shown and discussed by Dr. John Stoeckle, Associate Professor of Medicine and Dr. Aaron Lazare, Associate Professor of Psychiatry, Harvard Medical School.)

Reading: Henderson, L.J., "Physician and Patient as a Social System," New England Journal of Medicine, vol. 212 (1935), pp. 819-823.

Week X *The Technological Orientation of Twentieth Century Physicians in Diagnosing Illness*

Lecture 1: *Technology and Diagnosis*

Readings: Reiser, "The Shortcomings of Technology in Medical Decision Making," pp. 158-173.

Week X (continued)

Lecture 2: *Observer Variation and Error in Medicine*

Reading: Reiser, "Selection and Evaluation of Evidence in Medicine," pp. 174-195.

Week XI *The Organization of Medical Research in America*

Lecture 1: *Medical Research Before the Second World War*

Readings: "The Relation of American Medical Societies to Scientific Research," New York Medical Journal, vol. 52 (1890), p. 184.

Welch, William H., "An Address at the Formal Opening of the Laboratories of the Rockefeller Institute for Medical Research on May 11, 1906," Bulletin of the Johns Hopkins Hospital, vol. 17 (1906), pp. 247-251.

Osler, William, "Whole-Time Clinical Professors: A Letter to President Remsen," from Collected Reprints of Dr. Osler, 23-61, 1909-20, Sept. 1, 1911, pp. 4-14.

Lecture 2: *The Post-War Research Boom and Its Relation to Medical Education and Medical Care*

Readings: Bush, Vannevar, Science, the Endless Frontier, July 1945, United States Government Printing Office, Washington, D.C., pp. v-ix, 1-11, 43-58.

Research in the Service of Man: Biomedical Knowledge, Development, and Use; A Conference sponsored by the Subcommittee on Government Research and the Frontiers of Science Foundation of Oklahoma for the Committee on Government Operations, United STates Senate, held at Oklahoma City, Oklahoma, October 24-27, 1966, U.S. Government Printing Office, Washington, D.C., 1967.

Contributors:

Bennett, Ivan L. "Application of Biomedical Knowlege: The White House View," pp. 5-10.

Piel, Gerard, "The Public Stake in an Accelerated Program of Applying Biomedical Knowledge," pp. 16-23.

Weinberg, Alvin M., "Prospects for Big Biology," pp. 32-43.

Shannon, James A., "NIH--Present and Potential Contribution to Application of Biomedical Knowledge," pp. 72-85.

Week XII *Medical Care in Twentieth-Century America*

Lecture 1: *Responses to the Concept of Health Insurance in America*

Readings: Rubinow, I.M., "Sickness Insurance," American Labor Legislation Review, vol. 3 (1913), pp. 162-171.

Burns, Eveline M., "Policy Decisions Facing the United States in Financing and Organizing Health Care," Public Health Reports, vol. 81 (1966), pp. 675-683.

Lecture 2: *The Specialization of Medicine*

Reading: Reiser, "Medical Specialism and the Centralization of Medical Care," pp. 144-157.

Week XIII *The Automation of Medical Practice: Present and Future*

Lecture 1:

Readings: Reiser, "Telecommunication, Automation, and Medical Practice," pp. 196-226.

Reiser, "Conclusion," pp. 227-231.

RUTGERS UNIVERSITY

HEALTH AND THE ENVIRONMENT IN AMERICA: AN HISTORICAL OVERVIEW

History, 512:121 Fall Semester 1983 Prof. G. Grob

BOOKS:

Rene Dubos, MIRAGE OF HEALTH: UTOPIAS, PROGRESS, AND BIOLOGICAL CHANGE (Harper & Row paperback)
Thomas R. Dunlap, DDT: SCIENTISTS, CITIZENS , AND PUBLIC POLICY (Princeton University Press, paperback)
Judith W. Leavitt and Ronald Numbers, SICKNESS AND HEALTH IN AMERICA: READINGS IN THE HISTORY OF MEDICINE AND PUBLIC HEALTH (University of Wisconsin Press Paperback)
Sinclair Lewis, ARROWSMITH (paperback NAL)
William McNeill, PLAGUES AND PEOPLES (Anchor paperback)
Charles E. Rosenberg, THE CHOLERA YEARS: THE UNITED STATES IN 1832, 1849, and 1866 (University of Chicago Press paperback)
Richard H. Shryock, MEDICINE AND SOCIETY IN AMERICA 1660-1860 (Cornell University Press paperback)

ASSIGNED READINGS:

Although the schedule of readings will remain flexible, students should attempt to read the assignments prior to the specific topics covered in class.

EXAMINATIONS:

All students are required to take the regular semester and final examinations. The dates for the semester examination will be set early in the semester. There will be no makeup examinations for regularly scheduled examinations. Students who miss the examination will receive additional questions on the final examination, which will cover the work missed.

Any student who misses the final examination must provide a note from a physician before being permitted to take a makeup examination. The makeup examination will be given during the first week of the spring semester only.

The instructor is available immediately following each class or by special appointment. His regular office is Van Dyck Hall 305, and his campus telephone extension is 7905 or 7906.

COURSE OUTLINE & ASSIGNMENTS:

I. HEALTH, DISEASE, AND SOCIETY: AN INTRODUCTION
   A. Contemporary society and the problem of health
   B. Medical utopias
   C. The concept of disease
   D. Changing patterns of disease
      1. human longevity
      2. historic patterns of disease
      3. social determinants of disease
      4. conclusion

   READINGS:
   Dubos, MIRAGE OF HEALTH, entire book
   Leavitt & Numbers, SICKNESS AND HEALTH IN AMERICA, 3-38
   McNeill, PLAGUES AND PEOPLES, 1-175

II. THE ENCOUNTER OF NEW AND OLD WORLD ENVIRONMENTS
   A. Two environments
   B. New World population and old world disease patterns
   C. Syphilis: indigenous or imported?
   D. The transformation of the environment

III. COLONIAL SOCIETY AND THE PATTERN OF DISEASE
   A. Introduction
   B. Population and Colonial America
   C. Colonial disease patterns
   D. Colonial society and the reaction to disease
      1. Boston: a case study
      2. The great awakening
      3. An urban epidemic: Philadelphia and yellow fever in 1793

   READINGS:
   Shryock, MEDICINE AND SOCIETY IN AMERICA, 1-81
   Leavitt & Numbers, SICKNESS & HEALTH IN AMERICA, 39-53, 229-256
   McNeill, PLAGUES AND PEOPLES, 176-207

IV. HEALTH AND DISEASE IN AMERICA, 1800-1870
   A. Introduction
   B. Modernization and the demographic transition

C. Disease and social change
   1. Introduction
   2. Environmental change and disease: malaria as a case study
   3. The persistence of epidemics
      a. Introduction
      b. The dilemma of etiology
      c. Cholera
      d. Yellow Fever
   4. The impact of war, 1861-1865

D. The Medical Profession, 1800-1870
   1. The licensing controversy
   2. The rise of sectarianism
      a. Introduction
      b. Thomsonianism
      c. Homeopathy

E. The practice of medicine and the role of physicians modernization and social change: the public health movement in mid-nineteenth century America
   1. Introduction
   2. Demography, mortality, statistics, and disease: the origins of the quantitative mind
   3. The religious factor
   4. The sanitarian awakening

F. Conclusion

READINGS:
Shrylock, MEDICINE AND SOCIETY IN AMERICA, 82-174
Rosenberg, THE CHOLERA YEARS, entire book
Leavitt & Numbers, SICKNESS AND HEALTH IN AMERICA, 55-102; 129-137; 257-304; 313-373

V. HEALTH AND DISEASE IN AMERICA SINCE 1870

A. Introduction

B. Changing theories of disease

C. Disease in modern America
   1. Introduction
   2. The pattern of disease
   3. Disease in modern America
      a. Introduction
      b. Tuberculosis
      c. Pellagra
      d. Narcotics and the problem of addiction
      e. Influenza
      f. Poliomyelitis

4. The search for cures
    a. Control by public health measures
    b. Prevention by immunization
    c. Treatment with serum
    d. The development of antibiotics
    e. The newer vaccines

D. The Eugenics Movement: the use and misuse of science
    1. The concept of Eugenics
    2. The origins of American Eugenics
    3. The influence of Eugenics in American society, 1900-19
    4. The decline of Eugenics

E. Economic and industrial development and environmental impact: dilemmas of public policy

F. The medical profession and American society
    1. Introduction
    2. The impact of technology
    3. The rise of the hospital
    4. The professionalization of medicine
    5. The debate over health care
    6. Research and training: the role of the federal government
        a. Introduction
        b. The federal government and medical education
        c. Medical Research Policy

READINGS:
Dunlap, DDT, entire book
Lewis, ARROWSMITH, entire book
Leavitt & Numbers, SICKNESS AND HEALTH IN AMERICA, 103-128; 139-225; 305-312; 375-431
McNeill, PLAGUES AND PEOPLES, 208-257

VI. HEALTH, DISEASE, AND THE ENVIRONMENT: PRESENT AND FUTURE
   A. Introduction
   B. Morbidity and mortality differentials
   C. Population and welfare
      1. Population
      2. The consequences of positive population growth vs. zero population growth

VII. Conclusion: The Tragedy of Humanity

UNIVERSITY OF PENNSYLVANIA

DEPARTMENT OF HISTORY
FALL, 1982

HISTORY 161

AMERICAN ECONOMIC HISTORY
TUESDAYS AND THURSDAYS 1:30-3:00 Walter Licht

History 161 will meet twice a week for one and a half hour sessions. One class each week will be devoted to presentation of materials, the other to discussion of reading assignments. In depth analyses of readings will represent a major part of the course. Students will be expected to come to discussion sessions having completed the reading assignments thoroughly and carefully. Exams will include identifications from the assignments.

An in-class midterm will be given on Thursday, October 21, and an in-class final during final exams week. In addition, students will submit a five-six page paper on Tuesday, November 23. The paper will involve the writing of a research proposal in American economic history. Further information about the paper assignment will be provided in the coming weeks.

The following paperback books have been ordered at the Penn Book Center on Walnut near 38th Street. Starred (*) books are especially recommended for purchase. All books have been placed on reserve in the library.

Alfred Chandler, Strategy & Structure: Chapters in the History of American Enterprise, pages 1-162.

Robert Fogel, Railroads & American Economic Growth: Essays in Econometric History

*Ellis Hawley, The New Deal & the Problem of Monopoly

*Gabriel Kolko, The Triumph of Conservatism: A Reinterpretation of American History

*DouglassNorth, Economic Growth of the United States, 1790-1860

Edwin Perkins, The Economy of Colonial America

Glen Porter, The Rise of Big Business

Nathan Rosenberg, Technology & American Economic Growth, pages 1-116

*Gavin Wright, The Political Economy of the Cotton South

SCHEDULE OF LECTURES AND READINGS

September 9: Introduction to the Study of American Economic History

September 14: The Colonial Economy

September 16: Discussion: Edwin Perkins, The Economy of Colonial America

September 21: Toward Sustained Economic Growth

September 23: Discussion: Douglass North, Economic Growth of the United States, 1790-1860

September 28: Early Industrialization

September 30: Discussion: Nathan Rosenberg, Technology & American Growth, pp. 1-116
C. Earle and R. Hoffman, "The Foundation of the Modern Economy: Agriculture and the Costs of Labor in the United States and England, 1800-60" (xeroxes on reserve)
Susan Hirsch, "The Process of Industrialization" (xeroxes on reserve)

October 5: The Transportation and Communication Revolutions

October 7: Discussion: Robert Fogel, Railroads & American Economic Growth

October 12: The Political Economy of Slavery

October 14: Discussion: Gavin Wright, The Political Economy of the Cotton South

October 19: The Civil War and Its Impact

*October 21: IN-CLASS MIDTERM EXAM

October 26: Post-Bellum Agricultural Development

October 28: Discussion: R. Ransom and R. Sutch, "Debt Peonage in the Cotton South After the Civil War" (xeroxes on reserve)
R. Ransom and R. Sutch, "The Impact of the Civil War and of Emancipation on Southern Agriculture" (xeroxes on reserve)
C. Goldin and F. Lewis, "The Economic Cost of the American Civil War: Estimates and Implications" (xeroxes on reserve)
P. Temin, "The Post-Bellum Recovery of the South and the Cost of the Civil War" (xeroxes on reserve)

November 2: The Rise of the Large Scale Corporation

November 4: Discussion: Glen Porter, The Rise of Big Business

November 9: Late Nineteenth-Century Urban Growth and Development

November 11: The Rise of State Corporate Capitalism
Discussion: Gabriel Kolko, The Triumph of Conservatism

November 16: World War I and Its Impact

November 18: The Twenties and the Modern Economy
Discussion: Alfred Chandler, Strategy and Structure: Chapters in the History of American Enterprise, pp. 1-162 (book and xeroxes on reserve)

November 23: The Causes of the Depression
TERM PAPER TO BE SUBMITTED

November 30: **The New Deal**
Discussion: **Ellis Hawley, The New Deal & The Problem of Monopoly, Parts I-II**

December 2: **The New Deal**
Discussion: **Ellis Hawley, The New Deal & The Problem of Monopoly, Parts III-IV**

December 7: **World War II and the Post War Economy**

December 9: **The Historical Roots of Contemporary Economic Crises - Can Capitalism Survive?**
Discussion: **E. Rothschild, "Reagan and the Real America" (xeroxes on reserve)**
E. Rothschild, "The Philosophy of Reaganism" (xeroxes on reserve)
R. Heilbroner, "The Demand from the Supply Side" (xeroxes on reserve)
A. Przeworski and M. Wallerstein, "Democratic Capitalism at the Crossroads"

PRINCETON UNIVERSITY
Department of History

Spring Term, 1983 — HISTORY 386

Michael A. Bernstein
G-31 Dickinson Hall
452-4183

AMERICAN ECONOMIC DEVELOPMENT

Course Description: America as a raw materials producer, as an agrarian society, and as an industrial nation. Emphasis on the logic of American growth, the social and political tensions accompanying expansion, and twentieth-century transformations of American capitalism. There is no presumption that students have had previous training in either economics or statistics, although elements of both disciplines will be used in class and in some of the readings.

Course Readings: The following books have been ordered at the University Store:

S. Ratner, *et al.*; *The Evolution of the American Economy.*
D. North; *The Economic Growth of the United States, 1790-1860.*
P. Passell, S. Lee; *A New Economic View of American History.*

These works are also on reserve in Firestone Library. Other readings, mostly in journals and anthologies, are either on reserve at Firestone or available in the reserve room of Firestone Library.

Course Requirements: There will be two lectures and one preceptorial per week. Those readings starred on the assignment list are required, but it is expected that students will do at least one optional reading per class topic. A midterm and final examination, both of the take-home variety, will be given during the specified examination periods. They will account for 20% and 50% of the course grade respectively. A research paper, 5-10 pages in length, will be due just after the Spring Vacation and will account for 30% of the course grade. Potential paper topics will be circulated by the instructor early in the semester, but students are free to pursue their own topics provided they discuss them with the instructor in advance. A lively and informed contribution to discussions will be credited to the student's grade.

The following abbreviations are used in the reading list:

RSS	Ratner *et al.* text.
LP	P. Passell, S. Lee text.
N	D. North text.
JEH	Journal of Economic History.
WMQ	William and Mary Quarterly.
CHR	Canadian Historical Review
JPE	Jounral of Political Economy.
AER	American Economic Review.
RAEH	R. Fogel, S. Engerman (eds.); *The Reinterpretation of American Economic History.*
AH	Agricultural History.
JSH	Journal of Southern History

AHR	American Historical Review.
MVHR	Mississippi Valley Historical Review
AEG	L. Davis, *et al.*; *American Economic Growth*.
BHR	Business History Review.
CEH	The Cambridge Economic History.
EHR	Economic History Review
SEJ	Southern Economic Journal.
JSocH	Journal of Social History.

Class and Preceptorial Topics

I. America as a Colony

1) British Mercantilism and Colonial Settlement
2) The Export Economy of the Seaboard: New England
Precept: Economic Development in Long-Run Perspective

3) The Export Economy of the Seaboard: Middle Colonies and Virginia
4) Colonial Class Structure and Economic Function: The Revolution
Precept: The Constitution, Private Property, and the State

II. America as a Union of Economic Regions

5) Federal and State Mercantilism
6) Trade and Regional Growth
Precept: Sectoral Shift and Early Economic Development in the North

7) The Regions: The Northeast
8) The Regions: The South
Precept: The Economic Implications of Chattel Slavery

9) The Regions: The West
10) The Civil War: Economic Causes and Consequences
Precept: The Civil War and Economic Development

III. America as an Expanding Nation

11) The South: 1865-1940
12) The Spread of Commercial Farming
Precept: Underdevelopment in the American South, 1865-1940

13) The Transcontinental Railroads
14) The Growth of Large-Scale Industry: Technology and Organization
Precept: The Emergence of the Organized Labor Movement

15) Migration and the Labor Force
16) Mechanisms of Capital Expansion
Precept: Large-Scale Enterprise and its Regulation

17) The Politics of Expansion: Republicanism
18) Democracy and Dissent
Precept: Political Movements and Economic Policy from Grant to Hoover

19) Problems of the 1920s
20) Instability and Depression: The 1930's
Precept: The Great Depression in American Capitalism, 1929-1939

21) The New Deal
22) Post-War Prosperity and International Reconstruction
Precept: America's Foreign Economic Expansion in the Post-War Era: Politics and Economics

23) Fiscal Activism, Economic Intervention, and the Great Society
24) Stagflation and Industrial Retardation in the 1970's and 1980's
Precept: Reaction and Retrenchment: The End of the Keynesian Era?

Assignment List

1) British Mercantilism and Colonial Settlment

*RSS: Introduction and Ch. 1
*C. Nettles, "British Mercantilism and the Development of the 13 Colonies," JEH, 1952.
LP: Introduction and Ch. 1

2) The Export Economy of the Seaboard: New England

*RSS: Ch. 2
*K. Lockridge, "Land, Population, and the Evolution of New England Society," Past and Present, 1968
J. Henretta, "Economic Development and Social Structure in Colonial Boston," WMQ, 1965.

Precept: Economic Development in Long-Run Perspective

*D. Levine, "The Theory of the Growth of the Capitalist Economy," Economic Development and Cultural Change, 1975
Maurice Dobb, Studies in the Development of Capitalism, Ch. 1.
Karl Marx, Pre-Capitalist Economic Formations, (ed., E.J. Hobsbawm), pp. 67-120.

3) The Export Economy of the Seaboard: Middle Colonies and Virginia

*RSS: Ch. 3
*R. Sheridan, "The British Credit Crisis of 1772 and the American Colonies," JEH, 1964.

4) Colonial Class Structure and Economic Function: The Revolution

*RSS: Ch. 4
*M. Egnal, J. Ernst, "An Economic Interpretation of the American Revolution," WMQ, 1972.
LP: Ch. 2
M. Egnal, "Economic Development of the American Colonies," WMQ, 1975.
L. Harper, "Mercantilism and the American Revolution," CHR, 1942.

Precept: The Constitution, Private Property, and the State

*M. Horwitz, The Transformation of American Law, Ch. 2.
*A. Hamilton, J. Jay, J. Madison, The Federalist, #10
C. Beard, An Economic Interpretation of the Constitution, Ch. VI.
F. MacDonald, We the People: The Economic Origins of the Constitution, Ch. X

5) Federal and State Mercantilism

*RSS: Chs. 5, 7
*G. Taylor, The Trapsportation Revolution, Chs. II-III.
J. Miller, The Federalist Era, Chs. 3-6.
Alexander Hamilton; Letter to James Duane and Letter to Robert Morris; on reserve. From The Papers of Alexander Hamilton Vol. II
H. Scheiber, Ohio Canal Era, part I.

6) Trade and Regional Growth

*RSS: Ch. 9
*L. Schmidt, "Internal Commerce and the Development of National Economy before 1860," JPE, 1939.
N: Ch. IX.

Precept: Sectoral Shift and Early Economic Development in the North

*C. Clark, "Household Economy, Market Exchange and the Rise of Capitalism in the Connecticut Valley, 1800-1860," JSocH, 1979.
*P.W. Bidwell, "The Agricultural Revolution in New England," AHR, 1921.
H. Barron, "The Impact of Rural Depopulation on the Local Economy: Chelsea, Vermont, 1840-1900," AH, 1980.

7) The Regions: The Northeast

*RSS: Chs. 8, 10
*G. Taylor, The Trasportation Revolution, Chs. X-XI.
H.J. Habakkuk, "The Economic Effects of Labour Scarcity," in (S.B. Saul (ed.)), Technological Change: The United States and Britain in the Nineteenth Century.

8) The Regions: The South

*W. Parker, "The Slave Plantation in American Agriculture," in (A. Coats, R. Robertson (eds.)), Essays in American Economic History.
*E. Genovese, The Political Economy of Slavery, parts 1 and 4.
*R. Fogel, S. Engerman, "The Economics of Slavery," in RAEH.
A. Conrad, J. Meyer, "The Economics of Slavery," JPE, 1958.
N: Ch. X.

Precept: The Economic Implications of Chattel Slavery

*R. Russel, "General Effects of Slavery upon Southern Economic Progress," JSH, 1938.
*W.N. Parker, "Slavery and Southern Economic Development: An Hypothesis and Some Evidence," in (W.N. Parker (ed.)), The Structure of the Cotton Economy of the Antebellum South.

E.S. Morgan, "The Labor Problem at Jamestown, 1607-18," AHR, 1971.
U.B. Phillips, "The Economic Cost of Slaveholding in the Cotton Belt," Political Science Quarterly, 1905.

9) The Regions: The West

*RSS: Ch. 6.
*N: Chs. XI, XIII-XV.
*W. Parker, "From Northwest to Midwest," in (D. Klingaman, R. Vedder (eds.)), Essays in 19th Century Economic History.
LP: Ch. 7
F. Turner, "The Significance of the Frontier in American History," in (R. Billington (ed.)), Frontier and Section.
B. Hibbard, A History of the Public Land Policies, Chs. VI, VIII-XIII.

10) The Civl War: Economic Causes and Consequences

*C. Beard, M. Beard, The Rise of American Civilization, Chs. XVII-XVIII.
LP: Chs. 10-11
T. Cochran, "Did the Civil War Retard Industrialization?," MVHR, 1961.
S. Salsbury, "The Effect of the Civil War on American Industrial Development," in (R. Andreano (ed.)), The Economic Impact of the American Civil War.

Precept: The Civil War and Economic Development

*Barrington Moore, Jr., Social Origins of Dictatorship and Democracy, Ch. III.
R. Hofstadter, "The Tariff Issue on the Eve of the Civl War," AHR, 1938.
Louis M. Hacker, The Triumph of American Capitalism, Chs. XXIII-XXIV.

11) The South: 1865-1940

*E. Lerner, "Southern Output and Agricultural Income, 1860-1880," AH, 1959.
*W.N. Parker, "The South in the National Economy, 1865-1970," SEJ, 1980.
D. Dowd, "A Comparative Analysis of Economic Development in the American West and South," JEH, 1956.
G. Wright, "Cotton Competition and the Post-Bellum Recovery of the American South," JEH, 1974.

12) The Spread of Commercial Farming

*RSS: Chs. 11, 18.
*AEG: Ch. 11.
C. Danhof, Change in Agriculture, Chs. 4-6.
F. Shannon, The Farmer's Last Frontier, Chs. 7-9.

Precept: Underdevelopment in the American South, 1865-1940

*R. Ransom, R. Sutch, "Debt Peonage in the Cotton South after the Civil War," JEH, 1972.
R. Ransom, R. Sutch, "The 'Lock-In' Mechanism and Overproduction of Cotton in the Postbellum South," AH, 1975.

13) The Transcontinental Railroads

*RSS: Chs. 14, 19
*AEG: Ch. 13
R. Fogel, "Railroads and American Economic Growth," in RAEH.
LP: Ch. 13
A. Fishlow, "The Dynamics of Railroad Extension into the West," in RAEH.
L. Jenks, "The Railroad as an Economic Force in American Development," JEH, 1944.

14) The Growth of Large-Scale Industry: Technology and Organization

*RSS: Chs. 12, 17
*AEG: Ch. 7
*A. Chandler, L. Galambos, "The Development of Large-Scale Economic Organization in Modern America," JEH, 1970.
N. Rosenberg, "Technical Change in the Machine Tool Industry," JEH, 1963.
A. Chandler, The Visible Hand, part IV.

Precept: The Emergence of the Organized Labor Movement

*Norman Ware, The Labor Movement in the United States: 1865-1890, Ch. XII.
*David Montgomery, Worker's Control in America, Ch. 1.
John R. Commons, A History of Labor in the United States, vol. I: pp. 3-21, 335-56, 575-623; vol. II: pp. 156-91, 356-94, 521-37.
Daniel Nelson, Managers and Workers, Ch. 4.

15) Migration and the Labor Force

*RSS: Chs. 13, 21
*H. Gutman, "Work, Culture, and Society in Industrializing America," AHR, 1973.
AEG: Ch. 15.
H. Braverman, Labor and Monopoly Capital, Chs. 6-9.

16) Mechanisms of Capital Expansion

*RSS: Ch. 15
*AEG: Ch. 9
L. Davis, "Capital Markets and Industrial Concentration," EHR, 1966.
R. Sylla, "Federal Policy, Banking Market Structure, and Capital Mibilization in the U.S.," JEH, 1969.

Precept: Large-Scale Enterprise and its Reguation

*RSS: Ch. 16
*G. Kolko, The Triumph of Conservatism, Chs. 1-2.
AEG: Ch. 17.
T. McCraw, "Regulation in America," BHR, 1975.
Alan Neale, Antitrust Laws of the USA, Intro. and Ch. XV.

17) The Politics of Expansion: Republicanism

*RSS: Ch. 20
*G. Mowry, The Era of Theodore Roosevelt, Chs. 5-7.
LP: Ch. 14
Eric Foner, Free Soil, Free Labor, Free Men, Ch. 1.

18) Democracy and Dissent

*R. Hofstadter, The Age of Reform, Chs. VI-VII.
*Douglas North, Growth and Welfare in the American Past,
A. Mayhew, "A Reappraisal of the Causes of Farm Protest in the United States, 1870-1900," JEH, 1972.
LP: Ch. 15.
J. Hicks, The Populist Revolt, Chs. II-III, IX.

Precept: Political Movements and Economic Policy from Grant to Hoover

*W. Parker, "American Attitudes toward Business," (xerox)
*Lewis Gould (ed.), The Progressive Era, Chs. 3-4.
A. S. Link, "What Happened to the Progressive Movement in the 1920's?" AHR, 1959.

19) Problems of the 1920's

*George Soule, Prosperity Decade, Chs. VI, XIII, XV.
*AEG: Ch. 13
F. Allen, Only Yesterday, Ch. 7, 11-14.

20) Instability and Depression: The 1930's

*Broadus Mitchell, Depression Decade, Chs. I-II.
M. Friedman, A. Schwartz, A Monetary History of the U.S., Ch. 7.
LP: Ch. 16.
John K. Galbraith, The Great Crash: 1929, Chs. VI-X.

Precept: The Great Depression in American Capitalism, 1929-1939.

*G. McLaughlin, R. Watkins, "The Problem of Industrial Growth in a Mature Economy," AER, 1939, (Supplement).
*A. Hansen, "Economic Progress and Declining Population Growth," AER, 1946.
J. M. Keynes, "Some Economic Consequences of a Declining Population," Eugenics Review, 1937.

21) The New Deal

*W. Leuchtenberg, Franklin D. Roosevelt and the New Deal, Chs. 3-4, 6-7.
*E. Brown, "Fiscal Policy in the Thirties," AER, 1956.
Broadus Mitchell, Depression Decade, Chs. VII-VIII.
Herbert Stein, The Fiscal Revolution in America, Chs. 5-7.
Frances Piven, Richard Cloward, Regulating the Poor, Chs. 2-3.
D. Montgomery, Worker's Control in America, Ch. 7.

22) Post-War Prosperity and International Reconstruction

*Herbert Stein, The Fiscal Revolution in America, Chs. 8-9.
W.W. Rostow, "The Dynamics of American Society," in (R. Freeman (ed.)), Postwar Economic Trends in the United States.
Brian Tew, International Monetary Cooperation: 1945-70, Ch. 7.
B. Bernstein, A. Matusow, (eds.), The Truman Administration, Ch. 2.
T.G. Paterson, "The Quest for Peace and Prosperity," in (B. Bernstein (ed.)), Politics and Policies of the Truman Administration.

Precept: America's Foreign Economic Expansion in the Post-War Era: Politics and Economics

*Harry Magdoff, The Age of Imperialism, Ch. 5.
*S. M. Miller, et al., "Does the U.S. Economy Require Imperialism?," Social Policy, (September-October, 1970).
David Horowitz, (ed.), Corporations and the Cold War, selections by L. Gardner and C. Nathanson
W. Williams, The Tragedy of American Diplomacy, Ch. 6.

23) Fiscal Activism, Economic Intervention, and the Great Society

*Herbert Stein, The Fiscal Revolution in America, Chs. 15-16.
*James Tobin, The New Economics One Decade Older, Chs. 1-2.
Seymour E. Harris, Economics of the Kennedy Years and a Look Ahead, Ch. 4 and part V.
Paul Baran, Paul Sweezy, Monopoly Capital, Chs. 6-7.
Arthur M. Okun, "The Fiscal Fiasco of the Vietnam Period, in (A.M. Okun (ed.)), The Battle Against Unemployment.

24) Stagflation and Industrial Retardation in the 1970's and 1980's

*Alan S. Blinder, Economic Policy and the Great Stagflation, Ch. 3.
*E. Rothschild, "Reagan and the Real America," New York Review of Books, (February 5, 1982).
W. Nordhaus, "The New Brand of Economics," New York Times, (February 22, 1981), section 3, p. 2.

Precept: Reaction and Retrenchment: The End of the Keynesian Era?

*John M. Keynes, The General Theory of Employment. Interest and Money, Ch. 24.
*Friedrich A. Hayek, The Road to Serfdom, Chs. III, VII.
"Excerpts from the National Platform of the Republican Party", New York Times, (July 13, 1980), p. 14.
"Democratic Party Platform: 1976" and "Republican Party Platform: 1976", both in Donald B. Johnson, National Party Platforms, vol. II: pp. 915-28, 933-7, 965-75, 981-85.

NEW YORK UNIVERSITY
WASHINGTON SQUARE COLLEGE
DEPARTMENT OF HISTORY

Industrialization and the American Working Class

V57.0615, M-W 1:30-2:45

Fall 1980
Prof. D. Walkowitz

The following paperback texts may be purchased at the N.Y.U. bookstore:

I. Bernstein, Turbulent Years (Houghton Mifflin)
H. Braverman, Labor and Monopoly Capital (Monthly Review)
A. Dawley, Class and Community (Harvard)
E. Gurley Flynn, The Rebel Girl (New World)
H. Gutman, Work, Culture and Society (Vintage)
D. Nelson, Managers and Workers (Wisconsin)
W. O'Neill, Women at Work (Quadrangle)
J. Rayback, History of American Labor (Free Press)
C. Sigal, Going Away
G. Grob, "The Knights of Labor and The Trade Unions, 1878-1886." (Bobbs-Merrill Reprint)
J. Lemisch, "Jack Tar in the Streets" (Bobbs-Merrill Reprint)
G. Lerner, "The Lady and the Mill Girl" (Bobbs-Merrill Reprint)
D. Montgomery, "The Working Clases of the Pre-Industrial American City." (Bobbs-Merrill Reprint)
R. Radosh, "The Corporate Ideology of American Labor Leaders (Bobbs-Merrill Reprint)

SYLLABUS

Week	Topic/Assignment
1 (Sept. 17)	Introduction: methods/terminology Rayback, pt. 1
2 (Sept. 22, 24)	Protestant ethic and Colonial labor Economic Preconditions for Industrialization. Lemisch, "Jack Tar;" Dawley, intro. and Ch. 1
3 (Sept. 29, Oct. 1)	Industrial Capital and the Transformation of Work Discussion: Early Industrialization: Progress or Immiseration? Montgomery, "The Working Classes;" Rayback, ch. V; Dawley, chs. 2,3
4 (Oct. 6,8)	Early Industrialization: Origin of the Labor Force and the New Standard of Living. Lerner "Lady and the Mill Girl;" Dawley, 4-7
5 (Oct. 13, 15)	Maturing Industrial Society: Corporate Power and Technology. Discussion: Dawley. Rayback, ch. VI-VIII

6 (Oct. 20, 22)	Maturing Industrial Society: The Success Myth and Social Mobility. Film: "Molders of Troy;" Gutman, pts. I, III
7 (Oct. 27, 29)	Immigrant Workers Organize: Family Community, Factory. Discussion: Hegemony or Worker's Control? Gutman, pt. II,IV; Rayback, chs. IX-XII
8 (Nov. 3,5)	Protest and Reaction, 1860-1894 Mid Term Examination. Grob, "The Knights of Labor;" Dawley, ch. 8 and conclusion
9 (Nov. 10, 12)	Monopoly Capital and the Routinization of Work. Braverman, chs. 4-6, 11-14, Nelson, chs. 1-5; O'Neill, pt. 1
10 (Nov. 17, 19)	Early Radicalism: Socialists and the IWW. Discussion: Braverman, Flynn, The Rebel Girl; Rayback, XIII-XVIII
11 (Nov. 24, 26)	Workers' Control and Corporate Labor Radosh, "The Corporate Ideology;" Nelson, chs. 6-end; Rayback, XIX-XX
12 (Dec. 1, 3)	From Craft to Industrial Unionism Discussion: Nelson, Bernstein, 1-317; Rayback, XXI-XXII
13 (Dec. 8, 10)	The Left and Industrial Unionism Film: "The Inheritance;" Bernstein, finish, Rayback, XXIII-XXV
14 (Dec. 15, 17)	White Collar Labor in Welfare State Discussion: Proletarians or Professionals? Rayback, XXVI-end; Braverman, chs. 15-16, 18-19
15 (Jan. 5, 7)	The Mystification of the Working Class Sigal, Going Away; O'Neill, "Inside The Telephone Co."

This course will consist mostly of lectures though all students will be expected to participate in regular discussion sections that will meet on six occasions with either the instructor or the teaching assistant. The class will be divided into several discussion sections for those meetings where attendance will be taken. A discussion section evaluation will comprise about 1/6th of the final grade.

A midterm examination will make up another 1/6th, and a final exam and term paper will each count 1/3th. Review questions on which the final will be based will be handed out a week or two before the end of the semester.

The term paper should be a fully documented, original, analytic essay (perhaps 5-10 typewritten pages) on either of two topics.

1. "Class Consciousness and American Labor; A case study of... (the Knights of Labor, National Labor Union, IWW, AFL, CIO, a local union, or compare two of the proceeding).

2. The Impact of Industrialization: or a case study of technological development in a specific industry in a specific city.
ex: The Lynn shoemakers

A precis with bibliography must be typed and submitted to your discussion leader for approval. The paper is due December 15.

NEW YORK UNIVERSITY

Industrialization and the Working Class
in Comparative Perspective: 1780-1870

G57.1021
Spring 1982
M. Nolan & D. Walkowitz

Please purchase as many of the following paperbacks as possible.

Edward P. Thompson, The Making of the English Working Class
David Landes, Unbound Prometheus
Georges Rude, The Crowd in History
Karl Marx, Capital, vol. 1.
William Sewell, Work and Revolution
Alan Dawley, Class and Community
Thomas Dublin, Women at Work
Herbert Gutman, Work, Culture and Society in Industrializing America
James Henretta, The Evolution of American Society, 1700-1815
Eric Hobsbawm, Primitive Rebels
Joseph Rayback, History of American Labor
C.S. Doty, The Industrial Revolution

These books are also available in the Reserve Room of Bobst. All articles assigned and all excerpts from books not available in paperback are on reserve in Bobst and in the History Department, 19 University Place, 4th floor.

I. February 9: Introduction

Part I: The Industrial Revolution

II. February 16: Preindustrial Society

James Henretta, The Evolution of American Society, Chapters 1 and 6. (read Chap. 2 and 3 if you have time.)
Hans Medick, "The Proto-industrial Family Economy," Social History, Oct. 1976.
E. P. Thompson, "Patrician Society, Plebian Culture," Journal of Social History, Summer, 1974.
E. P. Thompson, "The Moral Economy of the Eighteenth Century Crowd," Past and Present, 1971.
I. Wallerstein, The Modern World System, Chapter 2.

III. February 23: The Nature of the Industrial Revolution, I

David Landes, Unbound Prometheus, Chapters 1-4.
Habbakuk, H. J., "Economic Effects of Labour Scarcity," in Saul, ed. Technological Change.
Neil Smelser, "Sociological History: The Industrial Revolution and the British Working-class Family," Journal of Social History, vol. 1, nol. 1 (on microfilm)

IV. March 2: The Nature of the Industrial Revolution, II

Karl Marx, Capital, Chapters I, VI, VII, X (sections 1, 2, 5, 6), XII, XIV, XV (sections 1, 3, 4, 8).

Part II: Work and Culture in Early Industrial Society

V. March 9: Social Consequences of the Industrial Revolution

C. S. Doty, The Industrial Revolution, pp. 11-21, 53-118.
E. P. Thompson, The Making of the English Working Class, Chapters VI-X.

VI. March 16: Technology and the Organization of Work

R. Samuel, "Workshop of the World," History Workshop Journal, Spring 1977.
Sidney Pollard, The Genesis of Modern Management, Chapter 5.
Stephen Marglin, "What Do Bosses Do?" Review of Radical Political Economics, 1974.
E. P. Thompson, "Time, Work Discipline and Industrial Capitalism," Past and Present, 1967.
Robert Bezucha, The Lyon Uprising of 1834, Chapter 1.

VII. March 23: Women and Work in Europe

Ivy Pinchbeck, Women Workers and the Industrial Revolution, Chapters III, V, IX, XI.
Joan Scott and Louise Tilly, "Women's Work and the Family in Nineteenth Century Europe,"
Barbara Taylor, "The Men are as Bad as Their Masters," Feminist Studies, Spring 1975.
O. Hufton, "Women and the Family Economy in Eighteenth Century France, French Historical Studies, Spring 1975.
E. Yeo and E. P. Thompson, The Unknown Mayhew, Chapters on "Slopworkers and Needlewomen," and "Dressmakers and Milliners."

VIII. March 30: Women and Work in the United States

Thomas Dublin, Women at Work, entire.
Christine Stansell, "The Origins of the Sweatshop: Women and Industrialization in New York City."

April 6: Spring Vacation

IX. April 13: Culture

E. P. Thompson, The Making of the English Working Class, Chapters XI and XII.
Herbert Gutman, Work, Culture and Society, essays on "Work, Culture and Society," and "Protestantism and the American Labor Movement."
David Montgomery, "The Shuttle and the Cross," Journal of Social History, Summer 1972.
Sean Wilentz, "Artisan Republican Ritual and the Rise of Class Conflict in New York City, 1788-1837."

Part III: Protest and Organization

X. April 20: Preindustrial Protest

Eric Hobsbawm, Primitive Rebels, entire.

XI. April 27: Protest in Transitional Societies

Georges Rude, The Crowd in History, entire.
Jesse Lemisch, "Jack Tar in the Streets," William and Mary Quarterly, XXV, July 1968.

XII. May 4: Working-class Formation in England

E. P. Thompson, The Making of the English Working Class, Part III.
John Foster, "Nineteenth Century Towns: A Class Dimension," in Dyos, The Study of Urban History.

XIII. May 11: Working-class Formation in France

William Sewell, Work and Revolution, entire.

XIV. May 18: Working-class Formation in the United States

Alan Dawley, Class and Community, entire.

SARAH LAWRENCE COLLEGE

Phyllis Vine
Center for Continuing Education
Fall, 1981

HISTORY OF WORK IN AMERICA

Books to Purchase (all paper)

James R. Green, The World of the Worker, (Hill and Wang)
Milton Cantor & Bruce Laurie, ed., Class, Sex and the Woman Worker, (Greenwood Press)
Studs Terkel, Working, (Avon)
Alan Dawley, Class and Community, (Harvard Univ. Press)
Harry Braverman, Labor and Monopoly Capitol, (Monthly Review)

PAPERS DUE: October 28; November 18.

September 9 - Introduction:

AGRICULTURAL SOCIETY

September 16:

(R) James A. Henretta, "Families and Farms: Mentalite in Pre-Industrial America," William and Mary Quarterly, vol. 35, no. 1, (January, 1978), 3-32.

(R) Calvin Martin, "The European Impact on the Culture of a Northeastern Algonquian Tribe: An Ecological Interpretation," William and Mary Quarterly, (Jan. 1974), 3-26.

(R) James Lemon, The Best Poor Man's Country, (Norton), 150-184.

INDUSTRIALIZATION

September 23:

(R) E.P. Thompson, "Time, Work-Discipline and Industrial Capitalism," in Past and Present, vol. 38 (1967), 56-97.

(R) Hugh Thomas, "Work and Leisure in Pre-Industrial Society," Past and Present, vol. 29 (Dec., 1964), 50-66.

September 30 - Library Tour

October 7:

Dawley, Class and Community (entire)

(R) On reserve in the Sarah Lawrence College Library

WORKERS AND UNIONS

October 14:

(R) Elizabeth Pleck, "Two Worlds in One," Journal of Social History, vol. 10 (1976), 178-195.

The following four articles in Cantor and Laurie, eds., Class, Sex and the Woman Worker:
Carol Groneman, "She Earns as a Child..." 83-101.
Miriam Cohen, "Italian-American Women in New York City," 120-144.
Alice Kessler-Harris, "Organizing the Unorganizable," 144-166.
Virginia Yans-McLaughlin, "Italian Women and Work," 101-120.

(R) Ros Baxandall, Linda Gordon & Susan Reverby, America's Working Women, (Vintage, 1976), 169-185.

October 21:

(R) Herbert Gutman, "Work, Culture and Society in Industrializing America," in Work, Culture and Society, (Vintage, 1977), 3-78.

James R. Green, The World of the Worker, (Hill and Wang), 1-66.

(R) Joyce L. Kornbluh, Rebel Voices: An IWW Anthology, (Univ. of Michigan Press, 1972 ed.), 1-13, 18-24, 35-56.

October 28: Papers Due: discuss

Reminder. There will be a film today: Of Babies and Banners which might run past 12:00 noon.

November 4:

(R) Booker T. Washington, "The Negro and the Labor Unions," Atlantic Monthly, (June, 1913), pages (to be announced).

(R) Paul Worthman, "Black Workers and Labor Unions in Birmingham, 1874-1904," Labor History, (Summer, 1969), 377-407.

(R) Herbert Gutman, "The Negro and the United Mine Workers," in Work, Culture and Society, (Vintage), 121-209.

SCIENTIFIC MANAGEMENT

November 11:

Harry Braverman, Labor and Monopoly Capital, (Monthly Review Press), 85-183.

James R. Green, The World of the Worker, (Hill and Wang), 67-132.

(R) Stephen Meyer, "Adapting the Immigrant to the Line: Americanization in the Ford Factory, 1914-1921," Journal of Social History, vol. 14, no. 1 (Fall, 1980), 67-83.

November 18: Papers Due

November 25:

(R) Helen Merrell Lynd and Robert Lynd, Middletown, (Harcourt, Brace & World, 1956 ed.), 21-93.

Stuart Ewen, Captains of Consciousness, (McGraw Hill, 1976), pages (to be announced).

(R) C. Wright Mills, White Collar, (Oxford, 1951 ed.), 161-189.

Braverman, Labor and Monopoly Capital, 257-374.

OUT OF WORK

December 2:

Studs Terkel, Hard Times, (Pocket Books, 1978 ed.), 156-176.

John A. Garraty, Unemployment in History, (Harper Colophon Books), 165-215.

Film: ALICE ADAMS

WORKING TODAY

December 9:

To be announced.

December 16:

Studs Terkel, Working, (Avon), any 100 pages.

Green, The World of the Worker, (Hill and Wang), 175-248.

HARVARD UNIVERSITY

Gary Gerstle

Social Studies 98, Fall 1982

SOCIAL HISTORY OF AMERICAN LABOR, 1776-1877

Week of September 27: Religious and Political Sources of Working-Class Culture

Perry Miller, "Declension in a Bible Commonwealth," Nature's Nation (Cambridge, 1967), pp. 14-49.

Bernard Bailyn, The Ideological Origins of the American Revolution (Cambridge, 1972), Chapters 1-5.

Week of October 4: Workers and the American Revolution

Eric Foner, Tom Paine and Revolutionary America (NY, 1976).

Thomas Paine, Common Sense and The Crisis (NY, 1973).

Week of October 11: Capitalism and Labor in Ante-Bellum America: An Introduction

Maurice Dobb, "Capitalism," Studies in the Development of Capitalism (NY, 1963), pp. 1-32.

G.R. Taylor, The Transportation Revolution, 1815-1860 (NY, 1963), pp. 3-14, 132-175, 207-300, 384-398.

Richard Hofstadter, "Andrew Jackson and the Rise of Liberal Capitalism," The American Political Tradition (NY, 1973), pp. 56-85.

Christopher Clark, "Household Economy, Market Exchange and the Rise of Capitalism in the Connecticut Valley, 1800-1860," Journal of Social History 13 (1980), pp. 169-189.

Week of October 18: The Emergence of New Social and Productive Relations

Paul Faler, Mechanics and Manufacturers in the Early Industrial Revolution (Albany, 1981), pp. 1-99.

Thomas Dublin, Women at Work (NY, 1979), pp. 1-85.

Nancy Cott, The Bonds of Womanhood (New Haven, 1978), pp. 1-62.

Week of October 25: A New Morality

E. P. Thompson, "Time, Work-Discipline and Industrial Capitalism," Past and Present 38 (1967), pp. 56-97.

Faler, Mechanics and Manufacturers, pp. 100-138.

Cott, Bonds of Womanhood, pp. 63-159.

The Diaries of N. B. Gordon, mill agent

Week of November 1: Resistance and Accomodation to the New Order, Part I

Faler, Mechanics and Manufacturers, pp. 139-233.

Cott, Bonds of Womanhood, pp. 160-206.

Seth Luther, An Address Delivered Before the Mechanics and Workingmen of the City of Brooklyn (1836)

Week of November 8: Resistance and Accomodation, Part II

Bruce Laurie, Working People of Philadelphia, 1800-1850 (Philadelphia, 1980).

Week of November 15: Immigrant Labor

Oscar Handlin, Boston's Immigrants: A Study in Acculturation, (Revised and Enlarged Edition; NY, 1977)

Eric Foner, "Class, Ethnicity and Radicalism in the Gilded Age: The Land League and Irish America," Marxist Perspectives 2 (Spring, 1978), pp. 6-55.

Week of November 29: Slave Labor

Eugene Genovese, Roll, Jordan, Roll (NY, 1974).

Week of December 6: The Ideology of Free Labor

Eric Foner, Free Soil, Free Labor, Free Men (NY, 1970).

Week of December 13: The Myth and Reality of Social Mobility

Stephan Thernstrom, Poverty and Progress (NY, 1973).

James Henretta, "The Study of Social Mobility: Ideological Assumptions and Conceptual Bias," Labor History 18 (1977).

Jeremy Brecher, Strike! (SF, 1972), Chapter 1.

HARVARD UNIVERSITY

Gary Gerstle

Social Studies 98, Spring 1983

SOCIAL HISTORY OF AMERICAN LABOR, 1877-1948

Week of February 7: The Rise of Corporate Capitalism

Daniel Nelson, Managers and Workers (Madison, 1975).

Harry Braverman, Labor and Monopoly Capital (NY, 1974), Introduction and Part I.

Week of February 14: Perspectives on the American Labor Movement

Selig Perlman, A History of Trade Unionism in the United States (NY, 1922), Parts I and III.

David Montgomery, "Workers' Control of Machine Production in the Nineteenth Century," in Montgomery, Workers' Control in America (Cambridge, 1980), 9-31.

Herbert Gutman, "Work, Culture and Society in Industrializing America, 1815-1919," in Gutman, Work, Culture and Society in Industrializing America (NY, 1977), 3-78.

Week of February 21: Knights of Labor: Visions and Realities

Gerald Grob, Workers and Utopia, Chapters 3-7.

Paul Buhle, "The Knights of Labor in Rhode Island," Radical History Review 17 (1978), 39-73.

Kenneth Kann, "The Knights of Labor and the Southern Black Worker," Labor History 18 (1977), 49-70.

Herbert Gutman, "The Workers' Search for Power: Labor in the Gilded Age," in H. Wayne Morgan, ed., The Gilded Age: A Reappraisal, 31-53.

Week of February 28: Socialism

Ray Ginger, Eugene V. Debs (NY, 1962), Parts I-III.

Irving Howe, "Jewish Labor, Jewish Socialism," in World of Our Fathers (NY, 1976).

Week of March 7: Ethnic Consciousness and Class Consciousness

David Brody, "The American Worker in the Progressive Era: A Comprehensive Analysis," in Brody, Workers in Industrial America (NY, 1980), 3-47.

Irving Howe, World of Our Fathers, pp. 1-286, 460-496.

Virginia Yans-McLaughlin, "A Flexible Tradition: South Italian Immigrants Confront a New Work Experience," Journal of Social History 7 (1974), 429-445.

Week of March 14: Women Workers and Black Workers

Alice Kessler-Harris, Out to Work: A History of Wage-Earning Women in the United States (NY, 1982), Part II.

Susan Porter Benson, "'The Customers Ain't God': The Work of Department-Store Saleswomen, 1890-1940," in Frisch and Walkowitz, eds., Working-Class America, 185-211.

William M. Tuttle, Jr., Race Riot: Chicago in the Red Summer of 1919, pp. 74-183, 208-241.

Week of March 21: Welfare Capitalism and the American Plan

Stuart Ewen, Captains of Consciousness: Advertising and the Social Roots of Consumer Culture (NY, 1976).

David Brody, "The Rise and Decline of Welfare Capitalism," in Brody, Workers in Industrial America, 48-81.

Week of March 28: A Novel of Immigrant Labor

Thomas Bell, Out of This Furnace: A Novel of Immigrant Labor in America (Pittsburgh, 1977).

Week of April 4: The Origins of Industrial Unions

James Green, The World of the Worker (NY, 1980), Chapter 5.

Irving Bernstein, The Turbulent Years: A History of the American Worker, 1933-1941 (Boston, 1969), Chapter 6, "Eruption."

David Brody, "The Emergence of Mass Production Unionism," in Brody, Workers in Industrial America, 82-119.

Ronald Schatz, "Union Pioneers: The Founders of Local Unions at General Electric and Westinghouse, 1933-37," Journal of American History 66 (1979).

Week of April 11: Class, Ethnicity and Industrial Unionism

Peter Friedlander, The Emergence of a UAW Local, 1936-39 (Pittsburgh, 1976).

Joshua Freeman, "Catholics, Communists and Republicans: Irish Workers and the Organization of the Transport Workers Union," in Frisch and Walkowitz, Working-Class America, 256-283.

Week of April 18: The Nature of New Deal Reform

William Leuchtenberg, Franklin D. Roosevelt and the New Deal, 1932-1940 (NY, 1963), Conclusion.

Ronald Radosh, "The Myth of the New Deal," in Radosh and Murray Rothbard, eds., New History of Leviathan (NY, 1972).

Theda Skocpol, "Political Response to Capitalist Crisis: Neo-Marxist Theories of the State and the Case of the New Deal," Politics and Society 10 (1980), 155-201.

Karl Klare, "Judicial Deradicalization of the Wagner Act and the Origins of Modern Legal Consciousness, 1937-1941," Minnesota Law Review 62 (1977-78), 265-339.

Week of April 25: World War Two and After

Bert Cochran, Labor and Communism: The Conflict that Shaped American Unions (Princeton, 1977), Chapters 7-13.

David Brody, "The Uses of Power I: Industrial Battleground," and "The Uses of Power II: Political Action," in Brody, Workers in Industrial America, 173-257.

James Green, The World of the Worker, Chapters 6-7.

UNIVERSITY OF MASSACHUSETTS
AT AMHERST

American Labor Since the Thirties — Fall, 1979
LRRC

Bruce Laurie

The following books may be purchased at the Logos book store in Amherst:

Irving Bernstein, The Turbulent Years.
Jeremy Brecher, Strike!
Richard Cloward and Frances F. Piven, Regulating the Poor.
Peter Friedlander, The Emergence of a U.A.W. Local, 1936-1939.
Alice and Staughton Lynd, eds., Rank and File.
Robert and Helen Lynd, Middletown.
____________, Middletown in Transition (optional).
Antomio Gramsci, Prison Notebooks.
J. Rifkin and R. Barber, The North Will Rise Again.
Raymond Williams, Marxism and Literature.

These books and the core reading assignments for each week are on reserve in the Reserve Reading Room of the Tower Library.
Each student is responsible for two papers.

Sept. 5: Introduction and Assignment of papers.

Sept. 12-19: Theory.

Readings: Karl Marx, The Communist Manifesto.
Antonio Gramsci, Prison Notebooks, 206-76, 381-472.
Raymond Williams, Marxism and Literature, 75-141.

Suggested: Alan Dawley and Paul Faler, " Workingclass Culture and Politics in the Industrial Revolution: Sources of Loyalism and Rebellion," Jour. of Soc. Hist., 9 (June, 1976), 466-80.

L. Althusser, Reading Capital.
____________, For Marx.
E.P. Thompson, The Poverty of Theory, 195-406.
Erik O. Wright, "Class Boundaries in Advanced Capitalist Societies," New Left Rev. (July-Aug.), 1976.

Sept. 26: Organized Labor and the Second Industrial Revolution.

Readings: James O. Morris, "The A.F. of L. in the 1920s: A Strategy of Defense," Ind. and Labor Relations Rev., 11 (July, 1958), 572-90.
Ronald Radosh, "The Corporate Ideology of American Labor from Gompers to Hillman," in Weinstein and Eakins, eds., For a New America.

Paper I: The Second Industrial Revolution.
Alfred D. Chandler, The Visible Hand.
____________, Strategy and Structure.
Richard Edwards, Contested Terrain.
Daniel Nelson, Managers and Workers.
Harry Braverman, Labor and Monopoly Capital.

Paper II: The A.F. of L. in the Twenties.

David Montgomery, Worker Control in America (if available).
_______________, "The 'New Unionism' and the Transformation of Worker Consciousness in America, 1909-1922," Jour. of Soc. Hist., 7 (Summer, 1974), 509-29.
I. Bernstein, The Lean Years.
M. Dubofsky and W. Van Tine, John L. Lewis.
Jean T. McKelvey, A.F. of L. Attitudes towards Production, 1900-1932.
C. Nyman, Union-Management Cooperation in the "Stretch-Out".
Paul. F. Gemmill, Present-Day Labor Relations.

Sept. 26: The Culture of Adjustment.

Readings: P. and S. Lynd, Middletown.
L. Tilly and J. Scott, Women, Work, & Family, 176-213.

Paper I: Consumerism.

Stuart Ewen, Captains of Consciousness.
Edward Filene, The Way Out: A Forecast of Coming Changes in American Business and Industry.
_____________, The Consumer's Dollar.
Dale Yoder, Labor's Attitudes in Iowa and Contiguous Territories.
R. Lynd, "Family Members as Consumers," Annals (March, 1932).
________, "The People as Consumers," in Report of the President's Research Committee on Social Trends.
J. Bodnar, "Immigration and Modernization: The Case of Slavic Peasants in Industrial America," Jour. of Soc. Hist., 9 (1976), 44-71.
R. Sklar, ed., The Plastic Age, 1917-1933.

Paper II: The Black Worker.
F. Henri, The Great Migration.
K. Kusmer, A Ghetto Takes Shape: Black Cleveland, 1870-1930.
G. Osofsky, Harlem: The Making of a Ghetto.
D. Katzman, Black Detroit.
S. Spero and A. Harris, The Black Worker.
Allan Spear, Black Chicago: The Making of a Negro Ghetto.

Oct. 3: The Social Basis of Politics, 1925- 1940.

Readings: S. Lubell, The Future of American Politics, 42-68.
M. Cantor, The Divided Left, 97-149, or J. Weinstein, Ambiguous Legacy, 57-86.

Paper I: The Roosevelt Coalition.
S. Lubell, The Future of American Politics.
R. Beyor, Neighbors in Conflict.
John Allswang, A House for all Peoples.
E. Kantowiscz, Polish American Politics in Chicago.
P. Kleppner, The Second Party System (approx. title).

Paper II: The Insurgents.

T. Harry Williams, "The Gentleman from Louisiana: Demagogue or Democrat?" Jour. of Southern Hist., 26 (Feb., 1960).

Joseph P. Shenton, " The Coughlin Movement and the New Deal," Pol. Sci. Qtly., 3 (Sept., 1958).

David H. Bennett, Demagogues of the Depression.
Geoffrey S. Smith, To Save a Nation.
Charles Tull, Father Coughlin and the New Deal.
R. Beyor, Neighbors in Conflict.

Oct. 10: New Deal Social Legislation.

Readings: I. Bernstein, The Turbulent Years, 1-36, 172-216, 318-51, 635-81.

Paper I: The Labor Front.

D. Fusfeld, The Economic Thought of the F.D.R. and the Origins of the New Deal.

G.N. Farr, Recent Labor Policy.

Thirty Hour Week Bill, Hearings before House Committee on Labor, 73 Cong., 1st Sess., 1933.

I. Bernstein, New Deal Collective Bargaining.
W. Millis and Brown, From the Wagner Act to Taft Hartley.
J.M. Eisner, William M. Leiserson.
(and any material on the Taylor Society and Morris Cook).
B. Rauch, This History of the New Deal, 1933-1938.

Paper II: Social Security.

D. Fusfeld, The Economic Thought of the F.D.R. and the Origins of the New Deal.

C. McKinley and R.W. Frase, Launching Social Security.
Daniel Nelson, Unemployment Insurance,
Edwin Witte, The Development of the Social Security Act.
Paul H. Douglas, Social Security in the United States,
(and relevant Congressional hearings, 1934-35).

Oct. 17: The Revolt of the Unorganized, 1933-35.

Readings: I. Bernstein, Turbulent Years, 37-171, 217-317
J. Brecher, Strike!, 144-77.
R. and H. Lynd, Middletown in Transition, 295-372, 402-86.

Paper I: Mobilizing the Unemployed

Roy Rosenzweig, "Organizing the Unemployed: The Early Years of the Depression, 1929-1933," Rad. Am., 10 (July-Aug., 1976), 37-62.

R. Rosenzweig,"Radicals and the Jobless: The Musteites and the Unemployed Leagues, 1932-1936," Lab. Hist., 16 (Winter, 1975), 52-77.

D. Leab,"'United We Eat': The Creation and Organization of the Unemployed Councils in 1930," Lab. Hist., 8 (Fall, 1967).

Roger Daniels, The Bonus March.
Thomas P. Jones, Five Cities.
L. Adamic, My America, 1928-1938.
Charles R. Walker, American City.
Ruth McKenney, Industrial Valley.
O. Milton Hall, "Attitudes and Unemployment: A Comparison of the Opinions of Employed and Unemployed Men," Archives of Psychology (March, 1934), 5-65.
P. Eisenberg and P. Lazarsfeld, "The Psychological Effects of Unemployment," Psy. Bulletin, 35 (1938), 358-80.
Homer W. Jones, Life, Liberty, and Property
E. Wight Bakke, Citizens without Work.

Paper II: The Left and Mass Production Workers.
S. Lynd, " The Possibility of Radicalism in the Early 1930s: The Case of Steel," Rad. Am., 6 (Nov.-Dec., 1972), 37-64.
S. Fine, The Automobile under the Blue Eagle.
B. Cochran, Labor and Communism.
M. Quin, The Big Strike.
P. Eliel, Waterfront and General Strikes.
Harry Dalheimer, A History of the Mechanics Educational Society of America.
J. Matles and J. Higgins, Them and Us.

Oct. 24: The Formation of the CIO

Readings: P. Friedlander, The Emergence of a U.A.W. Local, 1936-1939
I. Bernstein, The Turbulent Years, 352-634 (optional).
J. Brecher, Strike!, 177-217.
A. and S. Lynd, eds., Rank and File, 9-88.

Paper I: Auto and Steel.
C. Goldin and H. Ruttenberg, Dynamics of Industrial Democracy.
T.R. Brooks, As Steel Goes.
Vincent D. Sweeney, The U.S.W. Twenty Years After.
S. Fine, Sit Down!
Henry Kraus, The Many and the Few.
Clayton Fountain, Union Guy.
B. Cochran, Labor and Communism.
Jack Skeels, "The Backround of U.A.W. Factionalism," Lab. Hist, 2 (Spring, 1962).
(See also, UAW and USW settlements in the N.Y. Times.)

Paper II: A Critique of the C.P.U.S.A.
A. Richmond, A Long View from the Left.
Lewis Coser and Irving Howe, The American Communist Party.
Joseph Starobin, American Communism in Crisis, 1943-1957.
N. Glazer, The Social Basis of American Communism.
G. Charney, A Long Journey.
A. and S. Lynd, eds., Rank and File, 89-110.
H. Haywood, Black Bolshevik.
W. Record, The Negro and the Communist Party.

Oct. 31- Nov.7: Wartime and After,

Readings: J. Green, "Fighting on Two Fronts: Working-Class Militancy in the Forties" and N. Lichtenstein, "Defending the No-Strike Pledge: CIO Politics During W.W.II," Rad. Am., 9 (July-Aug., 1975).

A. and S. Lynd, eds., Rank and File, 149-264.

S. Lubell, The Future of American Politics, 106-30.

J. Brecher, Strike!, 221-32.

Paper I: The Labor Statesmen and the Crisis of Liberalism.

C. Wright Mills, The New Men of Power.

J. Seidman, American Labor from Defense to Reconversion.

M. Josephson, Sidney Hillman, Statesman of American Labor.

B.J. Widdick and I. Howe, The U.A.W. and Walter Reuther.

Walter Reuther, Selected Papers.

Joseph Gaer, The First Round: The Story of CIO-PAC.

James C. Foster, The Union Politic, The CIO Political Action Committee.

Paper II: Purging the Communists.

David Oshinsky, "Labor's Cold War: The CIO and the Communists," in R. Griffith and A. Theoharis, eds., The Specter.

Bert Cochran, Labor and Communism.

F. Marquart, An Automobile Worker's Journal.

M. McAuliffe, Crisis on the Left: Cold War Politics and American Liberals.

D. Caute, The Great Fear.

L. DeCaux, Labor Radical.

Aaron Abel, American Catholicism and Social Action, Ch. 8.

Ronald Radosh, Labor and the Cold War.

D. Saposs, Communism in American Unions.

Paper III: The Significance of Taft Hartley.

H.A. Millis and E.C. Brown, From the Wagner Act to Taft Hartley.

B. Selekman, et al., eds., Problems in Labor Relations.

Alton Lee, Truman and Taft-Hartley.

(Congressional hearings on the Taft-Hartley bill.).

Joseph Rosenfarb, The National Labor Policy and How it Works.

D.O. Bowman, Public Control over Labor.

Paper IV: Women Workers in War and Peace.

Laura Baker, Wanted: Women in Wartime Industry.

M. Banning, Women for Defense.

Chester Gregory, Women in Defense Work during World War II.

International Labor Office, The War and Women's Employment.

H. Dratch, "The Politics of Child Care in the 1940s," Science and Society (Summer, 1974).

William H. Chafe, The American Woman, 135-95.

Elsie Bond, "Day Care of Children of Working Mothers in New York State during the War Emergency," New York History, 26 (January, 1945), 51-77.

P. Quick, "Rosie the Riveter: Myths and Realities," Rad. Am., 9 (July-Aug., 1975).

Paper V: The Black Worker in Wartime.

F. Dalfiume, ed., The Negro in the New Deal and World War II.
M. Ward, Indignant Heart.
H. Garfinkel, When Negroes March.
Jervis Anderson, A Philip Randolph.
P. Foner, Organized Labor and the Black Worker.
Howard Sitkoff, "Racial Militancy and Inter-racial Violence during the Second World War," Jour. of Am. Hist. (Dec., 1971).
E. Rudwick, CORE: A Study in the Civil Rights Movement,
S. Rosen, "The CIO Era, 1935-1955," in J. Jacobson, ed., The Negro and the American Labor Movement.

Nov. 14: Capitalism in the Cold War.

Readings: A. Mkrtchian, U.S. Labour Unions Today, 9-67.
M. Reich, "The Evolution of the United States Labor Force," in Edwards, et al., eds. The Capitalist System, 174-83.
R. Edwards, Contested Terrain, 162-202.

Paper I: Capital, the State, and Labor: The Private Sector.

A. Mkrtchian, U.S. Labour Unions Today, 68-195.
W. Serrin, The Company and the Union.
R. and Estelle James, Hoffa and the Teamsters.
S. Brill, The Teamsters.
John Herring, The Fight to Challenge: People and Power in the Steelworkers.
Joseph Becker, The Story of SUB.
N. Lichtenstein, "Auto Worker Militancy and the Structure of Factory Life, 1935-1955" (unpublished ms).
Erik O. Wright, Class, Crisis, and the State.

Paper II: The Rise of Public Employe Unions.

H. Braverman, Labor and Monopoly Capital, 293-401.
A. Sturmthal, ed., White Collar Trade Unionism.
A. Levison, Working-Class Majority.
S. Zagoria, Public Workers and Public Unions.

Nov. 21: The New Labor Force and the New Frontier.

Readings: T. Lowi, The End of Liberalism, 3-91.
H. Baron and B. Hymer, "Institutional Racism and Urban Labor Markets," in Edwards, et al., eds., The Capitalist System, 297-305.
R. Cloward and F. Piven, Regulating the Poor, 224-84.

Paper I: The Great Society: A Critique.

L. Wittner, Cold War America, 168-294.
R. Cloward and F. Piven, Regulating the Poor.
M. Anderson, The Federal Bulldozer.

J. David Greenstone and Paul E. Peterson, Race and Authority in Urban Politics.

T. Lowi, The End of Liberalism, 168-294.

John A. Perrotta, "Machine Influence in Community Action Programs: The Case of Providence, Rhode Island," Polity, (Summer, 1977).

Paper II: Women in the Labor Force: Causes and Consequences.

F. Blau, "Women in the Labor Force: An Overview," in Jo Freeman, ed., Women: A Feminist Perspective.

Heidi Hartman, "Capitalism, Patriarchy, and Job Segregation by Sex," Signs, 1 (Spring, 1976), 137-70.

Janice Madden, The Economics of Sex Discrimination.

Shelia Rowbotham, Woman's Consciousness, Man's World.

Edna Raphael, "Working Women and their Membership in Unions," Monthly Labor Rev., 97 (May, 1974).

Annemarie Troger, "The Coalition of Labor Union Women: Strategic Hope, Tactical Despair," Rad. Am., 9 (1975), 85-110.

Kathleen McCourt, Working-Class Women and Grass-Roots Politics.

J. Brecher and T. Costello, Common Sense for Hard Times, 176-87.

Nov. 28: The Current Crisis and the New Right.

Readings: R. Edwards, Contested Terrain, 202-16.

J. O'Connor, "The Fiscal Crisis of the State," in R. Edwards, et al., The Capitalist System, 192-201.

Paper I: An Analysis of the Crisis.

J. O'Connor, The Fiscal Crisis of the State.

B. Commoner, The Poverty of Power.

T. Weisskopf, "The Problem of Surplus Absorption in a Capitalist Society," in Edwards, et al., The Capitalist System, 364-74.

P. Baran and P. Sweezy, Monopoly Capital.

S. Hymer and R. Rowthorn, "Multinational Corporations and International Oligopoly: The Non-American Challenge," in C.P. Kindleberger, The International Corporation.

C. Oglesby, The Yankee and Cowboy War.

S. Coontz, Productive Labor and Effective Demand.

Paper II: The New Right.

Trilateral Commission, The Crisis of Democracy.

I. Peppercorn, R. Quinby, and Greg Roberts, "The New Right" (mimeo).

A. Kopkind, "America's New Right," New Times, Sept. 30, 1977.

J. Diggins, Up from Communism.

George Nash, The Conservative Intellectual Movement in America since 1945.

(Also see recent editions of Public Interest and Commentary).

K. McCourt, Working-Class Women and Grass Roots Politics.

Jorge Corralejo, "Report on Proposition 14: Farmworkers vs Big Growers, Big Money, and Big Lies," Rad. Am., 11 (March-Apr., 1977).

Dec 5: A New Insurgency?

Reading: J. Brecher, Strike!, 233-93.

Paper I: The Beleaguered Blue Collar Worker.

R. Blauner, Alienation and Freedom.
J. Brecher and T. Costello, Common Sense for Hard Times, esp. Ch. 7.
R. Sennett and J. Cobb, The Hidden Injuries of Class.
P. Binzen, Whitetown.
J. Ryan, ed., White Ethnics.
H. Gintis, "Alienation in Capitalist Society," in Edwards, et al., The Capitalist System, 274-85.

Paper II: Recent Rumblings.
J. Brecher and T. Costello, Common Sense for Hard Times, 23-103.
S. Peck, "The Political Consciousness of Rank-and-File Leaders," in S. Lynd, ed., American Labor Radicalism,
D. Georgakas and M. Surkin, Detroit: I Do Mind Dying.
J. Green, "Holding the Line: Miners' Militancy and the Strike of 1978," Rad. Am., 12 (May-June, 1978).
F. Kashner, "Rank and File Revolt at G.E.," Rad. Am., 12 (Nov.-Dec., 1978).
John Lippert, "Shopfloor Politics at Fleetwood," Rad. Am., 12 (July-Aug., 1978).
............., "Fleetwood Wildcat: Anatomy of a Wildcat Strike," Rad Am., 11 (Sept.-Oct., 1977).
S. Weir, "Doug Draser's Middle-Class Coalition," Rad Am., 13 (Jan.-Feb., 1979).
(And anything available on citizens' lobbies)

Dec. 12: Wrap- Up.

Reading: J. Rifkin and R. Barber, The North Will Rise Again.

W. G. McLoughlin
Syllabus, Fall 1983 History 177

The History of Religion in America

Topic for 1983: The Conflict Between Personal Faith and Public Authority, 1609-1983

In all ages the personal faith of individuals and groups have on occasion come into conflict with public authority, whether that authority is that of a czar, a king, a republican legislature, or the democratic majority. During the first 200 years after the settlement of British North America, the religion of the King (Anglicanism) or that of the Puritans (Congregationalism) was the established, state supported religion in most colonies. Those who disagreed with these establishments were called heretics, non-conformists, dissenters, fanatics, and were persecuted (or at least, forced to pay taxes to support the established church). After the American Revolution, the principles of religious freedom and separation of church and state were written into the federal constitution, but nonetheless, most Americans continued (until the present-day) to believe that the United States was a Christian country. Christianity was defined by the majority in terms of Evangelical Arminianism. To this religious identity of what it meant to be "an American" was usually added that "this is a whiteman's country" and one which was founded upon Anglo-Saxons laws, institutions, values and ideals. (WASP'ism was the abbreviation for this "quasi-establishment" which permeated American culture. Those who were not WASPs, were expected to conform to the ideals of the majority or to suffer social prejudice, sometimes violence, and often legal inequities.) The purpose of this course is to trace the various ways in which individuals and minority groups with religious principles different from those of the majority have tried to reconcile their dual allegiance to their faith and to the public authority. It is a conflict very much alive today as disputes over religious schools, abortion, working on "the Sabbath," conscientious objection to war, prayer in the public schools, etc. indicate. How the majority has acted toward the divided allegiance of the minorities and how the minorities have tried to cope with their desire to be "loyal Americans" despite their religious differences, is the subject of the course.

Books to be purchased:

The basic text in the course is Sydney E. Ahlstrom, A Religious History of the American People (New Haven, 1972). It is available in the bookstore. Assignments in this text are included for each week of the course. Because this is not a lecture course, the text is essential to provide general background.

In addition, the following books are also available at the bookstore, and one must be purchased out of the choices for each week of the course as numbered.

I. Either E. S. Morgan, The Puritan Dilemma or Kenneth Lockridge, A New England Town.

II. Either Kai Erikson, The Wayward Puritans or William Sargant, Battle for the Mind.

III. Either E. S. Gaustad, The Great Awakening in New England or Ernest Tuveson, Redeemer Nation.

IV. Either Adreinne Koch, The Philosophy of Thomas Jefferson or Thomas Paine, The Age of Reason or Gustav A. Koch, The Religion of the Enlightenment.

V. Martin Marty, Righteous Empire.

VI. Either A. F. C. Wallace, The Death and Rebirth of the Seneca or Robert K. Berkhofer, The Whiteman's Indian or Robert K. Berkhofer, Salvation and the Savage.

VII. Either Oscar Handlin, Boston's Immigrants or Jay Dolan, The Immigrant Church: Catholics in New York City or Oscar Handlin, The Uprooted.

VIII. Either A. J. Raboteau, Slave Religion or Lawrence Levine, Black Culture and Consciousness.

IX. Either Richard Gambino, Blood of My Blood or Thomas Kessner, The Golden Door or Moses Rischin, The Promised City.

X. All students must buy both George Marsden, Fundamentalism and American Culture and the New Yorker Magazine, May 18, 1981 on Jerry Falwell.

XI. Either Milton Gordon, Assimilation in American Life or Will Herberg, Protestant, Catholic, Jew.

XII. Either Theodore Roszak, The Making of a Counter-Culture or E. S. Gaustad, Dissent in America.

NOTE: Copies of all these books are also on reserve in the Rockefeller Library. In addition, other reserve readings are noted below for each week.

Orientation Meeting: Thursday, Sept. 8:

Recommended reading: Clifford Geertz, "Religion as a Cultural System" in The Interpretation of Cultures. Robert Bellah, "America's Civil Religion," in Daedalus (Winter, 1967).

I. Week of Sept. 15: The Puritan Corporate Christian Community

Read either E. S. Morgan, The Puritan Dilemma or Kenneth Lockridge, A New England Town.

Read: Aaron B. Seidman, "Church and State in the Early Years of the Massachusetts Bay Colony," New England Quarterly, vol. 18 (1945) pp. 211-233.

For background on Puritanism and Calvinism read in the Ahlstrom textbook chaps. 5-14.

II. Week of Sept. 22: Social Deviance, Sects, Cults and Religious Brainwashing

Read Kai T. Erikson, The Wayward Puritans

Read William Sargant, Battle for the Mind, Intro. pp. 1-35 and chap. 5, 143-185.

Read Bryan Wilson, Religious Sects (N. Y., 1970) "Sects in Sociological Perspective," pp. 7-47.

Read David Williams, "Horses, Pigeons and the Therapy of Conversion: A Psychological Reading of Jonathan Edward's Theology" in Harvard Theological Review, vol. 74 (1981) pp. 337-352.

III. Week of Sept. 29: The First Great Awakening, Millennialism and the Breakdown of the Puritan Corporate Ideal

Read either E. S. Gaustad, The Great Awakening in New England or Ernest Tuveson, Redeemer Nation.

Read Rhys Isaac, "Evangelical Revolt: The Baptists' Challenge to Traditional Order in Virginia, 1765-1775," William and Mary Quarterly, vol. 31 (1974).

Read in the Ahlstrom textbook: chaps. 15-20 on the breakdown of the corporate state.

IV. Week of Oct. 6: Deism, the Enlightenment, and Separation of Church and State

Read either Adrienne Koch, The Philosophy of Thomas Jefferson or Thomas Paine, The Age of Reason or Gustav A. Koch, The Religion of the Englightenment.

Read Anson P. Stokes, Church and State in the United States, vol. I, chap. 4, section 8, pp. 292-358 on "Separation of Church and State" (esp. 341-343); xeroxed on reserve.

Read Henry F. May, The Enlightenment in America, Part III, pp. 153-304.

Read John F. Wilson's introduction to Church and State in American History, pp. ix-xx; xeroxed on reserve.

Read Gustav A. Koch, The Religion of the Enlightenment, chaps. 1 or 2 on Ethan Allen and Elihu Palmer

Read in the Ahlstrom textbook chaps. 22-24 on Deism, the Enlightenment and disestablishment.

V. Week of Oct. 13: The Second Great Awakening and the Rise of the New Quasi-Establishment

Read Martin Marty, Righteous Empire.

Read Henry Steele Commager, "The Blasphemy of Abner Kneeland," in the New England Quarterly, vol. 8 (1935) pp. 29-41; xeroxed on reserve.

Read "Commonwealth V. Kneeland," Suffolk County Court Records; xeroxed on reserve.

Read C. Peter Magrath, "Chief Justice Write & the Twin Relic," Vanderbilt Law Review, XVIII, 507-543.

Read "The Mormons, the Law and the Territory of Utah," by Orma Linford in The American Journal of Legal History, vol. 23, 1979; xeroxed on reserve.

Read in the Ahlstrom textbook chaps. 25-29, on the proliferation of sects in America during and after the Second Great Awakening.

VI. Week of Oct. 20: The Persecution and Survival of the Religion of Native Americans

Read either A. F. C. Wallace, The Death and Rebirth of the Seneca or Robert Berkhofer, The Whiteman's Indian or Robert Berkhofer, Salvation and the Savage.

Read the three Navajo Peyote Cases (1964, 1971, 1972) xeroxed on reserve: "Native American Church vs. Arizona Corporation Commissioners."

Read Peter Williams, Popular Religion in America, pp. 26-35.

Read "Resistance at Big Mountain" in Akwesasne Notes (Summer, 1981) xeroxed.

Read the references under "Indians" and "Indian Missions" in the Ahlstrom textbook (see index for pages).

VII. Week of Oct. 27: The Religious Difficulties of the European Immigrants after 1830

Read either Oscar Handlin, Boston's Immigrants or Jay Dolan, The Immigrant Church or Oscar Handlin, The Uprooted.

Read R. A. Billington, The Protestant Crusade, chaps. 1, 3, 12, 13, 15 on the rise of anti-Irish, anti-Catholic and Know-Nothing sentiment, 1830-1860.

Read Anson P. Stokes, Church and State in the United States, vol. I, chap. 12, "The Roman Catholic Adjustments to American Church-State Conditions," pp. 784-854.

Read John Higham, Strangers in the Land, chaps. 9, 10, 11 on Immigration restriction in the 1920s, pp. 234-331.

Read in the Ahlstrom textbook chaps. 31-38 on Nativism, xenophobia, and the religious difficulties of European immigrants.

VIII. Week of Nov. 3: Problems of Afro-American Religious Identity

Read either Albert Raboteau, Slave Religion or Lawrence Levine, Black Culture and Consciousness.

Read W. E. B. DuBois, "Of Our Spiritual Strivings" in Souls of Black Folk, chap. I.

Read E. D. Cronon, Marcus Garvey, chaps. 7-8.

Read The Autobiography of Malcolm X, chaps. 10, 11, 12 on his conversion to the Black Muslim faith.

Read in the Ahlstrom textbook chaps. 43 and 62 on the major black denominations.

IX. Week of Nov. 10: Jewish and Italian Religious Adjustments

Read one of the following: Richard Gambino, Blood of My Blood
Thomas Kessner, The Golden Door
Moses Rischin, The Promised City

Oscar Handlin, "American Views of the Jew," in American Jewish Historical Society Publications, vol. 40, (1950-51) xeroxed on reserve.

Milton Himmelfarb, "Secular Society, a Jewish Perspective," in Daedalus, Winter, 1967.

Louis D. Brandeis, "A Call to the Educated Jew," in The Menorah Journal, vol. I, Jan., 1915. Xeroxed on reserve.

Randolph S. Bourne, "The Jew and Trans-National America," in The Menorah Journal, vol. 2 (December, 1916) xeroxed on reserve.

Horace Kallen, "Democracy vs. the Melting-Pot," in Culture and Democracy in the United States (N. Y., 1924) xeroxed on reserve.

Read in the Ahlstrom textbook on the divisions between orthodox, conservative and reform Judaism, and the problems of other immigrant groups, chaps. 35 and 57.

X. Week of Nov. 17: Fundamentalists and Neo-Evangelicals

Read George Marsden, Fundamentalism and American Culture.

Read Martin Marty, A Nation of Believers, chaps. 4-5 on Fundamentalism and Pentecostalism.

Read Frances Fitzgerald, "The Rev. Jerry Falwell" in The New Yorker, May 18, 1981.

Read Ron L. Numbers, "Creationism in 20th Century America," vol. 218, Science (November, 1982) xeroxed on reserve.

Read court decision in Epperson vs. Arkansas," in Supreme Court Reports (1968) overthrowing the Tennessee evolution law. Xeroxed on reserve.

Read the Ahlstrom textbook chaps. 44-51 on the controversy between Fundamentalists and Liberal Protestants.

XI. Week of Dec. 1: Assimilation and the Rise of Unmeltable Ethnics

Read either Milton Gordon, Assimilation in American Life or Will Herberg, Protestant, Catholic, Jew.

Read John Dewey, A Common Faith, chap. 1, "Religion vs. the Religious" p. 1-28.

Read Michael Novak, The Rise of the Unmeltable Ethnics (N. Y., 1973) Preface to the Paperback Edition and chap. 1.

XII. Week of Dec. 8: Dissent, the Counter-Culture and Current Church-State Issues

Read either Theodore Roszak, The Making of a Counter-Culture or E. S. Gaustad, Dissent in America.

Philip B. Kurland, "Expanding Conceptions of Religious Freedom," in Wisconsin Law Review (1966) pp. 215-296; xeroxed on reserve.

Read the following cases which are xeroxed on reserve:
- Conscientious Objections cases: "The Seeger Case" as reflected in Welsh vs. U.S. (1970).
- Jewish Sabbath and Employment, "Braunfeld vs. Philadelphia" (1961).
- Seventh Day Adventists and employment, "Sherbert vs. Verner" (1963).
- Jehovah's Witnesses and the school flag salute, "West Virginia vs. Barnette" (1942).

Read Judge Raymond F. Pettine's decision on "The Nativity Scene on Public Property," (1981) xeroxed on reserve.

Read Larry Laudan's analysis of Judge Overton's decision in the Arkansas Creationism Case, "Science at the Bar," in Evolution, Morality and the Meaning of Life (Totowa, N. J., 1982) pp. 149-154, xeroxed on reserve.

Fall, 1983 HISTORY 177 Prof. W. McLoughlin

Some definitions of religion, culture, symbols, rituals

Clifford Geertz, The Interpretation of Cultures (New York, 1973):

52 "Culture is a set of symbolic devices for controlling behavior."

89 Sacred symbols synthesize a people's ethos.

89 "The culture concept to which I adhere has neither multiple referent nor, so far as I can see, any unusual ambiguity: it denotes an historically transmitted pattern of meanings embodied in symbols, a system of inherited conceptions expressed in symbolic forms by means of which men communicate, perpetuate, and develop their knowledge about and attitudes toward life."

"Sacred symbols function to synthesize a people's ethos--the tone, character, and quality of their life, its moral and aesthetic style and mood--and their world view--the picture they have of the way things in sheer actuality are, their most comprehensive ideas of order. In religious belief and practice a group's ethos is rendered intellectually reasonable by being shown to represent a way of life ideally adapted to the actual state of affairs the world view describes, while the world view is rendered emotionally convincing by being presented as an image of an actual state of affairs peculiarly well-arranged to accommodate such a way of life . . . it objectivizes moral and aesthetic preference by depicting them as the imposed conditions of life implicit in a world with a particular structure, as mere common sense given the unablerable shape of relation. On the other [hand] it supports these received beliefs about the world's body by invoking deeply felt moral and aesthetic sentiments as experiential evidence for their truth. Religious symbols formulate a basic congruence between a particular style of life and a specific (if, most often, implicit) metaphysic, and in so doing sustain each with borrowed authority of the other."

"Religion tunes human actions to an envisaged cosmic order and projects images of cosmic order onto the plane of human experience."

89-90 "Religion is a (1) system of symbols which acts to (2) establish powerful, pervasive, and long-lasting moods and motivations in men by (3) formulating conceptions of a general order of existence and (4) clothing these conceptions with such an aura of factuality that (5) the moods and motivations seem uniquely realistic."

90 religion confronts and confirms experience--it justifies existing preferences by objectifying them as reality imposed on circumstance and it evokes deep sentiments as experiential evidence for "reality"

91 rituals are the symbolic dimension of social events

96 religious activities involve (1) mood (intensity) and (2) motivation (action, service)

99 religion orders chaos

142 (Durkheim) belief and ritual reinforce the traditional social ties between individuals; social structure is strengthened and perpetuated through the ritualistic or mythic symbolization of the underlying social values. (Culture derives from social organization.)

142 (Malinowski) religion satisfies both cognitive and affective demands for a stable, comprehensible and coercible world; religion enables man to maintain an inner security in the face of natural contingency. (Social organization derives from culture.)

143 (Geertz) religion can be either supportive, harmonizing integrative (consoles, celebrates) or disruptive, disintegrative, disturbing (witchcraft, antinomianism, perfectionism); religion can preserve, transform, or destroy social order.

144 Culture is an ordered system of meaning and of symbols in terms of which social interaction takes place. A social system is the pattern of social interaction.

146 Culture is the fabric of meaning in terms of which human beings interpret their experiences and guide their action.
Social Structure is the form that action takes, the actual existing network of social relations (behavioral interaction, institutions).
Personality structure is the pattern of motivational interaction which leads individuals to desire to work within the system (provided they can see congruence between the logic of culture and the organic function of their place in it). Disorientation, alienation, anomie result from failure of congruence, from disjunction, or disruption between the culture, the social structure and the personality.

171 Max Weber "set forth a distinction between two idealized polar types of religions in world history, the 'traditional' and the 'rationalized,' which if it is overgeneralized and incompletely formulated is yet a useful starting point for a discussion of the process of genuinely religious change. . . . Traditional religious concepts (Weber also calls them magical) rigidly stereotype established social practices. Inextricably bound up with secular custom in an almost point-for-point manner, they draw 'all branches of human activity into the circle of symbolic magic' and so insure that the stream of everyday existence continues to flow steadily within a fixed and firmly outlined course. Rationalized concepts, however, are not so thoroughly intertwined with the concrete details of ordinary life. They are 'apart,' 'above,' or 'outside' of them and the relations of the systems of ritual and belief in which they are embodied to secular society are not intimate and unexamined but distant and problematic. A rationalized religion is, to the degree that it is rationalized, self-conscious and worldly-wise. . . ."

171-172 "Traditional religions consist of a multitude of very concretely defined and only loosely ordered sacred entities, an untidy collections of fuzzy ritual acts and vivid animistic images. . . .
Rationalized religions, on the other hand, are more abstract, more logically coherent and more generally phrased. [Religious problems in traditional religious systems] get inclusive formulations and evoke comprehensive attitudes. They become conceptualized as universal and inherent qualities of human existence. . . ."

Kenneth Burridge, New Heaven, New Earth (New York, 1969):

4-5 "An awakening of religious activity is a frequent characteristic of periods of social unrest." "All religions are basically concerned with power. . . . Religions are concerned with the systematic ordering of different kinds of power. . . . This entails a specific framework of rules grounded in an interplay between experience . . . and faith . . . received truths or assumptions give way to new truths. . . . These assumptions are community truths . . . which command a consensus. From them are derived the sets of moral imperatives . . . to which men . . . subject themselves . . . no religious movement lacks a political ideology [how wealth and power are distributed in a society].

Victor Turner, The Forest of Symbols (Ithaca, 1967):

7 Rituals of "life crisis" (birth, puberty, death, christening, graduation); rituals of affliction (misfortune in hunting illness, miscarriage, witchcraft).

19 "By ritual I mean prescribed formal behavior of occasions . . . having references to belief in mystical beings or powers. The symbol is the smallest unit of ritual which still retains the specific properties of ritual behavior."

"A symbol is a thing regarded by general consent as naturally typifying or representing or recalling something by possession of analogous qualities or by association in fact or thought."

20 "Symbols are essentially involved in social processes whereby groups become adjusted to internal changes and adapted to their external environment."

"The structure and properties of ritual symbols" can be inferred from
(1) external form and observable characteristics
(2) interpretations offered by specialists and laymen in the culture
(3) analytical contexts worked out by the anthropologist

"dominant symbols" are
(1) means to fulfil purposes of the ritual
(2) axiomatic values or references to these values (i.e., the stand for basic social values)

24 Ritual symbols sometimes mask (though analytical context discloses) powerful unconscious wishes of a kind considered illicit to express. Hidden social tensions are revealed to the observer which the informant does not articulate. The ritual (like dream fantasies) helps to release these tensions by censoring them in symbols which nevertheless have deep emotive (affective) power.

25 (Jung) "A sign is an analogous or abbreviated expression of a known thing. But a symbol is always the best possible expression of a relatively unknown fact, a fact [God, witch] however which is nonetheless recognized or postulated as existing."

HISTORY 177

Questions for Weekly Reports

Week:

Orientation: What are some of the different ways of defining the terms "religion", "church", "denomination", "sect", "cult"? Why do definitions differ among sociologists, anthropologists, historians, theologians? What is theology?

I. 1. Define "Puritan", "Puritanism" and "the Five Points of Calvinism"?
2. What was the relationship between church and state in Massachusetts Bay? Was Massachusetts a theocracy?
3. What does Morgan mean by "The Puritan Dilemma"?
4. In what sense was the Puritan experiment a utopian one based on the ideal of harmony and of community decision-making? Were the Puritans backward-looking or forward-looking?
5. Why did the people who lived in Puritan New England find Puritanism so satisfying? Why and when did it fail?

II. 1. Did Puritans treat dissenters any differently from the way dissenters are treated in any society?
2. What is social deviance? How is it measured today and how was it measured in the Massachusetts Bay Colony? Were the Indians dissenters?
3. What are some of the definitions of "religious conversion" and how does that take place? What is its function for society, for the church, for the individual?
4. Which of the various dissenting groups in seventeenth century were most severely persecuted and why? Which were least persecuted and why?
5. Is psychology or sociology more helpful in defining sects and cults? What are the strengths and weaknesses of Sargant's theories?

III. 1. What do you consider the main causes of the First Great Awakening?
2. What do you consider the most important results of the First Great Awakening?
3. How did the Awakening differ in different parts of the colonies?
4. What groups tended to support the Awakening and what groups opposed it and why?
5. Is religious enthusiasm (or religious zeal) a source of social liberation or a source of social confusion?

IV. 1. How do "the Five Points of Deism" compare or contrast with the "Five Points of Calvinism"?
2. What was "The Enlightenment" and how does it relate to Deism?
3. Who did more to separate church and state, the Deists or the Calvinists?
4. Why did disestablishment take place at different times in different states, and why was the First Amendment to the Constitution so little help in this?

IV. 5. What were the principal arguments for and aganist the separation of church and state?
6. What does "disestablishment" mean and what was the General Assessment tax which George Washington and Patrick Henry supported?

V. 1. What does Marty mean by the term "Righteous Empire"? Is is the same as WASPism?
2. Was Abner Kneeland imprisoned primarily for his religious dissent or for his sociopolitical deviance?
3. Why were the Mormons denied religious liberty?
4. What were the causes and results of the Second Great Awakening?
5. What are "The Five Points of Evangelical-Arminianism" and how do they differ from Calvinism and Deism? Who or what was chiefly responsible for their success in replacing Calvinism and Deism?

VI. 1. To what extent did the Handsome Lake religion revive the traditionalism of the Seneca Indians and to what extent did it assimilate traditional ways to Christianity?
2. Is the revitalization of the Seneca culture in any way similar to the revitalization which the Second Great Awakening brought to white American culture?
3. Did the missionaries to the Indians help them or did they simply serve as forces for their destruction as a people?
4. What were the main reasons for anti-Indian prejudice and how did the Indians try to counteract it? Why didn't they succeed in gaining religious equality?
5. Are Indians successfully asserting their identity today or are they still subject to persecution and discrimination and why? How did they resist Christianization?

VII. 1. Were the immigrants from Ireland persecuted primarily because of their Catholicism, their peasant conservatism, or their race?
2. In what ways did the European immigrants try to combat discrimination and how successful were they?
3. In what ways were Catholicism and Evangelical-Arminianism irreconcilable world views?
4. Was immigration restriction a wise move to ensure cultural order and stability, and if not, should immigration today be unrestricted? Why?
5. What is "Hansen's Law" and how valid do you think it is? Has it been true among your own family?

VIII. 1. What conscious or unconcscious tools of survival did Afro-Americans develop to protect their identities? What coping mechanisms did they develop?
2. How successful have Afro-Americans been in "integrating" into white-America?
3. What have been the most successful alternatives to integration?
4. What are "black separatism" and "black nationalism" and how do you evaluate these movements?

VIII. 5. Name the black leaders whom you believe have done the most for Afro-Americans and justify your choices. Which black leaders were least helpful and why?

IX. 1. Which group has had more difficulty retaining its identity and culture in America, the Jews or the Italians and why?
2. Were Italian immigrants really "social deviants"? Explain.
3. Were Jewish immigrants really "social deviants"? Explain.
4. What were the most effective ways by which Jews and/or Italians have maintained a balance between assimilation and a distinct identity?
5. How has the process of adjusting to America's "quasi-establishment" divided the Jews and/or the Italians among themselves?

X. 1. How do you account for the rise of Fundamentalism?
2. What are "The Five Points of Fundamentalism" and why are they considered so important by Fundamentalists?
3. Is Fundamentalism simply a continuation of nineteenth-century Evangelicalism or are the Neo-Evangelicals really different both from Fundamentalists and from nineteenth-century Evangelicals?
4. How do you account for the rise of Jerry Falwell and "The Christian Right" and what future do you think they have?
5. How important has the conflict between religion and science been in American culture and what are some of the key points of conflict?
6. What is a Liberal Protestant, and why did Brown University officially call itself a "Liberal Protestant institution" in 1952?

XI. 1. What is Will Herberg's opinion of assimilation and do you agree with it?
2. What is Milton Gordon's opinion of assimilation and do you agree with it?
3. What is Michael Novak's opinion of assimilation and do you agree with it?
4. How does John Dewey's, view of religion compare with Herberg's view of America's "culture religion"?

XII. 1. What is "the counter-culture" as Roszak defines it and has it disappeared?
2. What were the religious implications of the counter-culture and what influence did they have in the sixties and what influence do they have today?
3. Compare the counter-culture of the sixties with other counter-cultures in our history (say Greenwich VIllage in the 1920's or the Transcendentalists).
4. How do you account for the rise of so many cults and sects in the 1960's? Were they part of a breakdown of religious orthodoxy or the result of psychological difficulties or symptomatic of serious social dislocations and strains in American culture?
5. In what sense were the 1960's revitalization movement in American culture?

XII. 6. How do you account for the reaction against the counter-culture and its cults?

7. What does the Nativity Scene case in Pawtucket, RI tell us about the problems of dissent and quasi-establishment today?

XIII. 1. Are Americans on the whole more or less tolerant toward dissent (or social deviance) today than in previous generations? Where do Americans draw the line against tolerance today?

2. Has the concept of religious freedom expanded or contracted in recent years? And why?

3. Has the Supreme Court helped or confused the definition of separation of church and state?

4. What do you consider the three most difficult questions surrounding religious freedom today and why?

5. What do you consider the three most difficult problems facing an individual in maintaining his or her personal identity in America today? And why?

6. In your opinion will there be increasing or decreasing tolerance for dissent in your generation and why?

Themes of the Course

1. The Protestant Ethic and its relation to "The Success Myth," "The American Dream," and the rise of bourgeois capitalism. Sometimes called "The Work Ethic" or "The Calvinist Ethic."

See Max Weber, The Protestant Ethic and the Spirit of Capitalism
Richard H. Tawney, Religion and the Rise of Capitalism
Daniel T. Rodgers, The Work Ethic in Protestant America
and many others.

2. Millennialism and the belief in progress. This includes personal perfectionism and social perfectibility, various forms of millennial thought (pre-millennialism and post-millennialism).

See Ernest Tuveson, Redeemer Nation
James W. Davidson, The Logic of Millennial Thought
Ernest R. Sandeen, The Roots of Fundamentalism
and many others.

3. The Chosen or Covenanted People (sometimes referred to as "God's New Israel") and its relationship to "the mission of America" to lead the world to the millennium, to "manifest destiny," to westward expansion, to Christian Nationalism (the Cross and the Flag), and to assimilationism. (Also related to WASPism.)

See Martin M. Marty, Righteous Empire
Albert K. Weinberg, Manifest Destiny
Frederick E. Merk, Manifest Destiny and Mission
Conrad Cherry, God's New Israel
and many others.

4. The higher law concept (sometimes associated with God's revealed or divine laws, sometimes with Natural Law or the laws of nature). This includes the concept of "America's civil religion" and the belief in judgment by God against people, groups, or nation's who break the higher law as well as the right to revolt or practice civil disobedience in the name of the higher law.

See Russell E. Richey and Donald G. Jones, American Civil Religion
Robert N. Bellah, The Broken Covenant
H. Richard Niebuhr, The Kingdom of God in America
John F. Berens, Providence and Patriotism in Early America
and many others.

5. Revivals and Great Awakenings (or revitalization movements) and their relationship to basic reorientations in the American belief-value system. Revivalism as "an organizing process" and church recruiting process.

See William G. McLoughlin, Revivals, Awakenings and Reform
Anthony F. C. Wallace, The Death and Rebirth of the Seneca
Kenelm Burridge, New Heaven, New Earth
William G. McLoughlin, Modern Revivalism
and many books on individual revivalists and specific "Awakenings"

History 177 - Themes of the Course

6. The Melting Pot and the Salad Bowl, the problem of acculturation or assimilation of Native Americans and immigrants into the dominant belief-value system of this culture. The shift from WASPism to religious pluralism and the recurring periods of xenophobia, nativism, and 100% Americanism. This also includes ecumenical efforts to bridge denominational divisions, and recurrent anti-Semitism.

See John Higham, Strangers in the Land
Oscar Handlin, The Uprooted and Boston's Immigrants
R. A. Billington, The Protestant Crusade
Will Herberg, Protestant, Catholic, Jew
and many others (esp. Robert F. Berkhofer, The White Man's Indian).

7. Religion and Science, compatibility and incompatibility. The shift from the belief that religion and science were integral parts of God's universal order to an anti-clerical view that religionists were inimical to science and conversely that science was inimical to religion. Related to deism, the Enlightenment, Darwinism, agnosticism, and various sociological and psychological analyses of religious thought, action and belief.

See Henry F. May, The Enlightenment in America
Richard Hofstadter, Social Darwinism in American Thought
Stewart G. Cole, The History of Fundamentalism
and many others.

8. Sectarianism, cults and the proliferation of new denominations, including schismatics who break off from older denominations as well as groups which spring up under new charismatic prophets or from new religious ideas.

See Ernet Troeltsch, The Social Teachings of the Christian Churches
Elmer T. Clark, The Small Sects in America
Charles R. Braden, These Also Believe
as well as many studies of individual sects, cults and schismatics.

9. The separation of church and state, the right of dissent (or free exercise of religion), disestablishment. The shift from conformity of belief and worship, to toleration, to religious equality. The concept of voluntary support for religion and the supposed "high wall of separation" in view of frequent breaches of it

See Anson P. Stokes, 3 vols. Church and State in the United States
Leo Pfeffer, Church, State and Freedom.
John F. Wilson, Church and State in American History
and many others, including Norman F. Furniss, The Fundamentalist Controversy.

10. Religion and social reform. Efforts of religious leaders to involve churchgoers in working toward social change or even toward hristian Socialism, as well as the reactions against such efforts. This includes the stands taken by churches and church people to equal rights for blacks, women, Indians, "foreigners," and workingpeople as well as religious support for civil disobedience, pacificism, non-violence.

See Charles C. Cole, The Social Ideas of the Northern Evangelists
Charles H. Hopkins, The Rise of the Social Gospel
Donald B. Meyer, The Protestant Search for Political Realism
Kenneth Bailey, Southern White Protestantism in the Twentieth Century
as well as many books on individual reform movements and reform eras.

History 177 - Themes of the Course

11. Black religion in America. The formation of black churches and the various means by which black religious leaders have sought racial equality.

See Albert J. Raboteau, Slave Religion
Carter G. Woodson, The History of the Negro Church
C. Eric Lincoln, The Black Muslims in America
E. David Cronon, Marcus Garvey
as well as many biographies of leading black religious spokesmen.

12. Social sources of denominationalism. The relationship between religious affiliations and social classes or other kinds of division within the nation.

See H. Richard Niebuhr, The Social Sources of Denominationalism
Charles Y. Glock and Rodney Stark, Religion and Society in Tension
Andrew M. Greeley, The Denominational Society
Martin E. Marty, A Nation of Behavers
as well as studies of individual denominations and their origins.

13. Unbelief, Humanism, and non-Judeo-Christian groups in America. There has always been a sizable number of Americans who belonged to no church and who in fact rejected the Judeo-Christian tradition. Among these were native Americans, Oriental immigrants, deists, and agnostics. Also many positive thinkers were non-churhgoers.

See Martin E. Marty, Varieties of UnBelief
Theodore Roszak, The Making of a Counter-Culture
Robert E. Berkhofer, Salvation and the Savage
Gustav A. Koch, Republican Religion
Arthur E. Christy, The Orient in American Transcendentalism
and many others.

14. Psychological and Sociological (and anthropological) studies of religion and conversion, which deal with the meaning of religious conversion, the function of religion for individuals and groups, and the definition of religion.

See Hadley Cantril, The Pyschology of Social Movements
Clifford Geertz, Interpretation of Culture
William Sargant, Battle for the Mind
William James, The Varieties of Religious Experience
and many others.

The best bibliographies of religion in America are:

Nelson Burr, et al., A Critical Bibliography of Religion in America (2 vols.)
H. Shelton Smith, etc., American Christianity (2 vols.)

UNIVERSITY OF CALIFORNIA, LOS ANGELES

History 177C
MWF 12 noon

D. W. Howe
Spring 1979

HISTORY OF RELIGION IN THE UNITED STATES

This course considers the religious dimension of peopl'e experience in the United States. A number of religious traditions which have been important in this country will be examined, and attention devoted to relating developments in religion to other aspects of American culture. The purpose of the course is not to indoctrinate students in any particular religious or anti-religious viewpoint, but to examine the role religion has played in American life over the centuries of our history.

There will be one midterm and one final examination, covering the assigned reading and lecture. One short paper (no more than 6 pages) is also required, as described on the second page of this syllabus.

My office is at Bunche 5345; office hours are Mondays & Fridays, 1:30-2:30 p.m.

Topics to be treated this quarter are as follows. Dates in parentheses indicate when each assigned reading should be completed.

I. Traditional Religions of Western Civilization

Nathan Glazer, AMERICAN JUDAISM (second edition) (April 6)
John Cogley, CATHOLIC AMERICA (April 13)

II. Protest-antism

Edmund S. Morgan, THE PURITAN DILEMMA (April 20)
Sidney Ahlstrom, ed., THEOLOGY IN AMERICA, chap. II - You may omit items 1, 3, 4, 9, 11, 18, 19, 21, 23 and 29 (April 27)

Midterm examination on topics I and II - May 4

III. Evangelical Religion

Franklin Frazier and C. Eric Lincoln, THE NEGRO CHURCH AND THE BLACK CHURCH (May 11)
Ahlstrom, Chap. III (May 18)

IV. Religion in a Secular Society

Ray Ginger, SIX DAYS OR FOREVER? (May 25)
Ahlstrom, pp. 332-56 and 362-70 (June 1)
Ahlstrom, chap. XIII (June 8)

The final examination in this course is scheduled for Friday, June 15, from 11:30 a.m. to 2:30 p.m. It will cover topics I through IV. A description of this examination, giving specific advice on how to study for it, will be distributed toward the end of the quarter.

Each student will write a paper of no more than 6 pages. There are two options for the nature of this paper, both described below. Papers are due May 30.

Option I.

Attend a religious service which is not of your own tradition or faith. Write a sensitive and perceptive essay describing what is going on. You may choose to emphasize a particular aspect of the situation, e.g., social, theological, liturgical, historical. If you wish, you may compare the service with those you are accustomed to, or describe your own perspective on it. You must make an effort to relate the service you describe to some of the other work in the course. Further advice on writing the paper will be distributed later.

Option II.

Write an essay on one of the books listed below. All of them are on Reserve at the College Library (Powell). If you can obtain a copy otherwise, however, you may find that more convenient. You are urged to select and read your book as early as possible, to make sure you obtain the one of your choice. You may structure the paper however you wish, provided it includes: (a) a description of the contents of the book, (b) an evaluation of the author's interpretation of the subject, and (c) an attempt to relate the book to some other assigned work in this course. Further advice on writing the paper will be distributed later.

Where the subject-matter of a book is not evident from the title, I have indicated it in parentheses.

- William Sloan Coffin, ONCE TO EVERY MAN (autobiography of a liberal Protestant minister)
- Stephen Gottschalk, THE EMERGENCE OF CHRISTIAN SCIENCE IN AMERICAN RELIGIOUS THOUGHT
- Irving Howe, WORLD OF OUR FATHERS (Judaism; this is a long book, and if you read 300 pages it will suffice for the paper.)
- Whitney Cross, THE BURNED-OVER DISTRICT (evangelical Protestant movements in the 19th-century)
- Laurence Veysey, THE COMMUNAL EXPERIENCE:: ANARCHIST & MYSTICAL COMMUNITIES IN 20th-CENTURY AMERICA
- Joseph R. Washington, Jr., BLACK SECTS AND CULTS
- Garry Wills, BARE RUINED CHOIRS (Roman Catholicism in recent years)

Students wishing to supplement the readings or lectures with a textbook are referred to Sydney Ahlstrom, A RELIGIOUS HISTORY OF THE AMERICAN PEOPLE, which is on two-hour reserve at the College Library (Powell). Use of this textbook is entirely optional.

TABLE OF CONTENTS

VOLUME I

VOLUME III

Documents have been reproduced from the originals as submitted.

WOMEN'S HISTORY

A. SURVEY COURSES

B. THE TWENTIETH CENTURY

C. ETHNIC WOMEN'S HISTORY - AFRO-AMERICAN AND CHICANO

D. WOMEN AND RELIGION

E. WOMEN AND EDUCATION

F. SOCIAL HISTORY, WOMEN AND WORK

G. THEORY AND METHODOLOGY

Documents have been reproduced from the originals as submitted.

RYAN LIBRARY-IONA COLLEGE
1 0001 002 139 802